THE HARD WAY

THE HARD WAY

Writing By The Rebels Who Changed Sports

Edited By Will Balliett and Thomas Dyja
Foreword by Jim Bouton

A Thunder's Mouth Press/
Balliett & Fitzgerald Book
New York

First Edition

Compilation copyright © 1999 by Will Balliett & Thomas Dyja
Foreword copyright © 1999 by Jim Bouton
Introductions copyright © 1999 by Thomas Dyja

Published by
Thunder's Mouth Press
841 Broadway, 4th Floor
New York, NY 10003

and

Balliett & Fitzgerald Inc.
66 West Broadway, Suite 602
New York, NY 10007

Distributed by Publishers Group West

Book design: Sue Canavan

frontispiece photo: © Transcendental Graphics

Manufactured in the United States of America

ISBN: 1-56025-280-8

Library of Congress Cataloging-in-Publication Data

The hard way: writing by the rebels who changed sports / edited by
   Will Balliett and Thomas Dyja.
      p. cm.
   Includes bibliographical references.
   ISBN 1-56025-280-8
   1. Athletes—United States Biography.   2. Sports—United States
History.   I. Balliett, Will.   II. Dyja, Tom.
GV697.A1H347   1999
796′.092′273—dc21
   [B]   99-23962
                                                               CIP

To all those still working toward a level playing field.

CONTENTS

JIM BOUTON
FOREWORD

In the beginning there were the players—people who loved to run and throw, hit and catch, jump or dive. Then came the folks who liked to watch; people who shouted and cheered, laughed and cried—and they were called fans. Last of all came the owners and promoters, the agents and lawyers who figured out how to make a living off the first two groups.

With a product and customers already in place, making a profit from sport has been relatively simple. Making *obscene* profits requires some help. This comes in the form of special legislation, anti-trust exemptions, amateur by-laws, university policies and procedures, international rules and regulations designed to abridge the freedom of a singular class of people—athletes.

Rights taken for granted by the average citizen, but denied to athletes, include: the right to transfer from one college to another without being penalized, to choose an employer, to bargain for one's talent in a free market, to obtain due process, to exercise free speech, among others. Imagine the following scenarios: General Motors drafts an engineer from M.I.T., prevents him from speaking with other auto companies, and requires him to work in Ypsilanti for six years. A doctor has his license suspended for a non-medical act of civil disobedience. An actress is kicked out of college and her school is put on probation because she accepts money from an agent. Outrageous, you say? Unconstitutional? Un-American? Not in Sportsworld.

It is precisely these kinds of restrictions, drafted by team owners, endorsed by college presidents, enforced by sports governing bodies, affirmed by judges, and supported by the media, that have become accepted without question by the general population, including many of the athletes themselves! Which is part of the problem. Because athletes are the only ones who can change the system.

But it puts them in a catch-22. In order to prove damages in a court of law they must forgo playing, which lack of activity then damages their careers. What college football player is going to sit out a few years while he sues the NFL on the constitutionality of the draft? What high school kid is going to risk college eligibility by suing the NCAA? How many amateur athletes can even afford a legal fight against one of the sports' governing bodies? It's an unpopular, expensive, career-ending war with an uncertain result.

And the hardest part can be battling your fellow players. The athlete who takes a stand, signs a petition, promotes a union, or simply raises a fist to make a point is frequently branded as a "troublemaker" by the very teammates who stand to benefit. Or a "clubhouse lawyer."

Or in my case, "the Communist."

In the 1960s, with the Yankees and then the Seattle Pilots, our bullpen discussions would occasionally veer from women and guns to financial matters such as the minimum salary ($7,000). "It should be at least $25,000," I'd say, mounting my soapbox. "Baseball is a monopoly with special tax breaks and publicly financed stadiums. Plus we're not only the work force, *we're the product*!" The player's eyes would roll at this point and a coach would say, "Now that's Communist thinking."

Athletes are basically conservative people who succeeded by being team players. Many grew up in small towns where "union" was a bad word, or on city streets where the guy who popped off drew hostile fire. Athletes don't want to be *in* court, they want to be *on* the court. Play the game, see who's best, go get 'em tomorrow. If they liked arguing they would have been lawyers.

Of course, folks who spend all their time developing one set of skills are often lacking others. Too many players, especially in my day, were marginally educated, socially unsophisticated, and economically naive, Like bird dogs bred to hunt, players were bred to play, and were grateful for the opportunity.

And the owners took advantage of us. Contract negotiations were a joke. High school educated players with no business smarts would sit across the table from experienced general managers who got paid, in part, from what they saved on the players. No lawyers allowed. And no agents, of course (who wanted 10% of S7,000?). We weren't even allowed to have our fathers present!

In many ways it's a class war. Extremely wealthy individuals, called "sportsmen," buy professional teams or Olympic committee memberships, as a hobby. The athletes are "property" to be bought and sold for fun and profit, like horses. (It's not uncommon for team owners to also own race horses—the prohibition against gambling connections being limited to athletes.)

At least today the players are treated as well as the horses. And not just at mealtime. A friend recently commented that ballplayers are making more leaping catches against the outfield walls, and wondered why. The answer is the heavy padding on the walls, demanded years ago by the Player's Association. In the bad old days, players crashed into cement and steel, breaking bones and ending careers. Pete Reiser of the old Brooklyn Dodgers was a famous example. And it was only after Mickey Mantle tore up his knee, catching his spikes in the metal grid of an outfield drain, that they covered the drains with rubber caps. Today's players are *thoroughbreds*. We were ploughhorses.

The class difference between athletes and the people who control their careers has never been more apparent than at the Olympics. In 1968 I signed a petition to ban South Africa from the Olympics because they fielded an all-white team. Then I was asked to join a group going to Mexico City to lobby the matter with Olympic officials. I thought it would be a piece of cake. The Americans would recognize a Yankee pitcher, see the obvious injustice of the situation and do the right thing. The piece of cake turned out to be a bitter pill.

Olympic officials not only didn't want to expel South Africa, they didn't even want to *hear* about it. Alerted to our presence at the hotel where they were meeting, the officials did everything possible to avoid us. When American delegate Dennis Roby saw me in the lobby he ducked behind a potted plant and raced for the elevator. That's when I set a new Olympic record for fifty-yards-across-a-carpeted-lobby.

Although we didn't get an official hearing at the '68 Olympics, mounting pressures would eventually force the expulsion of South Africa until they fielded a more representative team. What was clear to me in Mexico City was that aristocratic Olympic Committee officials had more in common with each other than with the athletes they were supposedly representing. Which explains why you often read of amateur athletes not getting due process from the various sports federations. It's the limo-and-luxury-suite team versus the bus-and-dormitory team. The '68 Olympic officials simply couldn't expel a member of their own club.

In spite of the obstacles, many battles have been won. Title IX has leveled the playing field for women, professional sports unions have achieved a measure of economic justice, and the color line has been rubbed out, at least on the field. But more still needs to be done, particularly in the areas of race relations in professional sports management, a better deal for boxers, and a bill of rights for amateur athletes just to name a few. Still, whatever gains are made in the future will be owed to the victories of past wars. This book celebrates those battles and the warriors who fought them.

Jack Johnson, Jesse Owens, and Jackie Robinson risked not only their careers but their lives for what they believed in. Babe Didrickson Zaharias (I still remember my grandmother imitating Babe's golf stroke) and Billie Jean King were role models for generations of women. Curt Flood sacrificed his baseball career in the losing cause that benefits today's players. Thanks to Marvin Miller (who belongs in the Hall of Fame in his own category—*Savior*), baseball players achieved a measure of free-agency, which then spread to basketball, football and hockey.

Others, such as myself, contributed in less significant ways. I wrote *Ball Four* because I wanted to share the fun in baseball, not to change the system. It didn't take any courage. And I certainly never imagined that it would be used as evidence against the owners because it exposed their abuses against the players. Call me an unintentional warrior. But I'm happy to be on the team.

THOMAS DYJA

INTRODUCTION

Conflict is at the core of all sport, a simple fact which horrifies those who scream about winner-take-all mentalities and violence. Of course, conflict is at the core of all drama, too, and the three essential conflicts of drama—Man against Man, Man against his environment, and Man against himself—are exactly what draw sports lovers out to stadiums and into easy chairs around the world. If you don't believe that a good ballgame has more art to it than most "art," watch a tape of the Packers and Cowboys struggling through the bitter cold of the 1967 Ice Bowl, or the last out of any no-hitter.

Still, the conflict of sports feels somehow unreal; children won't starve to death if a team wins or loses, weather patterns won't change if a goal isn't scored. In fact, for much of the twentieth century the business of sports was run with a near phobia for real life-changing

1

conflict. During the game, message pitches and hard fouls were OK; but the structure of how the games were run, who ran them and for what end could not be questioned by athletes or the press. Baseball and football players had more in common with Roman gladiators than they did with any boys-of-summer dreams promulgated by starstruck beatwriters.

What binds the people represented in *The Hard Way* is that they all in some way turned the ritualized conflict of sports, this supposedly tamer version of the daily struggle to live, into something more meaningful, and not just for themselves, but for society as a whole. While thousands of athletes in various sports snuggled into the status quo, believing (not without reason) that a paycheck for playing a sport beat a paycheck for pounding rivets or shuffling papers, people such as Jack Johnson and Curt Flood stood up and burned with indignity, like fires on a mountain, and asserted their right to exercise their talents as they saw fit. What set Jackie Robinson apart from Joe Louis, what really brought African-Americans into the mainstream of sports and prepared the nation for the Civil Rights Movement, was that Robinson didn't apologize for his presence, didn't accomodate. And only eleven weeks after Robinson broke the color-barrier in the National League, Bill Veeck, president-owner-operator of the Cleveland Indians, sent Larry Doby out to pinch hit, breaking the color line in the American League. The pieces by these writers that we've included in *The Hard Way* all recount the remarkable struggles they faced in creating level playing fields in the business where level playing fields are quite literally essential.

The other athletes in this book also made their voices heard on topics besides jump shots and spit-balls. For those of us who grew up in the sixties and seventies, people such as Jim Brosnan, Jim Bouton, Dave Meggyesy, and Dock Ellis stepped out of the incessant Huntley-Brinkley drone about seemingly far away upheaval and put the spirit of a new generation directly in our faces. Like the players who struggled against racism, their battle was sometimes as much against their fellow athletes and the locker-room mentality as it was against the

2

corporate structures of sports. Their books rocked the way we viewed sports and its heroes, as did the groundbreaking media revolution initiated by Roone Arledge. Whether some of the ground should have been broken at all (Just how necessary is Hank Williams, Jr., to *Monday Night Football*, anyhow?) is another argument altogether, but at the very least his focused and aesthetically imaginative style of broadcasting brought a new kind of honesty to sports coverage. Marvin Miller's union tactics, once considered brash, introduced the now-obvious concept that athletes who risked their livelihoods and sometimes even their lives deserved the right to collective bargaining just as much as the plumber watching in the stands.

Our range in *The Hard Way* goes from sport-specific to global politics. Dick Button and George Halas risked the status quo to change the paths of figure skating and football—now the two most popular TV sports in the nation—by pushing their respective pursuits into the sky just as air travel and later space travel became commonplace. On a larger scale, Jesse Owens made the coming conflict between fascism and the rest of civilization richly apparent at the 1936 Berlin Olympics by confronting Hitler with pure skill. Along with his gold medals, he showed by the way he won them that brotherhood was a more powerful weapon than tyranny. Sisterhood also had a major role: Babe Didrikson Zaharias and Billie Jean King were both Goliaths in the battle of the sexes as they proved that women can be as physically and emotionally talented on the playing field as men.

And so, even with all of this said, why do these people matter, with sports nowadays somehow more pointless than ever and too important all at once? Perhaps it is ultimately this confusion as to whether sports are a trivial afterthought or a secular religion which made the hard ways of people such as Jackie Robinson and Billie Jean King vital to our culture. By taking such high-minded concepts as equality and fairness into the everyday world of yesterday's box scores and this afternoon's game, by bringing their struggles into places where scoundrels are known to hide, they proved that no place was too insignificant for justice, that fair deals and equal

INTRODUCTION

chances are not simply the province of the courts, but the business of every man and woman. If Dennis Rodman's taste for cross-dressing has made one drunken basketball fan think better of bashing a homosexual, then all the piercing and the hair dye has been worth it.

These athletes also have something else in common—they created some great reading. While some selections are unabashedly as-told-to's, we make no excuses; there is art in drawing out incidents and motivations, and presenting them in a way that lasts. On the other hand, writers as naturally gifted as Jim Brosnan and Jim Bouton come along about as often as perfect games.

Jackie Robinson

I Never Had It Made

The long road to racial equality has been paved with many lives, but Jackie Robinson's (1919–1972) achievement may have marked the most important milestone of them all. Major league baseball—thought to express so much about our country and our culture—had no place for African-Americans until Robinson bravely took the field in his Brooklyn Dodgers uniform. To break the color barrier in baseball was to put integration squarely in front of the American people. In this excerpt from his autobiography, Robinson recounts the pain of that first season in the major leagues.

Jackie Robinson, Jr., was born in November, 1946. If there is anything to the theory that the influences affecting expectant parents have important impact on the developing child, our baby son was predestined to lead a very complicated and complex life.

Rachel had had problems during her pregnancy that I was not aware of. She accepted them with uncomplaining courage because of her conviction that, since I had a job to do in baseball that was demanding and difficult, I should be as free as possible to deal with it without the further complications of family worries. She was determined, therefore, that, while she shared my problems with me, she would keep me from knowing about her own fears and anxieties. She did a good job of keeping her problems to herself. It wasn't until after Jackie was born that I learned that Rae had occasionally experienced fevers seemingly unconnected with the normal process of pregnancy. Her temperature would rise to 103 and 104 degrees and she would take sulfa drugs and aspirin to bring her fever down. She had insisted on traveling with me during the first season with Montreal because she knew I needed her. Often I would come home tired, discouraged, wondering if I could go on enduring the verbal abuse and even the physical provocations and continue to "turn the other cheek." Rachel knew exactly how I felt, and she would have the right words, the perfect way of comforting me. Rachel's understanding love was a powerful antidote for the poison of being taunted by fans, sneered at by fellow-players, and constantly mistreated because of my blackness.

In the eighth month of her pregnancy, I insisted that Rachel go home to Los Angeles to have the baby. Two weeks after she returned to her mother's home, I was able to get back to Los Angeles and be there the night she went into labor. When the time came, I got her to the hospital fast and our boy was born with unusual speed. We'll never forget that day—November 18, 1946.

The big question, as spring training for the 1947 season became imminent, was whether Branch Rickey would move me out of the minor league and up to the Brooklyn Dodgers. Because of my successful first season with Montreal, it was a question being asked in sportswriting and baseball circles. Even those who were dead set against a black man coming into the majors knew there was a strong possibility that Mr. Rickey would take the big step.

Mr. Rickey had to move cautiously and with skill and strategy. Rae and I never doubted that Mr. Rickey would carry out his intention, but we lived in suspense wondering when. In the latter part of January I was ordered to report back to the Montreal Royals for spring training in Cuba. I would not be able to afford to take Rachel and the baby with me. I had to go it alone.

Although we could not understand Mr. Rickey's reasons for the delay in bringing me up to the Dodgers, we believed he was working things out the best way possible. We thought it was a hopeful sign that both the Dodgers and the Royals would be training in Havana. It could be reasonably expected that the racist atmosphere I had had to face in Florida and other parts of the United States would not exist in another country of non-whites. The Royals now had three more black players—Roy Campanella, a catcher; Don Newcombe and Roy Partlow, both pitchers. I learned, on arriving in Havana, that we black players would be housed in separate quarters at a hotel fifteen miles away from the practice field. The rest of the team was living at a military academy, and the Dodgers were head-quartered at the beautiful Nacional Hotel. I expressed my resentment that the Cuban authorities would subject us to the same kind of seg-regation I had faced in Florida and was promptly informed that liv-ing arrangements had not been made by local authorities but by Mr. Rickey. I was told that he felt his plans for us were on the threshold of success and he didn't want a possible racial incident to jeopardize his program. I reluctantly accepted the explanation.

I was told I must learn to play first base. This disturbed me because I felt it might mean a delay in reaching the majors. However, it was felt that the Dodgers, in order to become contenders for the pennant, had to strengthen the first base position.

The fact that I had been assigned to first base aroused fear in the Dodger camp. They sensed that Mr. Rickey was planning to bring me up to the Dodgers. Some of the players got together and decided to sign a petition declaring they would not play with me on the team. Ironically, the leak about the planned revolt came from a Southerner, Kirby Higbe, of South Carolina. Higbe had a few too many beers one night, and he began feeling uncomfortable about the conspiracy. He revealed the plot to one of Mr. Rickey's aides and Mr. Rickey put down the rebellion with steamroller effectiveness. He said later, "I have always believed that a little show of force at the right time is necessary when there's a deliberate violation of law. . . . I believe that when a man is involved in an overt act of violence or in destruction of someone's rights, that it's no time to conduct an experiment in education or persuasion."

He found out who the ringleaders were—Hugh Casey, a good relief pitcher from Georgia; Southerner Bobby Bragan, a respected catcher; Dixie Walker of Alabama; and Carl Furrillo. Walker had deliberately taken a trip so he wouldn't appear to be in on the scheme. The ringleaders were called in individually, and Mr. Rickey told each one that petitions would make no difference. He said he would carry out his plan, regardless of protest. Anyone who was not willing to have a black teammate could quit. The petition protest collapsed before it got started.

Mr. Rickey was very direct with me during those early 1947 spring training days. He told me I couldn't rest on the victories I'd had with Montreal. I should, in fact, forget them as much as possible. My league record meant nothing. The true test would be making the grade on the field against major league pitching.

"I want you to be a whirling demon against the Dodgers," he said. "I want you to concentrate, to hit that ball, to get on base by *any means necessary*. I want you to run wild, to steal the pants off them, to be the most conspicuous player on the field—but conspicuous only because of the kind of baseball you're playing. Not only will you impress the Dodger players, but the stories that the newspapermen send back to the Brooklyn and New York newspapers will help create demand on the part of the fans that you be brought up to the majors."

With this kind of marching order, I simply had to give my best. I batted .625 and stole seven bases during seven Royals-Dodgers games. Not even this made the Brooklyn players ask for me as Mr. Rickey had hoped. He had wanted, when promoting me, to appear to be giving in to tremendous pressure from my teammates-to-be.

When this strategy failed, Mr. Rickey, a resourceful man, arranged to have Manager Leo Durocher tell the sportswriters that his Brooklyn team could win the pennant with a good man on first base and that I was the best prospect. Leo would add he was going to try to convince Mr. Rickey to sign me. That plan failed, too, because on April 9 before it could be carried out, Baseball Commissioner Chandler suspended Durocher for a year "for conduct detrimental to baseball." Durocher and the commissioner's office had been in conflict for some time. The commissioner's office had challenged Leo's "questionable associations" off the playing field. Durocher had hit back by noting that some very well-known gangsters had been seen near the Yankee dugout during a Dodger-Yankee game. He said no one had done anything about that. This sparked an exchange between the commissioner's office, Durocher, Mr. Rickey, and Yankee President Larry MacPhail. It had been common belief that the storm had blown over. Ironically, on the same April morning that Mr. Rickey hoped to make his move, Durocher was suspended.

Quickly, Mr. Rickey saw that signing the first black in the major leagues would virtually wipe the Durocher story, a negative one, off the front pages. His action would cause controversy, but he believed it would be like a shot in the arm to the club. On the morning of April 9, 1947, just before an exhibition game, reporters in the press box received a single sheet of paper with a one-line announcement. It read: "Brooklyn announces the purchase of the contract of Jack Roosevelt Robinson from Montreal. Signed, Branch Rickey."

That morning turned into a press Donnybrook. The sportswriters snatched up telephones. The telegraph wires relayed the message to the sports world.

Less than a week after I became Number 42 on the Brooklyn club, I played my first game with the team. I did a miserable job. There was an overflow crowd at Ebbets Field. If they expected any miracles out of Robinson, they were sadly disappointed. I was in another slump. I grounded out to the third baseman, flied out to left field, bounced into a double play, was safe on an error, and, later, was removed as a defensive safeguard. The next four games reflected my deep slump. I went to plate twenty times without one base hit. Burt Shotton, a man I respected and liked, had replaced Durocher as manager. As my slump deepened, I appreciated Shotton's patience and understanding. I knew the pressure was on him to take me out of the lineup. People began recalling Bob Feller's analysis of me. I was "good field, no hit." There were others who doubted that I could field and some who hoped I would flunk out and thus establish that blacks weren't ready for the majors. Shotton, however, continued to encourage me.

Early in the season, the Philadelphia Phillies came to Ebbets Field for a three-game series. I was still in my slump and events of the opening game certainly didn't help. Starting to the plate in the first inning, I could scarcely believe my ears. Almost as if it had been synchronized by some master conductor, hate poured forth from the Phillies dugout.

"Hey, nigger, why don't you go back to the cotton field where you belong?"

"They're waiting for you in the jungles, black boy!"

"Hey, snowflake, which one of those white boy's wives are you dating tonight?"

"We don't want you here, nigger."

"Go back to the bushes!"

Those insults and taunts were only samples of the torrent of abuse which poured out from the Phillies dugout that April day.

I have to admit that this day of all the unpleasant days in my life, brought me nearer to cracking up than I ever had been. Perhaps I should have become inured to this kind of garbage, but I was in New York City and unprepared to face the kind of barbarism from a northern team that I had come to associate with the Deep South. The abuse coming out of the Phillies dugout was being directed by the team's manager, Ben Chapman, a Southerner. I felt tortured and I tried just to play ball and ignore the insults. but it was really getting to me. What did the Phillies want from me? What, indeed, did Mr. Rickey expect of me? I was, after all, a human being. What was I doing here turning the other cheek as though I weren't a man? In college days I had had a reputation as a black man who never tolerated affronts to his dignity. I had defied prejudice in the Army. How could I have thought that barriers would fall, that, indeed, my talent could triumph over bigotry?

For one wild and rage-crazed minute I thought, "To hell with Mr.

11

Rickey's 'noble experiment.' It's clear it won't succeed. I have made every effort to work hard, to get myself into shape. My best is not enough for them." I thought what a glorious, cleansing thing it would be to let go. To hell with the image of the patient black freak I was supposed to create. I could throw down my bat, stride over to that Phillies dugout, grab one of those white sons of bitches and smash his teeth in with my despised black fist. Then I could walk away from it all. I'd never become a sports star. But my son could tell his son someday what his daddy could have been if he hadn't been too much of a man.

Then, I thought of Mr. Rickey—how his family and friends had begged him not to fight for me and my people. I thought of all his predictions, which had come true. Mr. Rickey had come to a crossroads and made a lonely decision. I was at a crossroads. I would make mine. I would stay.

The haters had almost won that round. They had succeeded in getting me so upset that I was an easy out. As the game progressed, the Phillies continued with the abuse.

After seven scoreless innings, we got the Phillies out in the eighth, and it was our turn at bat. I led off. The insults were still coming. I let the first pitch go by for a ball. I lined the next one into center field for a single. Gene Hermanski came up to hit and I took my lead.

The Phillies pitcher, a knuckle expert, let fly. I cut out for second. The throw was wide. It bounced past the shortstop. As I came into third, Hermanski singled me home. That was the game.

Apparently frustrated by our victory, the Phillies players kept the heat on me during the next two days. They even enlarged their name-calling to include the rest of the Brooklyn team.

"Hey, you carpetbaggers, how's your little reconstruction period getting along?"

That was a typical taunt. By the third day of our confrontation with these emissaries from the City of Brotherly Love, they had become so outrageous that Ed Stanky exploded. He started yelling at the Phillies.

"Listen, you yellow-bellied cowards," he cried out, "why don't you yell at somebody who can answer back?" It was then that I began to feel better. I remembered Mr. Rickey's prediction. If I won the respect of the team and got them solidly behind me, there would be no question about the success of the experiment.

Stanky wasn't the only Brooklyn player who was angry with the Phillies team. Some of my other teammates told the press about the way Chapman and his players had behaved. Sports columnists around the country criticized Chapman. Dan Parker, sports editor of the New York *Daily Mirror*, reported:

> Ben Chapman, who during his career with the Yankees was frequently involved in unpleasant incidents with fans who charged him with shouting anti-Semitic remarks at them from the ball field, seems to be up to his old trick of stirring up racial trouble. During the recent series between the Phils and the Dodgers, Chapman and three of his players poured a stream of abuse at Jackie Robinson. Jackie, with admirable restraint, ignored the guttersnipe language coming from the Phils dugout, thus stamping himself as the only gentleman among those involved in the incident.

The black press did a real job of letting its readers know about the race baiting which had taken place. The publicity in the press built so much anti-Chapman public feeling that the Philadelphia club decided steps must be taken to counteract it. Chapman met with representatives of the black press to try to explain his behavior. The Phillies public relations people insisted, as Ben Chapman did, that he was not anti-Negro. Chapman himself used an interesting line of defense in speaking with black reporters. Didn't they want me to become a big-time big leaguer? Well, so did he and his players. When they played exhibitions with the Yanks, they razzed DiMaggio as "the Wop," Chapman explained. When they came up against the Cards, Whitey Kurowski was called "the Polack." Riding opposition players was the Phils' style of baseball. The Phils could give it out and they could take it. Was I a weakling who couldn't take it? Well, if I wasn't a weakling, then I shouldn't expect special treatment. After all, Chapman said, all is forgotten after a ball game ends.

The press, black and white, didn't buy that argument. They said so. Commissioner Happy Chandler wasn't having any either. His office warned the Phils to keep racial baiting out of the dugout bench jockeying.

A fascinating development of the nastiness with the Phils was the attitude of Mr. Rickey and the reaction of my Brooklyn teammates. Mr. Rickey knew, better than most people, that Chapman's racial prejudice was deeper than he admitted. Bob Carpenter, the Phils' president, had phoned Rickey before game time to try to persuade him not to include me in the lineup. If I played, Carpenter threatened, his team would refuse to play. Mr. Rickey's response was that this would be fine with him. The Dodgers would then take all three games by default. The Dodgers' president wasn't angry with Chapman or his players. As a matter of fact, in later years, Mr. Rickey commented, "Chapman did more than anybody to unite the Dodgers. When he poured out that string of unconscionable abuse, he solidified and unified thirty men, not one of whom was willing to sit by and see someone kick around a man who had his hands tied behind his back—Chapman made Jackie a real member of the Dodgers."

Privately, at the time, I thought Mr. Rickey was carrying his "gratitude" to Chapman a little too far when he asked me to appear in public with Chapman. The Phillies manager was genuinely in trouble as a result of all the publicity on the racial razzing. Mr. Rickey thought it would be gracious and generous if I posed for a picture shaking hands with Chapman. The idea was also promoted by the baseball commissioner. I was somewhat sold—but not altogether—on the concept that a display of such harmony would be "good for the game." I have to admit, though, that having my picture taken with this man was one of the most difficult things I had to make myself do.

There were times, after I had bowed to humiliations like shaking hands with Chapman, when deep depression and speculation as to whether it was all worthwhile would seize me. Often, when I was in this kind of mood, something positive would happen to give me new strength. Sometimes the positive development would come in response to a negative one. This was exactly what happened when a clever sports editor exposed a plot that was brewing among the St. Louis Cardinals. The plan was set to be executed on May 9, 1947, when Brooklyn was to visit St. Louis for the first game of the season between the two clubs. The Cards were planning to pull a last-minute protest strike against my playing in the game. If successful, the plan could have had a chain reaction throughout the baseball world—with other players agreeing to unite in a strong bid to keep baseball white. Stanley Woodward, sports editor of the New York *Herald Tribune*, had learned of the plot and printed an exclusive scoop exposing it. Ford Frick reacted immediately and notified the Cardinal players in no uncertain terms that they would not be permitted to get away with a strike.

"If you do this you will be suspended from the league," Frick warned. "You will find that the friends you think you have in the press box will not support you, that you will be outcasts. I do not care if half the league strikes. Those who do it will encounter quick retribution. They will be suspended and I don't care if it wrecks the National League for five years. This is the United States of America, and one citizen has as much right to play as another."

"The National League," Frick continued, "will go down the line with Robinson whatever the consequence. You will find if you go through with your intention that you have been guilty of complete madness."

The hot light of publicity about the plot and the forthright hard line that Frick laid down to the plotters helped to avert what could have been a disaster for integration of baseball. Many writers and baseball personalities credited Woodward with significant service to baseball and to sportsmanship.

While some positive things were happening, there were others that were negative. Hate mail arrived daily, but it didn't bother me nearly as much as the threat mail. The threat mail included orders to me to get out of the game or be killed, threats to assault Rachel, to kidnap Jackie, Jr. Although none of the threats materialized, I was quite alarmed. Mr. Rickey, early in May, decided to turn some of the letters over to the police.

That same spring the Benjamin Franklin Hotel in Philadelphia, where my teammates were quartered, refused to accommodate me. The Phillies heckled me a second time, mixing up race baiting with childish remarks and gestures that coincided with the threats that had been made. Some of those grown men sat in the dugout and pointed bats at me and made machine-gunlike noises. It was an incredibly childish display of bad will.

I was helped over these crises by the courage and decency of a teammate who could easily have been my enemy rather than my friend. Pee Wee Reese, the successful Dodger shortstop, was one of the most highly respected players in the major leagues. When I first joined the club, I was aware that there might well be a real reluctance on Reese's part to accept me as a teammate. He was from Ekron, Kentucky. Furthermore, it had been rumored that I might take over Reese's position on the team. Mischief-makers seeking to create trouble between us had tried to agitate Reese into regarding me as a threat—a black one at that. But Reese, from the time I joined Brooklyn, had demonstrated a totally fair attitude.

Reese told a sportswriter, some months after I became a Dodger, "When I first met Robinson in spring training, I figured, well, let me give this guy a chance. It may be he's just as good as I am. Frankly, I don't think I'd stand up under the kind of thing he's been subjected to as well as he has."

Reese's tolerant attitude of withholding judgment to see if I would make it was translated into positive support soon after we became teammates. In Boston during a period when the heckling pressure seemed unbearable, some of the Boston players began to heckle Reese. They were riding him about being a Southerner and playing ball with a black man. Pee Wee didn't answer them. Without a glance in their direction, he left his position and walked over to me. He put his hand on my shoulder and began talking to me. His words weren't important. I don't even remember what he said. It was the gesture of comradeship and support that counted. As he stood talking with me with a friendly arm around my shoulder, he was saying loud and clear, "Yell. Heckle. Do anything you want. We came here to play baseball."

The jeering stopped, and a close and lasting friendship began between Reese and me. We were able, not only to help each other and our team in private as well as public situations, but to talk about racial prejudices and misunderstanding.

At the same time Mr. Rickey told me that when my teammates began to rally to my cause, we could consider the battle half won; he had also said that one of my roughest burdens would be the experience of being lonely in the midst of a group—my teammates. They would be my teammates on the field. But back in the locker rooms, I would know the strain and pressure of being a stranger in a crowd of guys who were friendly among themselves but uncertain about how to treat me. Some of them would resent me but would cover the resentment with aloofness or just a minimum amount of courtesy. Others genuinely wouldn't know how to be friendly with me. Some would even feel I preferred to be off in a corner and left out. After the games were over, my teammates had normal social lives with their wives, their girls, and each other. When I traveled, during those early days, unless Wendell Smith or some other black sportswriter happened to be going along, I sat by myself while the other guys chatted and laughed and played cards. I remember vividly a rare occasion when I was invited to join a poker game. One of the participants was a Georgia guy, Hugh Casey, the relief pitcher. Casey's luck wasn't too good during the game, and at one point he addressed a remark directly to me that caused a horrified silence.

"You know what I used to do down in Georgia when I ran into bad luck?" he said. "I used to go out and find me the biggest, blackest nigger woman I could find and rub her teats to change my luck."

I don't believe there was a man in that game, including me, who thought that I could take that. I had to force back my anger. I had the memory of Mr. Rickey's words about looking for a man "with guts enough not to fight back." Finally, I made myself turn to the dealer and told him to deal the cards.

Traveling had its problems but being at home with Rachel and little Jackie was great even if our living conditions left something to be desired. If we had been living away from our home base, the club would have found some type of separate living arrangement for us. But in the excitement of converting me into a Dodger, no one seemed to have given a thought to our accommodations. We were living—three of us—in one room in the McAlpin Hotel in midtown Manhattan. It was miserable for Rae. In that one room that seemed constantly overrun with newsmen, she had to fix the baby's formula, change his diapers, bathe him, and do all the things mothers do for small babies. We had no relatives in New York and no one to turn to for babysitting. Rae brought our son out to the ball park for the first game I played with the Dodgers. She was determined not to miss that game. Never having lived in the East, she brought little Jackie dressed in a coat which, in California, would have been a winter coat. He would not have been able to stand the cold, dressed as he was, if Roy Campanella's mother-in-law hadn't kept him with her under her fur coat. Rae warmed bottles at a hot dog stand. At four and a half months, Jackie began what was to be the story of his young life—growing up in the ball park. He came to many games with his mother, and when he was old enough, he became very popular with some of the Dodger players who would keep him on their laps and play with him.

Before the season ended, we did manage to escape from the hotel. We found a place in Brooklyn where there was a small sleeping room for little Jackie, a bedroom, and use of a kitchen for us. We had no place to entertain the few friends we were making, but it certainly beat living in the hotel and we were grateful.

We were glad, too, that we could see some tangible results from our sacrifices. Not only were the other black players on the Dodger team winning acceptance, but other teams started to follow Mr. Rickey's example. Larry Doby became the first black player in the American League, signing on with the Cleveland Indians, and Willard Brown and Henry Thompson had been hired by the St. Louis Browns.

The Dodgers won the pennant that year, and when our club came home in September from a swing across the West, we were joyfully received by our fans. Their enthusiasm for me was so great that I once went into a phone booth to call Rae and was trapped in that phone booth by admirers who let up only when policemen arrived on the scene to liberate me.

Getting a hero's welcome in September made me remember how bad the beginning of my first season with the Dodgers had been. At that time I still wasn't looking like any kind of winner, even though the increasing acceptance of my teammates had begun to help me out of a terrible slump. I seriously wondered if I could ever make the Rickey experiment a success. Both Manager Burt Shotton and Mr. Rickey believed I would eventually come through. Clyde Sukeforth with his quiet confidence helped as much as anybody else.

During the season I was under even greater pressure than in my Montreal days. It was there that I had earned a reputation for stealing bases, and the pressure eased when I began stealing them again. Late in June, in a night game at Pittsburgh, with the score tied 2-2, I kept a careful eye on pitcher Fitz Ostermueller. I noticed he had become a little careless and relaxed. I began dancing off third base. Ostermueller paid me the insult of winding up, ignoring my movements as antics. The pitch was a ball. Easing open my lead off third, I made a bold dash for home plate and slid in safe. That put us in the lead 3-2. It was the winning run of the game. As I ran I heard the exhilarating noise that is the best reward a player can get. The roar of the crowd.

After I made that comeback, I think Mr. Rickey was as happy as I was. He said to some friends at the time, "Wait! You haven't seen Robinson in action yet—not really. You may not have seen him at his best this year at all, or even next year. He's still in his shell. When he comes out for good, he'll be compared to Ty Cobb."

Mr. Rickey's words meant a great deal to me but not as much as something he did. Howie Schultz, the player who had been mentioned as a possible replacement for me during the bad days of my slump, was sold by the club.

That 1947 season was memorable in many ways. Some of the incidents that occurred resulted in far-reaching changes for the club. In late August we played the St. Louis Cardinals. In one of the last games, Enos Slaughter, a Cards outfielder, hit a ground ball. As I took the throw at first from the infielder, Slaughter deliberately went for my leg instead of the base and spiked me rather severely.

It was an act that unified the Dodger team. Teammates such as Hugh Casey of the poker game incident came charging out on the field to protest. The team had always been close to first place in the pennant race, but the spirit shown after the Slaughter incident strengthened our resolve and made us go on to win the pennant. The next time we played the Cards, we won two of the three games.

I had started the season as a lonely man, often feeling like a black Don Quixote tilting at a lot of white windmills. I ended it feeling like a member of a solid team. The Dodgers were a championship team because all of us had learned something. I had learned how to exercise self-control—to answer insults, violence, and injustice with silence and I had learned how to earn the respect of my teammates. They had learned that it's not skin color but talent and ability that counts. Maybe even the bigots had learned that, too.

The press had also changed. When I came up to the majors, the influential *Sporting News* had declared that a black man would find it almost impossible to succeed in organized baseball. At the end of the season, when they selected me as Rookie of the Year, that same publication said:

> That Jackie Roosevelt Robinson might have had more obstacles than his first year competitors, and that he perhaps had a harder fight to gain even major league recognition, was no con-

cern of this publication. The sociological experiment that Robinson represented, the trail-blazing that he did, the barriers he broke down, did not enter into the decision. He was rated and examined solely as a freshman player in the big leagues—on the basis of his hitting, his running, his defensive play, his team value.

Dixie Walker summed it up in a few words the other day when he said: "No other ballplayer on this club with the possible exception of Bruce Edwards has done more to put the Dodgers up in the race than Robinson has. He is everything Branch Rickey said he was when he came up from Montreal."

Rachel and I moved again. She had managed to find more satisfactory living quarters in Brooklyn, where we had our own kitchen and living room and even a guest bedroom. I was delighted when I learned that the man I had admired so much as a youngster, the Reverend Karl Downs, wanted to visit us. I had kept in touch with Karl over the years. Before I'd gone into service, he had left Pasadena to become president of Sam Houston State College in Texas. When I left UCLA, I heard from Karl who said he was on the spot. He needed a coach for his basketball team. There was very little money involved, but I knew that Karl would have done anything for me, so I couldn't turn him down. I went to Texas and took the job but could only stay for a few months before financial pressures caught up with me. When Rachel and I were married, Karl, insisting on paying his own expenses, had set aside all his duties in Texas to fly to Los Angeles and officiate at our wedding. I was delighted by the prospect of his visit to Brooklyn.

One day, during his visit, Karl had come out to see one of the games. Suddenly he felt sick and decided to go back home to rest and wait for us. I had no idea his sickness was serious. That evening when I reached home, Rachel had taken him to the hospital. Several days later, apparently recovered, Karl had returned to Texas. In a few days, he was dead.

Karl's death, in itself, was hard enough to take. But when we learned the circumstances, Rae and I experienced the bitter feeling that Karl Downs had died a victim of racism. We are convinced that Karl Downs would not have died at that time if he had remained in Brooklyn for the operation he required.

When he returned to Texas, Karl went to a segregated hospital to be operated on. As he was being wheeled back from the recovery room, complications set in. Rather than returning his black patient to the operating room or to a recovery room to be closely watched, the doctor in charge let him go to the segregated ward where he died. We believe Karl would not have died if he had received proper care, and there are a number of whites who evidently shared this belief. After Karl's death the doctor who performed the operation was put under such pressure that he was forced to leave town.

Karl Downs ranked with Roy Wilkins, Whitney Young, and Dr. Martin Luther King, Jr., in ability and dedication, and had he lived he would have developed into one of the front line leaders on the national scene. He was able to communicate with people of all colors because he was endowed with the ability to inspire confidence. It was hard to believe that God had taken the life of a man with such a promising future.

I especially missed Karl at the opening day of the 1947 world series. Seventy-five thousand fans, many of whom were black, turned out for that first series game. During the game, the fans were very kind to me, and there was an avalanche of crowd approval in the first inning as I drew a base on balls from Frank Shea and stole second. Pete Reiser hit a ground ball to shortstop and I tried for third, but I was caught in the run down. Fortunately my stops and starts gave Reiser a chance to reach second and, from that position, to score the first run of the game. In that series, our team was the underdog. We were up against that spectacular New York Yankees team that included some of the greats in baseball: Joe DiMaggio, Tommy Henrich, Yogi Berra, Johnny Lindell, Phil Rizzuto, and George McQuinn. We fought hard, but the Yankees were a great baseball club. Even though we lost we still felt we had acquitted ourselves well.

Bill Veeck
VEECK . . . AS IN WRECK

For all the showmanship and publicity that controversial president, owner and operator Bill Veeck (1914–1986) whipped up for his various baseball teams in the majors and minors, he was always committed to a generous vision of the game. After an attempt to buy the Philadelphia Phillies and stock it largely with African-American players, he found himself in 1947 as the general manager of the Cleveland Indians, where he signed Larry Doby, the first black player in the American League. In this excerpt, Veeck recounts his attempt to break the color barrier, and the struggles of Doby, who suffered the same kind of abuse as Jackie Robinson, but without the comfort of being called "The First."

When I signed Larry Doby, the first Negro player in the American League, we received 20,000 letters, most of them in violent and sometimes obscene protest. Over a period of time I answered all. In each answer, I included a paragraph congratulating them on being wise enough to have chosen parents so obviously to their liking. If everyone knew their precious secret, I told them, I was sure everyone would conform to the majority. Until that happy day, I wrote, I was sure they would agree that any man should be judged on his personal merit and allowed to exploit his talents to the fullest, whether he happened to be black, green, or blue with pink dots.

I am afraid irony is lost on these people, but that's not the point I want to make here. A year later, I was a collector for what is now called the Combined Jewish Appeal. This time I got something close to 5,000 violent and sometimes obscene letters. In answering, something very interesting happened. The names began to have a familiar ring. I became curious enough to check our files and I found they were to an astonishing degree—about 95 percent—the same people. A year after that, I converted to Catholicism. About 2,000 anti-Catholics were concerned enough about my soul to write me violent and again often obscene letters. All but a handful of them were already in our anti-Negro and anti-Semitic files.

So I am one man who has documentary proof that prejudice is indivisible. The jackal, after all, doesn't care what kind of animal he sinks his teeth into.

I have always had a strong feeling for minority groups. The pat curbstone explanation would be that having lost a leg myself, I can very easily identify myself with the deprived. Right? Wrong. I had tried to buy the Philadelphia Phillies and stock it with Negro players well before I went into the service. I think we live in a time when we psychoanalyze everybody's motives too much and that it is entirely possible to look at something which is ugly and say "This is ugly" without regard to conditioning, environment or social status. My only personal experience with discrimination is that I am a left-hander in a right-handed world, a subject on which I can become violent.

Thinking about it, it seems to me that all my life I have been fighting against the status quo, against the tyranny of the fossilized majority rule. I would suppose that whatever impels me to battle the old fossils of baseball also draws me to the side of the underdog. I would prefer to think of it as an essential decency. If someone wants to argue the point I won't object, although we'd have a better chance to be friends if he didn't.

Let me make it plain that my Philadelphia adventure was no idle dream. I had made my offer to Gerry Nugent, the president of the fast-sinking club, and he had expressed a willingness to accept it. As far as I knew I was the only bidder. The players were going to be assembled for me by Abe Saperstein and Doc Young, the sports editor of the Chicago *Defender*, two of the most knowledgeable men in the country on the subject of Negro baseball. With Satchel Paige, Roy Campanella, Luke Easter, Monte Irvin, and countless others in action and available, I had not the slightest doubt that in 1944, a war year, the Phils would have leaped from seventh place to the pennant.

I made one bad mistake. Out of my long respect for Judge Landis I felt he was entitled to prior notification of what I intended to do. I was aware of the risk I was taking although, to be honest, I could not see how he could stop me. The color line was a "gentleman's agreement" only. The only way the Commissioner could bar me from using Negroes would be to rule, officially and publicly, that they were "detrimental to baseball." With Negroes fighting in the war, such a ruling was unthinkable.

Judge Landis wasn't exactly shocked but he wasn't exactly overjoyed either. His first reaction, in fact, was that I was kidding him.

The next thing I knew I was informed that Nugent, being in bankruptcy, had turned the team back to the league and that I would therefore have to deal with the National League president, Ford Frick. Frick promptly informed me that the club had already been sold to William Cox, a lumber dealer, and that my agreement with Nugent was worthless. The Phillies were sold to Cox by Frick for about half what I had been willing to pay.

Word reached me soon enough that Frick was bragging all over the baseball world—strictly off the record, of course—about how he had stopped me from contaminating the league. That was my first direct encounter with Mr. Frick.

There is a suspicion, I suppose, that if I tried to buy the Phillies and stock it with Negro players, it was only because, showman that I am—promoter, con man, knave—I was grabbing for the quick and easy publicity and for the quick and easy way to rebuild a hopeless team. I am not going to suggest that I was innocent on either count.

On the other hand, I had no particular feeling about making it either an all-Negro team or not an all-Negro team. The one thing I did know was that I was not going to set up any quota system—a

principle which cost me my original backer. As always, I was operating from a short bankroll. The most obvious backer, it seemed to
me, was the CIO, which had just begun a campaign to organize Negro
workers in the South.

The CIO was ready and eager to give me all the financing I needed.
The money, in fact, was already escrowed when the CIO official I was
dealing with asked for my assurance that there would always be a
mixed team on the field. (I don't like to duck names, but there was a
promise from the beginning of the negotiations that his name would
not enter into any of the publicity.) The only assurance I am willing
to give anybody, ever, is that I will try to put the best possible team
on the field.

I had another potential—and logical—backer, Phillies Cigars, who
had already indicated a willingness to bankroll me. Ford Frick lowered the boom.

What offends me about prejudice, I think, is that it assumes a totally
unwarranted superiority. For as long as I can remember I have felt
vaguely uneasy when anybody tells me an anti-Negro or anti-Semitic
or anti-Catholic joke. It only takes one leg, you know, to walk away.

✣ ✣ ✣

All this is background, a presentation of credentials to the signing of Larry Doby and Satchel Paige. When I came to Cleveland, I
was almost sure I was going to sign a Negro player. We had four or
five Negro friends sending us reports from the beginning. At the
start of the 1947 season, I hired a Negro public relations man, Lou
Jones, so that he could familiarize himself with the league ahead of
time and serve as a companion and a buffer to the player we signed.
I spoke to the Negro leaders of the city and told them I was going to
hold them responsible for policing their own people in case of trouble. (There was nothing for them to be responsible for, of course. We
never had one fight in Cleveland in which a Negro was involved.)

I moved slowly and carefully, perhaps even timidly. It is usually overlooked, but if Jackie Robinson was the ideal man to break the color line, Brooklyn was also the ideal place. I wasn't that sure about Cleveland. Being unsure, I wanted to narrow the target areas as much as possible; I wanted to force the critics to make their attacks on the basis of pure prejudice—if they dared—and not on other grounds. To give them no opportunity to accuse us of signing a Negro as a publicity gimmick, I had informed the scouts that I wasn't necessarily looking for the best player in the Negro leagues but for a young player with the best long-term potential. And I only wanted to sign one Negro because, despite those glowing credentials I have given myself, I felt that I had to be in a position to extricate the club fairly easily in case we ran into too many problems.

The player whose name kept floating to the top was Larry Doby, the second baseman of the Newark Eagles. Still moving with great caution, I told Rudie to have Bill Killifer follow Doby for a few games without leaking what he was doing. Rudie followed instructions so well that he didn't even leak word to Killifer. He just told Bill to go down to Atlanta over the weekend, scout Newark and call us back with a rundown of all their players. Bill, logically enough, arrived in Atlanta under the impression that he was supposed to scout the Newark team in the International League. Upon looking through the paper and seeing that Newark wasn't in town, he did what any sensible man would do at the end of a wild-goose chase. He got stiff.

By the time Rudie tracked him down two days later, the Newark Eagles were in New Orleans. Bill eventually turned in a favorable report on Doby, and I scouted him myself, back in Newark, just before we bought him.

I had always felt that Mr. Rickey had been wrong in taking Jackie Robinson from a Negro club without paying for him. Contract or no, the owner of a Negro club could not possibly refuse to let a player go to the major leagues. It meant too much to the whole race. For anyone to take advantage of that situation, particularly while talking about equal rights, was terribly unfair.

I offered Mrs. Effa Manley, the owner of the Newark club, $10,000 for

Doby's contract, plus an additional $10,000 if he made our team. Effa was so pleased that she told me I could have the contract of her short-stop, who she thought was just as good, for $1,000. Our reports on the shortstop were good too. We had eliminated him because we thought he was too old. To show how smart I am, the shortstop was Monte Irvin.

To make it as easy as possible for Doby, I had decided to make the announcement on the road. Lou Jones picked him up in Newark and brought him to the Congress Hotel in Chicago to meet me and the press. In the taxi, on the way to the park, I told Larry, "If you have any troubles, come and talk them over with me. This is not the usual con, I mean this. It will take some time for the other fellows to get used to you. You have to accept that. You may have to go it alone for awhile. That's why Lou Jones is here."

A couple of the players made their objections known; I found far-away places to send them. Predictably, they were players of little tal-ent and therefore the most threatened economically. Joe Gordon, a club leader, was the player who welcomed Doby with the most open heart and became his friend and confidant. That didn't surprise me at all. Some of the writers disapproved, although not in print and not to me personally. That did surprise me.

In his first day in uniform, July 3, 1947, Doby saw action as a pinch hitter and struck out. During that whole first year, he was a complete bust. The next year, however, when Tris Speaker and Bill McKechnie converted him into a center fielder, Larry began to hit and one of our weak positions suddenly became one of our strongest.

Some of the players who had not seemed overjoyed at having Larry on the team became increasingly fond of him as it became apparent that he was going to help them slice a cut of that World Series money. The economics of prejudice, as I have discovered many times, cuts both ways.

And when Doby hit a tremendous home run to put us ahead in the fourth game of the World Series, it could be observed that none of the 81,000 people who were on their feet cheering seemed at all con-cerned about—or even conscious of—his color.

Doby was as close to me as any player I have ever known, although it took awhile before he would stop in the office to talk over his troubles. I am extremely fond of Larry and of his wife, Helyn, and their children. After all that is said, I have to add, in all honesty, that he was not the best man we could have picked for the first Negro player in the league. I don't say that from the club's point of view, since we could not have won without him, but from his.

Larry had been an all-sports star in Paterson, New Jersey. A local hero. He had never come face-to-face with prejudice until he became a big-leaguer. Prejudice was something he knew existed, something which he had accommodated himself to in his youth if only in the knowledge that it was going to keep him out of organized baseball. He had not been bruised as a human being, though; he had not had his nose rubbed in it. It hit him late in life; it hit him at a time he thought he had it licked; and it hit him hard.

We did not train in Florida. I had moved our training quarters to Arizona, not so much in preparation for Doby as out of an unpleasant experience with the Milwaukee Brewers. The Brewers' regular training headquarters were in Ocala, Florida. Our clubhouse was way out in left field, and the Jim Crow section was between the clubhouse and the edge of the stands. I was rather naïve about segregation. In those day it wasn't really publicized that much, as I suppose many Northern soldiers who took back seats in buses found out.

Being much the same age as most of my players, I would pitch batting practice, go to the clubhouse for a shower and then come out to watch the game. I emerged one day after the game had started, saw a few Negroes sitting in the bleachers and sat down with them, as is my custom, to barber a little as we watched the game.

Within a few minutes, the sheriff came running over to tell me I couldn't sit there.

I said, "I can't? I am . . . Why can't I?"

He told me it was for Negroes only.

I may have been naïve but I wasn't so naïve that I couldn't understand the meaning of a simple declarative sentence. Still, I continued to play it innocently. I said, "I'm not bothering them. I'm enjoying our talk and they don't seem to resent me too much. They won't mind if I stay here."

He kept trying to explain that the rules hadn't been laid down for their benefit, while the people around me, who seemed to be fairly well informed on that point, kept snickering gleefully.

"Well," I said finally, "then you'd better get your deputy and throw me out, because that's the only way I'm going to leave."

"You'd better get out," he said, "or I'll get the mayor."

There was a threat to make the blood run cold.

The mayor came bustling over, in short order. "You read our contract," I told him. "Our contract says we're leasing the ball park and we have sole control over it. As such, I may throw you out."

I got the usual stuff then about a violation of a city ordinance taking precedence over all private contracts.

"I don't know anything about that," I told him. "What I do know is that if you bother me any more we'll move our club out of Ocala tonight. And we'll tell everybody in the country why."

Here *was* a threat to make his blood run cold. We had taken over a little hotel, the Ocala House, for six weeks; if we left, the hotel and the town would both be hurt.

I sat there every day, just to annoy them, without ever being bothered again. Nevertheless, I had already made up my mind to get out of Florida. By arranging for the Giants to come to Arizona with us, I was able to move the next team I had down South, the 1947 Indians, to Tucson.

At Tucson, I discovered, the bleachers weren't segregated but the hotel was. We weren't able to talk the management into allowing Larry to stay with us his first year, although we did make it clear—and they agreed—that in the future they would take all of our players, regardless of race, creed or previous condition of servitude. It was easy enough for me to tell Larry that these things took time. It was true enough to say that we had, after all, broken through one color barrier even if he was going to have to wait a year. It was easy for me, because it was he who was being told to be patient and to wait.

For Larry, it was a bad spring for him all around. In addition to everything else, he wasn't hitting at all. Toward the end of training, Boudreau was beginning to mutter out loud that it might be a good idea to have him spend a year in the minors.

Doby made the team in Houston, our first exhibition game after we broke camp. But that was not a very happy day for him either.

The Giants and Indians were traveling north together, through Texas, with exhibition games scheduled for Houston, Dallas, Fort Worth and a couple of other cities. Knowing that Texas had a law against mixed participation on the field, we protected ourselves—and gave ourselves the leverage we needed to battle back—by booking an alternative schedule through New Mexico and Nevada.

The Texas games were all sellouts long before we arrived, due in some part at least to the attraction of a colored player. Still, as we had anticipated, the state officials threatened to cancel our games if we put Doby on the field. "Fine," we said. "We had a feeling you might say that, so we made an alternative schedule."

Once again, we found little disposition on the part of the promoters to let their racial theories keep them from making a few dollars. The games went on. We had even brought along a couple of extra colored boys from our minor-league teams to make it clear that we intended to play whom we wished.

We'd have done better, I suppose, to have taken the alternative route. It's hard to say. Doby was treated very badly in Houston, beginning with when he couldn't get a cabdriver to take him to the park. When he came to the plate for the first time, he was roundly booed. Larry took one pitch and then he hit what may very well be the longest ball I have ever seen hit in my life and was certainly the longest ball ever hit in Houston. Everybody in the park stood up and cheered as he rounded the bases. Larry hit two home runs, two doubles and a triple that day and made a couple of sensational catches in center field. In every succeeding year, he was greeted in Houston like a favorite son.

But Larry was not a man to shake off those earlier slights and insults that easily. He was always very sensitive. If he wanted to dispute an umpire's call, he would back off and point to the back of his hand, as if to say, "You called that on me because I'm colored."

When he was knocked down, he would sometimes throw his bat out to the mound. There was no doubt, understand, that he was right in thinking he was being thrown at because he was colored. All colored players were thrown at for years, a practice arising from an old coach's tale that Negroes didn't have the guts to come up off the ground and dig back in. It is usually called, with a delicacy unusual in baseball, "taking their power away." (Here, again, notice the rationalization of an economic prejudice. Having drawn the color line, we had to tell ourselves that the Negro, after all, didn't have it in him to make the grade anyway.) Some of them, like Luke Easter, would get up laughing and, as often as not, knock the next pitch out of the park. Larry may have hit the next pitch out of the park, but he wasn't laughing.

It was a very real and bitter and gnawing battle for Larry all the way. He had suffered such a shock that he was possessed by the idea that he had to fight the battle for integration for his kids, Larry Jr. and Christine, so that they would never be bruised as badly as he had been.

Knowing how he felt about it, I'd make sure that when I took him and his family to dinner we would go to a high-class white restaurant—to a far better place, in fact, than I would normally care to go myself.

Unless I'm very much mistaken, it was Larry who broke the color line in the Miami restaurants in the spring of 1955 when I was operating the Miami ball club. Clure Mosher, a television sportscaster, had called to ask me to appear on his show. Doby happened to be in the city for the ballplayers' golf tournament, and so I agreed on condition that all the Dobys would appear with me and that the station would find a good place for us to eat afterwards. Mosher, an ex-All-American football player, was all for it. He reserved a table for us at a very expensive restaurant named "Out of This World." Just in case we ran into any trouble, the station manager, Big Ed Little, who was about 6 foot 6, came along with us. As we entered the restaurant, he was protecting our rear. I was carrying the baby.

We couldn't have spent a more delightful evening. The owner greeted us himself and seated us at a table where we were not overly conspicuous but still visible to everybody in the room. Six or eight parties stopped by as they were leaving, the women as well as the men, just to tell Larry they had enjoyed seeing him play—an indirect way, really, of telling him they were delighted to see him in the restaurant. In every way, we were left with the unmistakable impression that the owner and the customers had been waiting for someone to do what Larry was doing.

It was important to Larry to make this kind of breakthrough, because the problem was always on his mind. Speaking purely about his career as a ballplayer, it was too much on his mind. Not that he wasn't a very good player. He led the league in home runs twice. In 1954, when the Indians won the pennant, he led in both home runs and runs batted in.

With all that, his inner turmoil was such a constant drain on him that he was never able to realize his full potential. Not to my mind, at any rate. If Larry had come up just a little later, when things were just a little better, he might very well have become one of the greatest players of all time.

Jack Johnson

IN THE RING AND OUT

At a time when Confederate veterans were still plentiful and Jim Crow laws were not even necessary given the assumption of black inferiority, boxer Jack Johnson (1878–1946) had the courage to knock out white fighters and marry white women, all to the nation's increasing distress. Here he lays out the difficult road he followed to finally take the heavyweight title.

I chased Burns around the world in order to get him into the ring with me. It was a two-year job. When I finally faced him in Sydney, New South Wales, December 26, 1908, and won the championship, the occasion was a notable one in the history of the prize ring. It was unlike any other event in the boxing world, because it marked the first time that a man of my race had ever won the title. It was the first championship contest ever waged off American soil, and for the first time in ring annals, the promoter of the fight and the manager of one of the contestants served also as referee. My suggestion that Hugh McIntosh serve in the latter capacity was one of the last of countless concessions that I had made in my effort to get at Burns, who had side-stepped me for months, and who had imposed conditions, some of which were almost impossible, and none of which a man less eager than I, would have considered for a moment. I trailed Burns from New York to London, from London to Paris and back, and from London to Australia. Always he made excuses or whenever he did show a willingness to meet me, it was under terms which denied me any possible advantage, and virtually removed every inducement excepting the possibility of gaining the title. I was the object of much ridicule on the part of Burns and his friends and he had openly insulted me so many times by uttering unprintable remarks and by calling me 'yellow,' that, had I met him personally he would have fared worse than he did in the ring at Sydney. But he was careful to avoid a personal meeting and hurled his insults at long range. For many months prior to the fight, there had been much bitterness between us. As the fight approached the tension increased, and a day or two before the ring meeting, came near assuming a rough and tumble clash, when he attempted to hit me with a chair.

My intensive chase after Burns began when I left San Francisco early in 1907, and went to New York, where Burns then was. I sought to arrange a meeting with him for the purpose of discussing a match, but he declined to meet me and soon afterward left for England. In the meantime, I engaged Sam Fitzpatrick as my manager, and we launched our campaign to go after the world title. Hattie McLay had joined me, and financed by her father, she, Fitzpatrick and I took up Burns' trail and followed him to London. He deftly escaped meeting me, but indulged in a lot of ill-flavored remarks and threats concerning me. Soon after my arrival in London, I made several music hall engagements, which kept me so busy that I had little opportunity for training or keeping myself in shape.

Fitzpatrick was busy in planning bouts for me, and despite the unfavorable fighting condition I was in, made a match with Ben Taylor, who was then England's most promising heavy-weight, having defeated every possible contender. This match was based upon the craziest terms under which I ever fought, and in view of the important prospects at stake, I thought Fitzpatrick had suddenly lost his senses. Taylor was in fighting trim and was much heavier than I.

I was in poor shape, yet Fitzpatrick had consented to terms which provided that to win, I must knock Taylor out in ten rounds; that the rounds were to go only two minutes each; and that we should use six-ounce gloves. Had I lost this fight, and there was a chance that I might, it would have meant a sudden end to my theatrical engagements, for I would have ceased to be an attraction. Furthermore it would have placed me in a class which would have prevented serious consideration of me as a contender for the title.

There was nothing for me to do but abide by Fitzpatrick's silly arrangements and I entered the ring with Taylor with my chance at the championship at stake. Fortunately, I was able to comply with the terms and knocked Taylor out in the eighth round. Hardly had I finished this fight when Fitz had another ready for me. It was Fred Drummond* whom I beat in a fairly fast go at Plymouth. The results of these fights were to raise me considerably in the esteem of the British public, which began to sit up and take more notice of me. The press and boxing authorities, if they ever had favored Burns, now became more friendly toward me, and recognized my claim on the privilege of meeting Burns, and backed me in those claims, taking occasion to direct much severe criticism upon the title holder.

I filled a few more theatrical engagements in London and Paris, while Burns left for Australia. I did not linger long in England, for my quarry having flitted, it was necessary for me to resume the pursuit. Accordingly, my party and I also set sail for Australia, where I eventually cornered Burns and arranged for our fight. It was my second visit to the Antipodes, and there were many friends to greet me. On my first visit, I had polished off Felix and Lang, two Australian fighting boys who were well thought of. This had won for me the respect of boxing enthusiasts, but there were not many who believed I had a chance with Burns, who was a prime favorite, because on two occasions he had knocked out Bill Squires, another Australian, who at one time had been a seven-days' wonder to the kangaroos. Because of his

*No record exists of this alleged bout.

two defeats of Squires, Burns was considered unbeatable and was the prime betting favorite, the average odds against me being two to one.

In addition to Burns' popularity, and the belief that I could not defeat him, the rumor became prevalent that there was some crooked work abroad; that it was framed that I should lose, and that I was not to have a fair chance in the ring. These rumors helped sustain the betting odds, and friends and others who really believed I could whip Burns, bet their money on my opponent in the belief that the decision would go against me, despite whatever showing I made. I felt too, that there was something astir and knew that I should have to watch my step in the selection of the referee. This was no pleasant combination of circumstances under which to contest for the championship in a strange country, but I was determined that nothing would prevent me from going through, because I already had sacrificed most of the usual rights and privileges accorded a challenger, and had agreed to accept a trivial sum of money—$5,000 whether I won or lost, while Burns was to get $35,000 win or lose.

My, but I did train for that fight! My training camp was at Botany bay, and in my camp were Duke Mullins, chief adviser and second; Bobby Bryant, Leo O'Donnell, Rudolph Unholz, the Walker brothers, Jack and George, and other boxers, all of whom served me well as sparring partners, seconds and general aids. My condition was superb. I do not recall another pre-fight period in my life when I felt better or was more fit to enter the ring. My lungs were in especially fine condition, and no matter how strenuously I exerted myself it seemed that I never got winded. Although we were engaged in the serious business of preparing to fight the world champion, we had a gay time at that camp, and indulged in strange and at times rather frivolous amusements. We performed stunts that amazed the Australians and caused them to shake their heads as if they doubted our sanity.

In two of these stunts, I was the sole performer, and the manner in which I performed indicated the excellent condition of my breathing equipment. Half in jest, I had wagered with some of my friends that I could outrun a kangaroo. The wager was taken and it was up to me to back my assertion. Accordingly, we stirred up a kangaroo and the chase began. These animals, it is generally known, are able to cover distance with ease and the one with which I raced was no exception. How far I chased him, I do not know. Both of us were developing high speed, and each was determined to endure, but the poor kangaroo finally gave up and toppled over dead. He had completely exhausted all his strength and vitality. As for me, I was little the worse for the chase.

On another occasion, a greased razor-back pig was turned loose for me to catch. He was a long, tall and lanky member of his species, built like a race horse. Furthermore, he was undomesticated and valued his liberty exceedingly high. He had no wish to be coddled and manifested a rather vicious nature. Once turned loose, he endeavored to put as much space as possible between himself and mankind. But as speedy as he was, he was unable to out-run me. After a pursuit that included many turns, twists and other maneuvers, I grasped his oily body, and despite his struggles subdued him.

Imitating hounds in speed and cunning, Duke Mullins, Bobby Bryant and myself ran a jack-rabbit to death. These rodents are considered about the last word in animal speed and are used in Australia in hound chases. Our race with the rabbit took place on a half-mile dog racing track within an enclosure. The rabbit was turned loose with the three of us in pursuit. Our victim resorted to all his clever tricks in eluding his enemies, and traveled so fast at times that he looked like a streak, but he was not clever nor fast enough to escape us, although he ran until he fell exhausted.

These are not imaginary tales but are actual occurrences and were reported in the Sydney newspapers. These and other events at my camp were a source of much discussion among Sydney folk and because of the unusual things which we did in the course of enjoying ourselves, attracted many people daily to our camp, wondering what we would do next. They got a lot of entertainment out of it and my friends and acquaintances increased in number. Most of my training was done in the early morning. I did lots of road work but comparatively little boxing, giving my attention largely to ball and bag punching. This method of training also caused the Australians to marvel. They were not accustomed to such procedure. They were certain that I was not training properly and that I was most neglectful. They were convinced that I could not possibly be in shape for the fight, and this belief having gained circulation, also added to the conviction that Burns would have the best of me.

I never was sure of getting Burns into the ring until I faced him inside of the rope. After the fight agreement was signed and our training camps were established, Burns continued his old tactics of sidestepping and making excuses. He was not satisfied with the terms of the contract, even after he signed them. He had many complaints to make, and persisted in opposing various details of arrangements for the fight. I expected him to call the fight off any day. I myself remained silent and either ignored his objections or consented to measures that would remove them, so eager was I to insure his presence in the ring at the appointed time. I do not exaggerate when I say it was almost necessary to drag him into the ring, but once in the ring he was a game and determined fighter and he took the punishment I gave him gamely and tried hard to defend his title.

The fight was the greatest ever held in Australia. Twenty-five thousand spectators attended, thousands of them having formed in line twenty-four hours before the fight began in order to get seats. Although in the midst of strangers, many of whom were semi-hostile toward me, I was not in the least perturbed. I felt no doubt of the outcome, and had I not intended to give the crowd its money's worth, I could have finished Burns in the first few rounds. Then, too, I figured that Burns had something coming to him, and I proposed to extend his punishment over a considerable length of time. I certainly wished to give him his $35,000 worth. He found out after the first few blows that he was done for, but he kept coming, and I heartily commend him for his gameness. His blows had no strength and I do not recall that they as much as stung me. Certainly he never jarred me. I hit him at will, whenever I wished, but I never exerted my whole power on him.

In addition to his gameness Burns fought cleanly. Neither of us used any foul or tricky tactics, which made it easy for the inexperienced and somewhat nervous referee. Once or twice he tried to separate us in the clinches, but lacking the strength for such effort, he gave it up and left us to work out of them of our own accord. Once in a clinch, he grabbed my wrist, which enabled Burns to land a blow on my face, but since it did not hurt me I made no complaint. Burns on the contrary complained many times and frequently appealed to the referee. My defense completely baffled Burns. I led brisk lefts and rights to his body and face, and administered an awful punishment to him.

I found my opponent easier than I had anticipated. I kept up a continual conversation with Burns and with those at the ring side, as I usually do in the ring. Once with my hands at my side, I extended my chest and chin inviting Burns to hit me. I made openings for him and called his attention to them. 'Find that yellow streak,' I told him. 'You have had much to say about it; now uncover it.' At first, Burns tried to answer my sallies, but he soon desisted, his remarks being scarcely audible.

The intervals between rounds gave me a chance to scan the crowd and pick out unusual types of faces, or watch the changing expressions that flitted across the countenances of the spectators as they concentrated their attention on us. I even had opportunity to examine the outlying landscape and the immediate structure around the ring. As my gaze wandered out into the surrounding territory, I saw a colored man sitting on a fence watching the fight with open mouth and bulging eyes. My glance returned to him again and again. He was one of the very few colored people present, and he became a sort of landmark for me. I became more and more interested in him, and soon discovered that mentally, he was fighting harder than I was.

Whenever I unlimbered a blow, he, too, shot one into the air landing it on an imaginary antagonist at about the same spot where I
landed on Burns. When I swayed to avert a blow from Burns, the
fighter on the fence also swayed in the same direction and at a similar angle. When I ducked he also ducked. But his battle came to an
inglorious end when it was necessary for me to make an unusually
low duck. He attempted to follow the movement and fell off the
fence. This incident so amused me that I laughed heartily, and Burns
and the spectators were at a loss to know what had so aroused my
mirth. Jack London, the late story writer, and Mrs. London were
ring-side spectators and I think it was at this time that London got
the idea of the golden smile with which he often described me later
and which was so frequently mentioned in after years.

In the ninth and tenth rounds Burns was in a bad way. It would
have been easy to have disposed of him, but so long as he invited
more punishment I ladled it out to him as thick as he could stand it
without going under. I eased up considerably in the last rounds, but
in the fourteenth I decided to put an end to it. Just as I stepped
out with this intention, I caught the eye of the police inspector. He
had said nothing, but I felt that he was going to and I desisted from
any further attack on Burns. I was not mistaken about the inspector's intention. 'This has gone far enough,' he said, and the fight
came to an end. I had gained the title of champion of the world.

Friends and acquaintances, many of whom had lost money on
Burns because of their fears that the fight would be unfair to me,
swarmed upon me as I left the ring and poured forth their congratu-
lations. Burns' friends helped him from the ring and hurried him to
a doctor. I had suffered no discomforts in the bout and there was
scarcely a scratch on me. After leaving my dressing room, I took a
plunge in the surf, followed it up with a motor drive, and that
evening entertained friends at dinner.

It was virtually necessary for me to wage two ring battles before I established undisputed claim to the championship. My fight with Burns really gave me the title, for he was the recognized champion. When I acquired his laurels, the question suddenly arose as to whether or not Burns was the champion. It was stoutly declared by some that Jeffries was the champion, because he actually had not lost the title in the ring, merely having voluntarily relinquished it to Hart, who had been defeated by Burns. It was upon this basis that Burns claimed the championship, and it never was questioned until I established my claim. At any rate I was not permitted to rest secure in the title. I was constantly harassed and criticized. Those who conceded, but resented my rightful claim to the title, started a turmoil by hunting a 'white hope' or one who would regain the title for the white race.

This hunt was a long and bitter one. All kinds of condemnation was heaped upon me—originating from no other cause than that I was not white. A large proportion of the public, or that part interested in boxing, at least, insisted that Jeffries still was the champion and that I must defeat him if I wished to retain the belt. I did not object to this proposal. I was willing to defend my claims against any man in the world. I lent my efforts and willingness to arrange a bout with Jeffries.

Babe Didrikson Zaharias

THIS LIFE I'VE LED

In an age of Mia Hamm and the WNBA, the wide-ranging adventures and triumphs of Babe Didrikson Zaharias (1914–1956), once considered the greatest female athlete ever, may seem quaint—here Babe tells how she won the 1932 AAU Track and Field meet as a one-woman team. But her domination of women's sports and her constant drive for success and excellence established for many the possibility that women could play the same games as men.

O nce when I was playing in the Celebrities Golf Tournament in Washington a few years ago, they put me on a program with Hildegarde the singer. We were up there at the microphone talking, and she said, "Babe, I can't understand why I don't hit a golf ball as far as you do. It seems to me I swing my club the same way."

I said, "Hildegarde, it's not enough just to swing at the ball. You've got to loosen your girdle and really let the ball have it!"

That line has probably been quoted as much as anything I ever said, although when writers have used it since, they've generally had me saying it to the reporters right after winning some big tournament or other. The stories about me sometimes get a little tall in the telling.

Anyway, that girdle crack was meant as a gag, and yet there was a lot of truth in it. My main idea in any kind of competition always has been to go out there and cut loose with everything I've got. I've always had the confidence that I was capable of winning out.

One time I really needed my confidence was when Employers Casualty sent me up to Chicago as a one-girl track team for those combined 1932 national championships and Olympic tryouts. The meet was being held at Dyche Stadium, the Northwestern University field, which is in Evanston, just outside Chicago.

I never can recite all the details of my performance that afternoon without checking the record book, but I can tell you everything that happened the night before in my hotel room in Chicago. I couldn't sleep. I kept having severe pains in my stomach. When I put my hand on it, the hand would just bounce up and down.

Mrs. Henry Wood was chaperoning me. She was our "team mother" at Employers Casualty. Naturally she wasn't doing any sleeping either, the way I was tossing around. She got worried and called the hotel doctor. She was afraid I might be coming down with an appendicitis attack or something.

The doctor came and examined me. He said, "There's nothing wrong with her. She's just all excited. The excitement is affecting the nerve center in her diaphragm." And that's what it was. I've found out since that whenever I get all keyed up like that before an event, it means I'm really ready.

We finally did fall asleep around dawn. And then we overslept. When we woke up, there was barely time for us to get ourselves ready and make it out to Evanston for the start of the meet.

We got down to the front of the hotel as quick as we could, and jumped into a taxicab. But when we told the driver we wanted to go to Dyche Stadium, he wouldn't take us. He said he just operated in Chicago.

So we got out of that cab and tried another one. This driver agreed to go to Evanston. What with the traffic and everything, though, it began to look like there wouldn't be time for me to dress out at the field. There was only one way we could make sure. Mrs. Wood held up a blanket around me and I changed into my track suit while we were riding along in the cab.

In spite of all those difficulties, it was one of those days in an athlete's life when you know you're just right. You feel you could fly. You're like a feather floating in air. I wasn't worried about the fact that of the ten individual events on the program I was entered in eight, including a couple I'd hardly ever done before, the shot put and the discus throw. I was going to be in everything but the fifty-yard and 220-yard dashes.

Mrs. Wood and I just did get there in time for the opening ceremonies. They announced each team over the loudspeaker, and then the girls on that team would run out on the track and get a hand. There were over 200 girls there. Some of those squads had fifteen or more girls. The Illinois Women's Athletic Club had twenty-two.

It came time to announce my "team." I spurted out there all alone, waving my arms, and you never heard such a roar. It brought out goose bumps all over me. I can feel them now, just thinking about it.

Some of the events that afternoon were Olympic trials. Others were just National A.A.U. events. But they all counted in the team point scoring. So they were all important to me if I was going to bring back the national championship for Employers Casualty.

For two-and-a-half hours I was flying all over the place. I'd run a heat in the eighty-meter hurdles, and then I'd take one of my high jumps. Then I'd go over to the broad jump and take a turn at that. Then they'd be calling for me to throw the javelin or put the eight-pound shot.

Well, there were several events I didn't figure to do too much in. One was the 100-meter dash, and I drew a blank there, although I just missed qualifying for the finals. I was edged out for third place in my semifinal heat.

But that was the only thing I got shut out in. Even in the discus, which wasn't a specialty of mine at all, I placed fourth to pick up an extra point. And I actually won the shot put, which was a big surprise. A girl named Rena MacDonald was supposed to be the best woman shot putter, but I beat her out with a throw of thirty-nine feet, six-and-a quarter inches.

I won the championship in the baseball throw for the third straight year. My distance was 272 feet, two inches. Then in three Olympic trial events I broke the world's record. In two of them it was a case of beating a record that I already held myself. I threw the javelin 139 feet, three inches, which was nearly six feet better than my old mark of 133 feet, five and-a-half inches. I won an eighty-meter hurdle heat in 11.9 seconds, a tenth of a second faster than my previous mark. In the finals of the eighty-meter hurdles I didn't do quite that well, but my time of 12.1 seconds was good enough to win.

In the high jump I was competing against a very fine specialist, Jean Shiley. When everybody had been eliminated except us two, they moved the bar up just a fraction above the world's record, held by a Dutch girl, Fraulein M. Gisolf. She'd cleared five feet, three-and-one-eighth inches. Now they had Jean Shiley and me try it at five feet, three-and three-sixteenths inches. Jean and I both got over. Neither of us could make it any higher that day, so we wound up in a first-place tie.

When I came off the field at the end of the afternoon, all puffing and sweating, Mrs. Wood was so happy and excited she was crying. She said, "You did it! You did it! You won the meet all by yourself!"

Colonel McCombs had that track meet doped out just about right. Of the eight events I entered, I placed in seven. I won five of them outright, and tied for first in a sixth. I scored a total of thirty points, which was plenty to win the national championship for Employers Casualty. The Illinois Women's Athletic Club was second with twenty-two points.

George Kirksey, who covered the meet for the United Press, said it was "the most amazing series of performances ever accomplished by any individual, male or female, in track and field history." Other sportswriters were saying the same sort of thing. This was when that stuff about me being a "super athlete" and a "wonder girl" started up.

Some friends took Mrs. Wood and me out that night, and we

danced until three o'clock in the morning. If I'm not mistaken, I had myself a workout the next day, to make sure that my muscles didn't tighten up or anything. I didn't need any rest in those days. I was just an eighteen-year-old kid. It got different later on, what with my cancer operation in 1953 and the back trouble I developed in the spring of 1955 and everything.

I've come back and won my share of golf tournaments, but a lot of the time recently I've felt I'd rather be at home with my husband, George Zaharias, working around the new house we built in Tampa, Florida.

George is the business head of the family, and for a while there he wasn't sure whether we should build. Then one morning at five o'clock, here's my big bear of a husband shaking me awake. "Honey," he says, "I've been thinking it over. You can have your house."

Anyway, winning that 1932 national-championship track meet singlehanded was the thing that first made my name big—that and the Olympic Games that followed. There were only five individual track and field events for women on the Olympic program that year. I was in three of them, which was the most they would allow one person to enter. I was in the javelin, the hurdles and the high jump.

The Olympics were held in Los Angeles a couple of weeks after the tryouts. We went out there in advance to start training. Mrs. Wood came back to Dallas with the trophies I'd won in Chicago, while I got on a train for Los Angeles with the other girls who had made the Olympic team.

I wasn't getting to sail across the ocean, the way I'd dreamed of doing when I first heard about the Olympic Games back in 1928. But a trip to Chicago, and then to Los Angeles, was almost the same as going overseas to me. I was as thrilled as any kid could be.

On the train going out, most of the girls sat around watching the scenery and playing cards and gabbing. I was busy taking exercises and doing my hurdle bends and stuff. I'd practice in the aisle. Several times a day I'd jog the whole length of the train and back. People in the other cars took to calling out, "Here she comes again!"

Other girls would say to me, "Why don't you take it easy for a while?" But I'd had my heart set on being in these Olympics for a long time. I wanted to be sure I was in shape now that I was finally getting there.

We had a stopoff in Denver so everybody could get off the train and work out. I was looking forward to seeing "The Mile High City." I was very young then, and hadn't been around much. I didn't realize the slogan came from the fact that Denver is a mile above sea level. It sounds silly now, but I expected to see a city that was built a mile up in the air.

They took us to a stadium there in Denver, and everybody went through their paces. I couldn't understand why I kept getting winded much quicker than I usually did. They explained to me that it was the effect of the high altitude. Years later Denver became my home for several years, and I found out that the altitude made a difference in the kitchen too. On a lot of dishes you couldn't go by the cooking times the ordinary recipe book called for. You had to make adjustments for that thinner air.

From Denver we went straight on to Los Angeles, and settled down there for regular workouts. The coach of the Olympic women's track and field squad was a man named George Vreeland. He wanted to improve my form in some of the events. Going over the hurdles, I bent my front leg more than you were supposed to, on account of having practiced over those hedges back home. And I didn't throw the javelin quite the way they said you should.

But I told the coach I was sorry, I wasn't going to change. My own coach, Colonel McCombs, had told me I should stick to my natural style. And I know today that he was right. There's no one way to do anything in athletics. You have to find the way that works best for you.

I don't believe Mr. Vreeland was too happy about my refusing to take any new instruction from him. But he accepted the situation. And he did say he admired my loyalty to the teachings of my coach.

While I was out there I got to meet a number of the Hollywood stars I'd seen on the screen. There was Clark Gable—he could really keep you laughing. And I spent some time with Will Rogers too. He was another wonderful fellow. Then there was Janet Gaynor and Norma Shearer and Norma Talmadge and Joe E. Brown.

It was a wonderful thrill to march into the Olympic Stadium in the parade on opening day, Monday, August first. To tell you the truth, though, I couldn't enjoy the ceremonies much after we got out there. We all had to wear special dresses and stockings and white shoes that the Olympic Committee had issued to us. I believe that was about the first time I'd ever worn a pair of stockings in my life; I was used to anklets and socks. And as for those shoes, they were really hurting my feet.

We had to stand there in a hot sun for about an hour and a quarter while a lot of speeches and things went on. My feet were hurting more and more. Pretty soon I slipped my feet out of my shoes. Then another girl did. By the end I think everybody had their shoes off.

They also issued us track shoes, but there I got permission to wear my own, which were all broken in and fitted me just right.

I was in the javelin throw that first day, and it didn't get started until late afternoon. Shadows were coming up over the stadium, and it was turning pretty cool. We all got out there to warm up. I was watching the German girls, because they were supposed to be the best javelin throwers. I could see that they'd been taught to loosen up by throwing the spear into the ground. I'd been told myself that this was the way to practice, but I never could agree. It seemed to me that this gave you the wrong motion. You'd feel a tug that wasn't right. I always thought you should warm up with the same swing you used in competition.

There were too many of us around for me to risk throwing any spears up into the air the way I wanted to. Rather than have no warm-up at all, I thought I'd practice that other way, throwing the javelin into the ground. I tried it, and I almost put it in a German girl's leg. I decided I'd better stop.

The event started. They had a little flag stuck in the ground out there to show how far the Olympic record was. It was a German flag, because a German girl had set the record. It was some distance short of my own world's record.

When my first turn came, I was aiming to throw the javelin right over that flag. I drew back, then came forward and let fly. What with the coolness and my lack of any real warm-up, I wasn't loosened up properly. As I let the spear go, my hand slipped off the cord on the handle.

Instead of arching the way it usually did, that javelin went out there like a catcher's peg from home plate to second base. It looked like it was going to go right through the flag. But it kept on about fourteen feet past it for a new Olympic and world's record of 143 feet, four inches.

In practice I'd made throws of close to 150 feet. Nobody knew it, but I tore a cartilage in my right shoulder when my hand slipped making that throw. On my last two turns, people thought I wasn't trying, because the throws weren't much good. But they didn't have to be. My first throw stood up to give me the gold medal for first place. A German girl, E. Braumiller, who was the defending Olympic champion in the event, came within nine inches of equaling me to place second. Another German girl, T. Fleischer, was third.

Two days later we had the qualifying heats for the eighty-meter hurdles. The Olympic record here was 12.2 seconds. The world's record, which I had set only a couple of weeks before in Evanston, was 11.9 seconds. I beat both those marks in winning my heat in 11.8 seconds.

The finals of the eighty-meter hurdles followed the next day, a Thursday. I was so anxious to set another new record that I jumped the gun, and they called us all back. Now in Olympic competition, if you jump the gun a second time they disqualify you. I didn't want that to happen, so I held back on the next start until I saw everybody taking off. It wasn't until the fifth hurdle that I caught up, and I just did beat out Evelyne Hall of Chicago. If it was horse racing, you'd say I won by a nose. Even with the late start, I set another new record with a time of 11.7 seconds.

Now all I needed was to win the high jump the next day to make a clean sweep of my three events. The high jump turned into another contest between Jean Shiley and myself, like the one we'd had in the Olympic tryouts. Both of us were better this day than we'd ever been. The cross bar moved up to five feet, five inches, which was nearly two inches higher than the record Jean and I had set in Evanston. We both cleared it. Now I'd beaten the world's record in all three of my Olympic events.

But there was still first place to be settled between Jean and myself. Since we were jumping off a tie, it was on a basis of one try only. They raised the bar another three-quarters of an inch. Jean Shiley gave it a real effort, but just missed getting across.

I took my turn. I went into my Western roll, kicking up and rolling over. I just soared up there. I felt like a bird. I could see that bar several inches beneath me as I went across. I was up around five-ten, higher than I had ever been, and it was a sensation like looking down from the top of the Empire State building. And then as I hit the ground, the bar came down after me.

Grantland Rice, who kept featuring me in his stories before and during the Olympics, described what happened this way. "There was a wild shout as Miss Didrikson cleared the cross bar by at least four inches. It was the most astonishing jump any woman ever dreamed about. But luck was against her. As the Babe fluttered to earth her left foot struck the standard a glancing blow, just six inches from the ground—and the cross bar toppled into the dust with her."

So they dropped the bar down to five feet, five-and-a-quarter inches to give us one last chance to break our first-place tie. Well, my Western roll was a little confusing to the judges. They weren't used to seeing it, especially with women jumpers. And the Western roll had to be performed just right to conform with the high-jump rules of the day. Your feet had to cross the bar first. If your head went over first, then it was a "dive" and didn't count.

We took our last jumps. Jean Shiley made hers this time. I made mine too. Then all of a sudden the judges disallowed my jump. They ruled that I had dived. Today it wouldn't matter which part of me went over first. You're allowed to get over the bar any way you possibly can, as long as you take off from the ground on one foot. But back there in 1932, the rule cost me my first-place tie.

There was a picture taken of that jump, and I think it proves my feet actually went over just ahead of the rest of me. I'd been jumping exactly the same way all afternoon—and all year, for that matter. I told the judges so, but they said, "If you were diving before, we didn't see it. We just saw it this time."

Up in the press box Grantland Rice could tell what was happening. He talked to me right afterwards, and said he thought I'd been given a bad deal. So did some of the other writers. That made me feel a little better about winding up in second place.

Then Grantland Rice gave me something new to think about. He invited me to play golf with him and some sportswriter friends out at the Brentwood Country Club. I was almost more excited about that than I had been about the Olympics themselves.

Jesse Owens

JESSE

While much of the history of black athletes in the twentieth century has been a part of

the story of the African-American struggle for equal rights, Jesse Owens's (1913–1980)

four gold medals at the 1936 Berlin Olympics stand for a global vision of human rights.

By beating the best of Aryan youth, Owens represented the rest of the world, all of us

outcasts from perfection because of our individuality. But Owens's victories were not

ultimately his greatest triumph; it was the generous, brotherly spirit with which he won,

as seen in this excerpt from his autobiography, that finally sets him apart.

I f I wasn't up to getting down on my knees and praying on the ship, showing in public what I believed seemed to be even more out of the question once I'd left the ship and arrived in Berlin. It was a godless city. Oh, there must have been some who believed, who secretly didn't go along with Hitler's ideas that he and his atheistic master race were superior to the rest of the world—but I and no one else would ever know it because they'd have to keep it secret. For some, though, it was impossible to keep their beliefs hidden. The Jewish people, for example, were known to have their own firm and devout religion. Before another Olympiad would ever take place, millions of them would be put to death by the German dictator for that religion.

But during the 1936 Olympics, Hitler had an even better target than the Jews—the United States Olympic team. First, a big part of

Hitler's superiority idea was that his Nazis should rule not just because they were better and smarter, but because they were stronger and healthier. Though Hitler himself was short, dark, and anything but athletic-looking, he constantly talked of his "tall, blond, blue-eyed, Aryan supermen." Every newspaper was filled with his braggings of how the German Olympic team would prove him correct by "vanquishing the inferior Americans."

But when Hitler said "inferior Americans," he meant more than that. Our track and field squad—and the running and jumping events seemed to get more publicity than all the other sports put together—in 1936 happened to be made up mostly of Negro stars. My buddy, Dave Albritton, was there. So was Ralph Metcalfe and others. And all of us came from pretty much the same background— Southern poor, physical laboring, God fearing. We were everything Hitler hated. Other people—the Jews, Poles, and all the others Hitler—hungered to have abjectly kneeling at his feet—at least didn't have their beliefs written on their very skins.

But, in particular, Hitler hated my skin. For I happened to have been the one who had set world records in the 100- and 200-yard dashes less than a year before, and had been dubbed "the world's fastest human" because of it. Even more, I happened to have broken the world broad-jump record by more than half a foot. Much before I was ever in the headlines, Hitler's critics outside of Germany—none was left inside—had challenged him to point to one person who was the super-strong, super-smart, super-everything Aryan superman. Hitler would have his henchmen answer that he was raising a race of his Aryan armies. But now, newspapermen from all over the world were asking him, "Who have you got to beat Jesse Owens?"

I wanted no part of politics. And I wasn't in Berlin to compete against any one athlete The purpose of the Olympics, anyway, was to do your best. As I'd learned long ago from Charles Riley, the only victory that counts is the one over yourself.

But Adolf Hitler wouldn't allow me that. He made the victory over myself and victory over another man one and the same when, finally, after years of being asked who was the supreme example of his Aryan superman, Hitler answered with a name.

Luz Long was that name.

It came as a shock to me that Hitler would name anybody. I'd heard of Long, of course. The Germans didn't let the rest of the world know exactly what their athletes were doing, so I had no idea how good he was. But there was no doubt that he was good. Our team had also heard that Hitler was keeping some super-athlete under wraps completely for the games. Obviously, Long was the one. I wondered what he looked like. And could he be the superman that Hitler claimed? One thing I did know: Luz Long had been groomed his entire life for this Olympiad, and for only a single event in it. The broad jump.

It was about fifteen minutes after I first set foot in Berlin's huge stadium on a muggy, August day, when I felt a strange, ominous chill run through me as my eyes scanned the athletes from other countries and then stopped cold on one who was wearing the German uniform. I knew it was Luz Long. And he indeed was a supreme example of Aryan perfection. Taller than I was by an inch, maybe two, the blue-eyed, sandy-haired Long was one of those rare athletic happenings you come to recognize after years in competition—a perfectly proportioned body, every lithe but powerful cord a celebration of pulsing natural muscle, stunningly compressed and honed by tens of thousands of obvious hours of sweat and determination. He may have been my archenemy, but I had to stand there in awe and just stare at Luz Long for several seconds.

Yet when he walked over to the broad-jump area to take a practice leap I knew—though it was the last thing I wanted to admit to myself—that he had the competitive spirit to match his body. Long didn't jump. He exploded with such an intensity, yet such ease. I was suddenly reminded of the race horses Charles Riley had taken me to see.

Long landed, laughing. One of the jumpers from another country came up to me. "You're lucky this is practice," he said matter-of-factly. "If they were measuring what that German did, it might be a new record."

And it might have been.

And, soon, too soon, they were measuring.

And for the first time in years I was falling short.

The broad-jump trials gave each athlete three tries to make a qualifying distance of 24 feet, 6 inches. I hadn't gone less than a foot further than that, practice or otherwise, for two years. And my first jump went much more than a foot further.

But I fouled.

In my eagerness to show Luz Long what I had, I'd been careless about measuring my steps to the take-off board. I'd gone over it.

Forget it, I said to myself. *You've fouled before. There are still two jumps left.*

I told myself that, but I didn't believe it. Second by second, home seemed farther away. Much more than the 6,000 miles. I wanted to be here, in Berlin, in the Olympics, but it wasn't my turf. It was Luz Long's turf. He was safe here. I was safe in Cleveland. Even in Oakville. Was poverty so bad after all? You didn't starve and at least it was familiar. That kind of empty stomach was a lot better than this kind— the kind I felt now—strange empty—the kind you knew wouldn't be filled at six o'clock dinner—the kind nothing would fill—

Stop thinking those thoughts! I screamed silently to myself. It took a few more unheard shouts, but I finally got myself together. I overcame the impulse to really fly. Instead, I measured my steps with absolute precision. Once. Then again. And as I jumped, when my name was finally called after all the waiting, I didn't try to break any records or outdo Luz Long. I tried just to qualify. That's all I wanted—just to get into the finals, and have three jumps again.

And I fell short by three inches. I was almost in a state of shock.

I had jumped less than twenty-five feet. I hadn't done that since since high school.

I put on my sweatshirt and tried to get off by myself. The reporters were buzzing around me like locusts. The press had always been good to me, and I tried to be as good as I could in return, but all my nerves now were like open wounds with each question cutting deeper and deeper. Finally, I'd answered their questions the best I could and they'd all gone to file their stories. All except one. He was an American writer I'd gotten to know pretty well.

"Jesse, off the record," he said when we were alone, "is it true about Hitler?"

"Is what true?"

"That he walked out of the stadium on you. Look—" The reporter pointed to Hitler's plush box in the first row center. It was glaringly empty. For a second I didn't know what to say. "I don't know," was all I could answer.

"That's what I heard, anyway," he said. "Anyhow, I'm going to file the story—won't quote you, though. It was right before your first practice jump. Saw it myself. Then I asked a couple of the German athletes, and they said that Hitler had made some vow not to look at you in action. Crazy?"

I nodded. But without much conviction. Was he crazy? I had just one jump left. And almost no time to get ready for it. The broad-jump preliminaries came before the finals of the other three events I was in—the 100-meter and 200-meter dashes, and the relay. How I did in the next ten minutes with this one remaining chance was, I knew, how I would do in the entire Olympics.

And, somehow, I sensed, in life itself.

What if I—I stopped myself from thinking it time and again, but it kept crashing through my mind—what if—what if—what if I didn't qualify? Hitler won't look so crazy, then. . . .

I fought, fought hard, harder . . . but, one cell at a time, panic crept into my body, taking me over. Any minute now—maybe any second—my name would be called for the final jump. I looked at Hitler's box. Empty. His way of saying that Jesse Owens was inferior. Around that box, filling every seat, were a hundred thousand Germans. All wanting Luz Long to beat me. And there laughing in a carefree way near the broad-jump pit, was Luz Long. He had only had to take one preliminary jump. Because he'd broken the Olympic record with it. Was he a superman? Even that idea began invading me.

I shook my body like an animal does to shake off water and walked back to the broad-jump area and, as I did, I heard a name called. Mine. Had to get ready because, after the man about to jump had jumped, it would be my turn. I glanced over at him. He was from England or France, I think, the champion of his own country, but he hadn't qualified in his first two jumps, either. And he probably wouldn't make it on this one.

I closed my eyes—didn't want to see him. Because I wasn't really seeing him, I was seeing myself. I heard the familiar sounds of his feet moving quickly toward the runway, the hush as he went up in the air, the disappointed murmurs when he came down far short.

Now it was my turn.

I opened my eyes, closed them once again. *I have to find strength somewhere, I said to myself. Have to reach into myself and find the strength to make it, to do my best.*

But there was nothing inside. I could find nothing. I was back in Oakville, except that this time I wasn't starting out in life, no matter how low, I was back there, ending up. I'd reached for the top, and fallen all the way to the bottom. Lower than I'd ever been, so low I'd never be able to get up again.

No.

No.

I can't let it happen. I can't—

But how? What? If I jumped with all my might, I'd foul. If I played it safe, I wouldn't go far enough. I've already lost. There's no way—

I must find a way.

Must.

Almost instinctively, I dropped down to my knees. *Pray. Must pray*, I whispered to myself.

But in front of a hundred thousand people?

"Jesse Owens!" It was the loudspeaker announcing my name for the second time.

I closed my eyes, one of my knees touching the ground. I must pray.

But what will they all think of me? *l must pray.*

Can't—

Must—

Can't—

But I must. Oh, God, I pleaded wordlessly with everything that was inside me. *Help me to pray. God, help me—*

But I couldn't. Couldn't.

"Jesse Owens!" They were calling my name for the last time. I had to get up, jump. But I hadn't prayed.

"Jazze Owenz!" Suddenly I felt a hand on my shoulder. It wasn't the loudspeaker calling my name a final time. It was a man standing right there next to me.

It was Luz Long.

✢   ✢   ✢

My archenemy. Or was he? The way his hand rested on my shoulder, the vibrations I felt as he looked at me and smiled, made me know somehow that, far from being my enemy, he was my friend.

Luz turned out to be the best friend I ever had. He turned out to be what you might call a messenger from God.

Any doubts I had left about him vanished the instant he spoke. "What has taken your goat, Jazze Owenz?" he asked.

In spite of all my panic, I had to smile. Almost laugh. But I couldn't speak.

"I Luz Long," he said, introducing himself. I nodded. "I think I know what is wrong with you," he went on, answering his own question. "You are 100 per cent when you jump. I the same. You cannot do halfway, but you are afraid you will foul again."

"'That's right," I said, finding my voice for the first time.

"I have answer," he said. "Same thing happen to me last year in Cologne."

There were literally only seconds left before I had to jump or default. Luz told me to simply remeasure my steps and jump from six inches in back of the take-off board giving it all I had. That way I could give 100 per cent and still not be afraid of fouling. He even laid his towel down at exactly the place from which I was to jump. It was so simple!

And it worked.

I could feel the confident energy surging back into my body as I stood still for that brief second before beginning my run. I went as fast as I ever had, took off, and felt almost like I was flying. When I came down, it was more than 26 feet—an Olympic record—from the take-off board. With the extra six inches, it surely would have been a new unofficial record.

But what did I care about records? I was in the finals!

I didn't know how to thank Luz Long. Because of him, because of his seeing past skin color, nationality, and Hitler's godless beliefs, I had what was most important to me in the world: A chance to rise from Oakville to champion of the entire world.

All I could offer in return was my friendship. I met with him that night, and we talked over coffee in the Olympic Village. We might've stayed up a little later than athletes should, who have to compete against the best from every country in the following days, but it was worth it for the bond between us gave a spiritual strength which was greater than the physical. Luz and I, it turned out, were very much alike. He was married and had one child, too. A son, Karl. He had come from humble beginnings. And he didn't believe Hitler's Aryan supremacy statements and was disturbed by the military aggressiveness of the German dictator. Still, it was his country and he felt that if he didn't fight for it, he would be putting his wife and child in danger.

I asked him about religion. He said that he did not have any, had never really known any. "Do you believe in God?" I questioned.

He held out his hands, palms up, as if to say he didn't know. Then he shrugged a little, as if to add that he had never really had any evidence that there was a higher power. He was so good, and all the truly good people I'd known till then believed in God. But even if Luz was a Nazi who might soon be my archenemy again, trying to kill my countrymen and even me, I felt that beneath that he was my brother. And even though he didn't believe in God, I believed in Luz Long. And nothing would ever change that.

We spent each night afterward talking, and the days competing. Because of him, I won the 100-meter dash and the 200-meter, breaking records in both, and helped to lead my team to victory—and a record—in the relay. But most of all, I was waiting for the high point: The broad jump. For here, once again, Luz and I would be competing against one another. Without him, I would have never been competing at all. Yet I somehow had to fuse that feeling with the will to do my best. For wasn't my love for Luz—and yes, I loved him—a love for the best that is within man, the best that was within me?

The day of the broad jump arrived. One by one, the other finalists fell by the wayside. Then, it was only Luz Long and Jesse Owens.

His first leap took the lead.

I beat it.

His second of three was even better.

I beat it by half an inch.

I watched him take a deep breath before his final leap. I watched his blue eyes look up into the sky, then down, fixing on a point which he knew—and I knew—would be well over an Olympic record. I could see him transforming the same beautiful energy which had enabled him to come to me and change the course of my life when I needed it most into the determination to do what had never been done before . . . to do what most men would call a miracle.

He stood perfectly still, as still as a statue, for an instant, and only his eyes moved as they looked skyward once more, and then he began his run. Fast from the beginning, not gradual like most, but then faster. His perfectly proportioned legs working like pistons now, his finely honed physique working like one total machine, all for one purpose, for one split second—

And then it happened. High. Higher than I'd ever seen anyone leap. But with so much power that it was not merely high, it was far. Incredibly far.

It seemed for a split second that he would never come down. But then he did, straining his body more than I'd ever seen any man strain, as if he were an eagle attempting at the last minute to rise above an infinite mountain . . . straining . . . moving forward as he fell downward . . . forward farther . . . forward . . . .

He landed!

Exactly in the spot on which his eyes had fixed.

Luz Long had set a new Olympic record.

I rushed over to him. Hugged him. I was glad. So glad.

But now it was my turn.

I took my time, measured my steps once, then again. I was tense, but that good kind of tense that you feel when you have to be tense to do your best. Deep, deep inside, under all the layers, there was a clear, placid pool of peace.

Now I, too, stood perfectly still.

I, too, looked up at the sky.

Then, I looked into Luz's blue eyes, as he stood off to the side, his face wordlessly urging me to do my best, to do better than I'd ever done. Looking into his eyes was no different than looking into the blue, cloudless sky.

I didn't look at the end of the pit. I decided I wasn't going to come down. I was going to fly. I was going to stay up in the air forever.

I began my run, also fast from the beginning, not gradual like most, but then faster.

I went faster, precariously fast, using all my speed to its advantage. And then!

I hit the take-off board. Leaped up, up, up—

. . . My body was weightless . . . I surged with all I had but at the same time merely let it float . . . higher . . . higher . . . into the clouds . . . I was reaching for the clouds . . . the clouds . . . the heavens—

I was coming down! Back to earth.

I fought against it.

I kicked my legs.

I churned my arms.

I reached to the sky as I leaped for the farthest part of the ground. The farthest—

I was on the earth once again. I felt the dirt and the sand of the pit in my shoes and on my legs. Instinctively, I fell forward, my elbows digging in, the tremendous velocity of my jump forcing sand into my mouth.

It tasted good. Because, almost instinctively, I sensed it was the sand from a part of the pit which no one had ever reached before.

Luz was the first to reach me. "You did it! I know you did it," he whispered.

They measured.

I had done it.

I had gone farther than Luz. I had set a new Olympic record. I had jumped farther than any man on earth.

Luz didn't let go of my arm. He lifted it up—as he had lifted me up in a different way a few days before—and led me away from the pit and toward the crowd. "Jazze Owenz!" he shouted. "Jazze Owenz!"

Some people in the crowd responded, "Jazze Owenz!"

Luz shouted it louder. "Jazze Owenz!"

Now a majority of the crowd picked it up. "Jazze Owenz! Jazze Owenz! Jazze Owenz!" they yelled.

Luz yelled it again. The crowd yelled it again. Luz again. And now the whole crowd, more than a hundred thousand Germans, were yelling, "Jazze Owenz! Jazze Owenz! Jazze Owenz!"

They were cheering me. But only I knew who they were really cheering.

I lifted Luz Long's arm.

"Luz Long!" I yelled at the top of my lungs. "Luz Long! Luz Long! Luz Long! Luz Long!"

Dick Button

DICK BUTTON ON SKATES

Best known now as the world's most opinionated and knowledgeable figure skating announcer, Dick Button brought the energy and athleticism of post-World War Two America to his then-earthbound sport. Under the guidance of his coach Gus Lussi, Button popularized a new vision of skating that emphasized speed, power and altitude. Here, Button describes the year-long struggle that led to his landing the first triple jump in competition.

The greatest efforts of my competitive skating career were climaxed in the Olympic Games of 1952 at Oslo. This was the realization of a double goal—to win a second Olympic Gold Medal as a fitting culmination to five years of international competition, and to do this in a dramatic fashion by presenting a triple jump for the first time.

The triple loop jump was the most formidable challenge I faced. It was a task which was physically painful and mentally frustrating. At times, in desperation, I was almost ready to concede that the jump was beyond my achievement. Then, almost magically, with the Olympic Games rushing on me, I became the first skater to jump from the ice and make three complete controlled revolutions before landing.

The story goes back to the summer of 1951 at Lake Placid, New York, when I discussed strategy for the Olympic Games with Gus Lussi. An Olympic free-skating program is given in five minutes, but plans must start months before. As early as July and August the pattern of preparing for the Championships was well established and by the time the mountains around Lake Placid took their fall plumage, two months had been spent training the figures and movements that I hoped would win another Olympic title.

Each year in the past I had tried to present a new jump, spin or combination. When Mr. Lussi and I went over all the moves mastered up to that time we decided that our answer for 1952 was not to be a variation on a move already standard.

Then for the first time, we begin to think seriously of triple revolutions—why not a triple jump? No one had ever done one in competition, and few had even suggested the possibility of such a feat. A triple jump captured my imagination. I had always been interested in new jumps and combinations. I recall how steadfastly Mr. Lussi and I had worked on a Button camel, or flying camel, and how jealously I had guarded it its first year for fear a rival would see it and beat me to the punch by skating it in an exhibition. That was not an idle fear. In skating, as in any field, once you have shown an original idea in public, opponents are sure to copy it if they can, and soon the new movement becomes a part of the standard technique.

Even the novices of today recognize many of the jumps and spins we introduced as a necessary part of every skater's repertoire. The double axel in 1948, the double loop-double loop in 1949, the triple-double-loop in 1950, the double axel-double loop and the double axel-double axel in 1951 were already being eyed by others, and to keep my place as leader in a fast moving sport I had yet to go forward.

Let me make a few words of explanation. A double jump required the skater to make two complete revolutions in the air (or two-and-one-half in the case of the double axel) between take-off and landing.

A triple-double jump simply means a double jump repeated three times in succession, without intermediary steps. But a triple jump by itself was distinctive and forbidding. It meant three complete revolutions in the air, and for all Mr. Lussi and I knew when we started on it, I might never succeed.

Almost feverishly we discussed the triple jump at Lake Placid. What type of jump should we select for the experiment? A triple salchow was talked up for a time, but no matter how well performed, it lacked the majesty and eye-appeal of higher jumps. These considerations led us to a triple loop jump as the basic triple jump to begin on. Others would follow if this was learned successfully.

There was only one problem—doing it. I was about to enter my senior year at Harvard and with graduate study to follow, there would not be time either during or after this coming season to practice school figures, study, and still work on free skating. If there was any time to learn triple revolution it was now.

I began daily work on triple revolution in the Olympic Arena at Lake Placid, while the hot summer sun shone outside. For days I tried to do three turns, but succeeded only in falling and soaking up the film of water that covered the ice.

I hated even to think that a triple loop was impossible for me. For relief I decided to resume work on simpler jumps, intending to tackle triple revolution later. Then the blow fell.

When I tried to do a simple axel I couldn't control my rotation. It was impossible to remain cool, for the harder I tried, the less sense of direction, of rotation, of control was in any jump. The rink whirled around my head, the skaters seemed out of focus and my eyes saw only the blurred lines of others every time I tried to get off the ice.

I muttered to Dudley Richards, a friend and competitor: "I've lost my jumps—I can't do anything right!" But Dudley could only good-naturedly clutch himself with laughter at the side of the rink and say that he would now win the World Championships.

It was not funny to me. Double salchows, axels, double flips, even single flips were "lost." But surely no one ever appeared more amusing than I did, wandering around the ice, looking for even a solitary double salchow. Visions of years of practice and hour on hour of work flashed across my mind. As each jump got progressively worse, I got progressively more frantic. Leaving the rink, I rushed to "Little Alps," Mr. Lussi's home in the mountains near Lake Placid. Mr. Lussi sat quietly as I blurted, "I can't do anything. I've lost every jump I have. I'll have to learn all over again!"

He calmed me down, and reminded me that it wasn't unusual for a skater who begins working on increased rotation to become "over-rotated." He explained that he had seen many cases of this loss of timing, and that the skater generally regained form in a few days. Finally he laughed, and explained that the thought of his champion pupil falling flat on the simplest jumps was as humorous to him as it was aggravating to me.

After several days my control at last returned, but only after the rank of "President of the Plumbers Union" had been bestowed upon me by the other skaters for the most wretched series of practice exhibitions.

But by this time the summer was almost over. Practice on dull school figures and working out a newer free skating program left little time for anything else. I hated to admit defeat but for the time it was safer, if not more creative, to work on other things.

The summer months faded into September and the Lake Placid skating rink was left devoid of feverish skaters working on gold medal tests and free skating. Harvard held its traditional invocation for the three hundred-sixteenth class and the autumn months gradually worked up into a fully-paced schedule.

Lectures in Cambridge called a halt, at least temporarily, to my skating preparation and more time than usual was spent on studying political philosophy, on bicycling to Wellesley, and on starting a senior honors thesis.

✣ ✣ ✣

Just before Christmas vacation, I decided to start work on a triple loop once more. As I warmed up one afternoon at the Boston Skating

Club, I felt there would be another hard session of many weeks. But I preferred to take the chance of a greater success or a greater fall, rather than maintain a cautious status quo.

Somewhat nonchalantly, I essayed a preparatory move I had worked out the summer before to get into position to feel the movement of the jump. Almost automatically, my skates left the ice, I whirled the full three revolutions and landed, shakily and poorly controlled to be sure, but cleanly. Without practice, or even extended concentration, I had . . . just . . . *done* it! The triple loop was mine. Like the double axel I first did cleanly only two days before the last Olympics, this provided an exhilaration that only other skaters who suddenly find a jump will appreciate.

I didn't really "have" the jump. I had done it once and that was all. Doing it again and again until it was fool-proof for Olympic Competition was not going to be easy. Had I known the many hours that it would take me to perfect the thing I might not have had the enthusiasm with which I sent off a telegram to Mr. Lussi.

Generally, I tried to keep a new jump secret, as I have pointed out. But it was different with the triple loop. I believed for valid reasons that it should have the fullest publicity possible and the Athletic Director at Harvard, learning about it, sent out a news release stating I would perform the new jump at the Olympic Games.

This departure from custom was made for two reasons. First, if a rival had not already begun work on a triple jump, I felt he did not have time to catch up with me before the Olympic Games.

Second, it would be wise to warn the judges that I was prepared to present a radical new jump at Oslo, otherwise it might go unrecognized; the judges might well ask themselves whether that was a triple revolution or an optical illusion.

When I was planning to introduce a new double jump at an earlier competition, Karl Schafer, former Olympic champion from Austria, had advised me, "If you want to do this double, by all means show it to the judges in advance, or let them know very definitely in advance what you intend. They may not believe it if not forewarned. I once jumped the double loop in competition. In exhibitions I didn't risk it, but friends continually complimented me on the double I had not skated. I left them their illusion."

Leaving Cambridge for Lake Placid, I began training in earnest after Christmas. My routine was broken only by occasional snow-ball fights and the annual crowning of the King and Queen of Winter. By this time Mother and Dad had made arrangements for me to train in Germany at Garmisch-Partenkirchen near the edge of the Bavarian Alps. A week later when we all flew from Idlewild to Germany, Mr. and Mrs. Lussi, Suzanne Morrow, the Canadian Champion, and a fast-rising young star—Muriel Reich—made up the rest of our party.

In Munich, the press insisted on the story of the triple loop. The photographers got together and pleaded with me to leap over my luggage, ". . . in a little triple just for the papers, please."

At Garmisch, our program was strict. I was on the ice in the morning from 7:30 to 11:45. Lunch and a massage took up the next two hours. Then I skated from two to four or five on one of the two huge ice surfaces in the stadium built for the Olympic Games of 1936.

After dinner I worked on my thesis for Harvard, by now titled, "International Socialism and the Schumann Plan." In shipping over the necessary material to finish writing it, I had paid a fortune in overweight, so that working on it now was more a matter of saving face than of desiring to desist from skating practice. In the many exhibitions that I was invited to give around Europe, it was always a part of my acceptance that I should be introduced to the leading socialists or other politicians instrumental in the plan to pool western Europe's coal and steel resources.

But all of these visits were to come much later—after the Olympics. In the meantime, at Garmisch, a severe snow storm had lasted for four days, making it almost impossible to skate. These four days I spent finishing the thesis. By the time the sun shone once more over the Kreuksick mountains, Mother had insured it for $1500 and mailed it to my tutor at Harvard. When he received it at the Boston Customs

House he told reporters it promised to be excellent from the outline I had submitted; but he later asked me where the devil I had the nerve to think any work of mine was worth $1500!

The triple loop was a lively subject of conversation among winter sportsmen at Garmisch. Many gathered at the stadium in the morning to watch our practice, among them John J. McCloy, then U. S. High Commissioner for Germany.

Unfortunately, it was one thing for me to do the triple loop separately, and quite another to try to integrate it into a free skating routine. I fell innumerable times a day, and these falls were jarring. Those at the rinkside looked on in amazement and asked "Can this be the Olympic Champion?"

Mother and Dad pleaded with me to quit the triple loop, because they felt it was too punishing. Once before, in 1948, Dad had tried to stop me when I persisted in landing on one hip rather than one skate while practicing a double axel. His point was that sport ceased as such when brutality entered.

Although it was not the most pleasant sensation, falling in itself has never really bothered me. I have always felt that if a person stops falling, he stops improving. It is a necessary part of progress.

But the continued falling here was more disastrous than hurt pride. The extraordinary stress of triple rotation strained the ligaments of my left leg only weeks before the Olympic Games. I consulted several doctors, who could prescribe only one remedy, massage and a drastic curtailment of practice for a few days.

All this time my free skating was in very poor shape. Introduction of the triple loop had caused me to miss timing on double jumps, and the rest of the skating, as in previous years, had reached a "low." I couldn't seem to do even an ordinary move well. When Suzanne Morrow laughingly predicted I would trip even on the simple mazurka jump, I promptly found myself fulfilling her prophecy. It was in this state that our party left Garmisch for Vienna to see the European championships and to skate an exhibition.

In the competition Helmut Seibt and Jeannette Altwegg were the winners and Seibt's feat naturally marked him as the chief European challenger for the Olympic Games.

Following the competition I had been invited to give an exhibition, and lively interest questioned whether I really could do a triple loop. I wanted to do well for two reasons. I knew it would be difficult to return to Vienna after the Olympics and I wanted to do my best before the ever-increasing audiences that had come to see our exhibitions since my first trip there, four years earlier. Also, I hoped my program would begin to pull itself out of the hole it was in.

But from this enlarged audience escaped an even larger groan when I fell—attempting the triple loop. This time, a fall *did* bother me. I hated to leave Vienna with a failure as her final impression of me. Immediately afterward I asked the management of the Wiener Eis Lauverein if it would be possible to schedule another exhibition for the following night. It would be possible, they answered. They would be delighted to accommodate another capacity crowd.

For the second exhibition I determined to stay on the ice all night, if necessary, to do the triple loop, and this firm resolve gave my skating a lift. I felt the improvement as the opening spins went well and a double lutz clicked cleanly. Then I approached the triple. A four-five-six step, a back crossing, and I strained my arms to lift and pull with more energy than I had summoned the night before. One . . . two . . . three turns in the air. The jump was clean and the landing strong. The rest of the program seemed a breeze; triple-double axels and triple-double loops were free yet controlled in the exhilarating lightness that followed the loop jump.

That one successful performance restored my bruised confidence, and we flew from Vienna to Oslo for the ultimate test in the Olympic Games. At the Norwegian capital, I stayed at the Royal Swedish Automobile Club. From the balcony, the setting sun colored the harbor that spread out below and, in the distance, Bislett Stadium, where the games would soon open, was coldly imposing in the darkness.

✤ ✤ ✤

On the second day of the Games, the men skated their school figures . . . starting early in the morning on the cold surface that shimmered back the sun's reflections. The judges were bundled up in straw boots twice the size of their feet, and muffs, hats, scarves, and gloves padded the outlines of their figures into Disney-esque forms.

The first few counters and rockers were run through rapidly. I took a lead on the first figure, and estimated that I was holding it. In the outdoor stadium, without hockey dashboards or stands close by, it was difficult to line up the edges of the eights.

I believed Helmut Seibt, Jimmy Grogan, and Hayes Alan Jenkins were following closely in their scores, but I could not say which had the advantage of the others. The bracket change bracket backwards was the final figure to be done. The judges raised their cards time after time as a skater finished either downcast or happy. For me it was the same as always. I was never fully satisfied with the figures laid down but was pleased that they were at least within what I liked to call championship level.

By the time the shadows had stretched to the length of a circle eight, the figures were over, and Mother told me she was sure I had the lead. She had become adept at taking down marks and working out the many details of scoring. Therefore I was not surprised when the statistics revealed my expected lead, with Seibt, Grogan, and Jenkins following in that order. There were nine firsts for me, 8 seconds and a third for Helmut while the point totals for the two of us were 1,000.2 and 957.7 respectively. I had a solid base to work on then. With two-thirds of the marking accounted for, I had only to execute the free skating with firmness and control, land my triple loop, and a second Olympic Gold Medal would be mine.

Many of the men worked out in Bislett that night just before the pair championships were held in the center of the huge ice surface. At first my knees were stiff after the long day spent on figures, and I faltered in my first try to do a triple loop. A professional teacher standing with Dad on the ice nearby immediately told him what was wrong with my form and how I should correct it. Dad, relating the story afterwards, said he had had to laugh. He told the teacher: "This is amusing. You saw a triple loop for the first time yesterday, and today you are an expert saying exactly what is wrong."

But by this time, the warmup had begun to tell, triple loops came easily, and the rest of the skating, with the knowledge that I was leading in the school figures, was lighthearted. It was necessary after a while for Mr. Lussi to admonish me sternly not to overdo lest I leave the title on the practice ice instead of in the championship area.

Removing my skates and pulling on a white polar coat, I watched the pairs. Early on the list were Karol and Peter Kennedy whose excellent performance would easily have won an Olympic title were it not for Ria Baran Falk and Paul Falk of Germany. Although many other pairs appeared, it was the battle between these that was to decide the winner.

From the start Ria and Paul Falk outshone any other pair I have ever seen. There are only a few skaters who attain the level of greatness and the Falks were of this number. Like Manolete, the Spanish bullfighter who scorned tricky passes and concentrated on simple classic moves that reached perfection, the Falks specialized on single jumps, simple lifts, and parallel skating that was always in unison. The exact matching of their styles and physiques made their complete similarity possible. They won first place.

On Mr. Lussi's insistence that I conserve energy for the free skating, I practiced little the following day and watched the ladies' school figures. Contrasting with the men there was a mass of color as the girls in bright dresses posed in line for photographers. Bronzed arms and legs were set off by every kind of skating costume, with the publicity-conscious doing their best to stand out as the most glamorous product since Sonja Henie. Had some spent more time on practice and less on primping, their scoring might quite possibly have been higher than it was.

✤　✤　✤

The days before the free skating event were usually spent by competitors in going over their entire program to build up wind, stamina and control to the highest level. Having spent five weeks training in Garmisch and another ten days before the Games, Mr. Lussi continually gentled me down. We both feared I would reach a peak too rapidly; for, once at a peak, an athlete can all too easily lose his "edge" fast.

Bislett presented a unique sight as my final test began. The tournament area was edged with snow, a brilliantly illuminated, square-cut diamond in the center of the vast ice expanse. Only the judges and photographers were at rinkside, and the stands, the spectators, seemed miles removed.

I had only a brief warm-up while the judges took their seats, and coaches called last minute instructions. A whistle blew shrilly, a little man carrying score cards slipped and slid across the band of ice rimming the competitive area, and the referee rose from his center chair. The men gathered around him as he reiterated to the skaters, in several languages, that should shoelaces break, they could start over; should they want more warm-up time, they could have it; and did they know the order of skating? Affirmative answers and nervous gestures answered him. Pulling on sweaters and coats, tucking hanging shoelaces into their boots, the skaters hurried back to the warmth of the dressing rooms to wait their turn.

Was I nervous? Let me put it this way: Yes. This was to be the crowning effort of years of practice. To be sure, I had a very substantial lead in school figures, but if I could not perform the triple loop, even though I should manage to win, the effort would be, in part, a failure. And there was always the chance that should I miss the triple loop and progress into cumulative errors in other moves, I would lose.

When the runner called my name, I tugged almost viciously at the laces of my boots, made the knots extra tight and went down the long runway to the rink. I looked around to see if Mother or Dad were there. Both as usual were so nervous that they could not sit near each other or with another skater; they were somewhere up in the stands.

Poor Mr. Lussi was absolutely white with anxiety. I winked reassuringly at him, but I knew perfectly well I would not enjoy the competition that night—it meant too much to me.

The scene confronting me as I stood there under the spotlights was unfamiliar and vaguely disturbing. Several judges sat in wire chairs at the edge of the snow line that described the perimeter of the skating area and a photographer now and then scurried to a new point of vantage. The audience—a mile away it seemed—was too far back in the darkness to get a feeling of contact. I regretted that Mother and Dad weren't sitting up close. I always enjoyed winking at them as I skated by although it shocked them for fear I would lose concentration.

Once again I heard my familiar competitive music. The beginning phrase always startled me out of the sluggish feeling that usually came over me before the competition began. I raised my arms, took an opening step and forced myself into the opening spin.

I thought over and over only that I had to take the program coolly. After thirty seconds, one axel and a double lutz, I had the feel of the ice. The next jump would tell whether weeks of work had been successful—whether I would be the first to do a triple jump in competition.

Would it work? Would it work? Now when I needed it most, would there be a hitch? The least fault in timing, the least rut in the ice at takeoff. . .

I took the four-five-six preparation step and moved toward the edge into the loop. I forgot in momentary panic which shoulder should go forward and which back. I was extraordinarily conscious of the judges, who looked so immobile at rinkside. But this was it. The edge cut the ice and my arms lowered, shoulders turning against the rotation to allow a grip that would follow through. My knees closed as my feet crossed in the air. The wind cut my eyes, and the coldness caused tears to stream down my cheeks. Up! Up! Height was vital. Round and around again in a spin which took only a fraction of a second to complete before it landed on a clean steady back edge. I pulled away breathless, excited and overjoyed, as applause rolled from the faraway stands like the rumbling of a distant pounding sea.

The rest of the program hardly mattered. I was let-down, serious, over-concerned, forgetting that this should be really all enjoyment. I finished the five minutes, now but an instant. Only when I left the ice did I realize I was exhausted.

Photographers popped flashbulbs; reporters asked questions. I had laced my boots so tightly that circulation had stopped. My feet were numb. Knots had to be cut before I could remove my boots.

The struggle was over, and even the closing ceremonies, so impressive to me four years before at St. Moritz, were now somehow anti-climactic, as I stood highest on the dais, with Seibt on the second level and Grogan on the third, to receive a second Olympic Gold Medal.

The championship had ended for me when I stepped off the center ice of Bislett Stadium, the gold medal secured by the first triple jump ever attempted in the athletic world's most significant competition.

George Halas

HALAS BY HALAS

In its early days, football had not yet shaken free of rugby, the English sport from which it grew, carrying on its hard-hitting, but ground-based style that usually produced three yards, a cloud of dust and a pile-up. Enter George Halas (1895–1983), innovative owner of the Chicago Bears. This excerpt from Halas By Halas *recounts the creation of the T-Formation, a new strategy which gave rise to the forward pass and the game as we know it.*

A s the 1929 season deteriorated, on its way to a miserable 4-8-2 ending, loss after loss drove home two lessons:

First, the time had come for me to stop playing. I was thirty-four. I no longer had speed. My muscles were no longer strong enough for me to shift supersized linesmen. Dutch had ceased playing regularly.

Secondly, the time had come for Dutch and me to stop coaching, or, more accurately, miscoaching. We had to put coaching under one mind. We decided to bring in someone who would pull the team together.

I wanted, first and foremost, an experienced coach who was a good teacher. I could think of no one who better met those qualifications than Ralph Jones, my freshman football coach and Varsity basketball coach at Illinois.

"Don't give out too much at one time," Jones used to say. "Give a little and let the student absorb that before giving more. If you give too much at once, you'll only confuse him."

Ralph Jones had left Illinois in the mid-twenties to become athletic director at Lake Forest Academy, a small but excellent secondary school in the north Chicago suburb. He was happy there but I persuaded him to come to the Bears.

It astonished everyone that the Bears should go to an academy for a coach. The announcement said we would pay Jones $10,000. Actually, the contract was for $7,500, but overstating salaries has rarely been disagreeable to employee or employers in many professions.

Ralph Jones was a sound strategist. He believed muscle, guts and spirit were not enough. He believed it also took brains to win games. Brainwork reduced the amount of profitless and painful crashing and thrashing about. Brainwork properly applied could add excitement and make the game more attractive.

"I'll give you a championship in three years," Jones said. I believed him.

In 1930, the line, on offense, formed up with guards 1 foot from the center, tackles 1 foot from the guards and the ends 2 feet from the tackles. On defense, the center moved back to become a linebacker and the other six bunched together closely. The tight formation led to pileup after pileup after pileup.

From time immemorial, the backfield had lined up in a T, the quarterback directly behind the center, the fullback directly behind him 4 or 5 yards with a halfback on each side. The ball went to the quarterback who pivoted and handed or lateraled to one of the backs. The other backs became blockers or receivers. The formation made sense for driving straight ahead. The objective then was power, power, power. Power in a tight backfield. Power in a tight line. Met by power on the defense. The result was crash, crash, crash—and boredom.

College coaches had tried to add opportunities for nimble runners and expert passers. At Notre Dame, Knute Rockne, the great Knute

Rockne, had created the Notre Dame box. The backfield lined up in a T and shifted to a box, either left or right, like this:

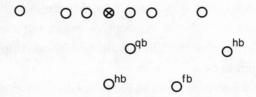

The center passed the ball to the back designated to run, pass or kick. The quarterback directed the team and called the signals. After the snap he became basically a blocker.

Pop Warner, the great Pop Warner, created the single wing and the double wing. Warner pulled the two guards back. The backs lined up in the T. On the shift, the two guards went together into the line on one side of the center, making four men on one side, two on the other. For running plays, the backs shifted into a lopsided version of Rockne's box. He called it a single wing. The backs and guards shifted to the same side, adding a lot of power to that side.

After the shift the single wing looked like this:

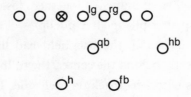

The double-wing shift ended like this:

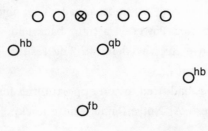

The halfbacks were in good position to go for passes. The box and the wings did add dimension to the game but I felt they were not much of an improvement over the T. I had grown up with the T. I had played it at Illinois, with the navy, with Hammond. I had used it with the Staleys. I kept it all through the twenties with the Bears, although I cannot recall how often critics denounced the Bears as an old-fashioned team.

Rules required that while signals were being called, a team could shift but the players had to hold the new position for a full second before the ball was snapped. That supposedly gave the defense time to adjust its positions. The shorter the pause, the more likely the defense would be caught unprepared. At Notre Dame, the one-second pause frequently was not much longer than the blink of an eye. The officials had a problem trying to determine when a second was a second.

Jones began by readjusting the offensive line. He increased the distance between center, guard and tackle from 1 foot to 1 yard and the distance between guard and end from 2 feet to 2 yards. The change gave the defense new opportunities to enter our backfield. To remove this gift, Jones needed to speed action in the backfield, to improve the blocking and to open holes in the line quickly. For plays coming through the line, the blockers should try not to bring down the assigned defense men but merely deflect them. For example: On a quick opening play between our right guard and tackle, our guard would hit their guard on the outside, moving him to the left, and our tackle would hit their tackle on the inside, moving him to the right. The two defense men would be out of action for only a few seconds but long enough for our back to get through with the ball.

To speed up action in the backfield and add diversity, Jones began applying a little-used rule which allows one man to move as soon as the signals begin and continue moving. The one-second halt after the shift does not apply to him. Jones saw tremendous opportunities in the rule. In Carl Brumbaugh and Red Grange he had ideal experimenters. They were smart. Brummy was a good passer, Grange a good receiver. Both could run and block.

Jones began by having Grange, playing left halfback, run to the right behind the line. By the time the ball was snapped he was outside our right end. He could take a lateral and run straight ahead, or he could run downfield to take a long pass, or he could come in behind the defense line to take a short pass, or he could join the end in blocking for another back coming around with the ball.

For variety, Jones would send the right halfback to the left.

One day, in a game against Green Bay, Brummy noted the defensive halfback followed Red, creating a gap in their secondary. Brummy told Red to go in motion but only as a lure. Brummy gave the ball to the fullback who went through an opening in the line, on through the gap and 54 yards for a touchdown.

In time Jones had so many plays the defense was totally confused.

"Playing football," said Red, "became a lot more fun."

Thus was born the modern T-Formation with man-in-motion. It broke the game wide open. Football became a game of brains. Instead of knocking men down, Jones tried to entice the defense into doing something helpful for us. Best of all, the public found our new brand of football exciting.

Jones worked out meticulous positioning. The quarterback was directly behind and tight up against the center. He placed his left hand, palm down, against the center's crotch, so the center could feel it and know the back was there. The right hand was about four inches below the left, palm up. On the count, the center would snap the ball into the quarterback's hands.

The quarterback would clamp both hands on the ball, pivot and move back to do whatever the play called for. He could hand the ball to one of the backs already charging forward for a quick opening play. He could pretend to hand it to a back, hide it, fade back and pass or hand it to another back. He could lateral it to one of the backs. If we needed a yard, he could do a quarterback sneak.

With the wing formation or the box, the center had to look back between his legs and pass the ball to the back. He would usually watch to make sure he had made a good pass. Only then would he be ready to block. By then, everybody else was in action. He had missed the explosive moment. Sometimes his pass to the back was faulty. That was costly.

With our T, the center could pass with his head up. On the count he became the first man to explode because he was the only one who knew the instant the play started. One of our great centers, George Trafton, began using only one hand to give the ball to the quarterback, increasing his readiness and ability to block. This is common procedure now.

For passes, Trafton would hand the ball with the laces in exactly the position Brummy wanted them. When throwing to a back for punts, field goals, or conversions, he could spiral the ball just enough to make it end up in the kicker's or holder's hands with the laces in the right position. It saved perhaps a half-second, but that was long enough to reduce the danger of a blocked kick.

We developed a simple system of signals. It was based on two two-digit numerals. The holes to the right were numbered 1-3-5-7-9; the holes to the left were 0-2-4-6-8. We numbered our backs in this manner: The left halfback was 2, the fullback 3, the right halfback 4. The first of the first two-digit numeral specified which back got the ball. The second number told where the hole should be opened. The second two-digit numerals told which back was going in motion and on what count the ball would be snapped.

If the quarterback called 31-26, plus some dead numbers added to disguise our real numbers, the fullback, 3, would get the ball from the quarterback and go through the 1 hole opened between center and right guard; the left half, 2, would go in motion to the right and the ball would be snapped on the count of 6.

The success of any play depends upon the ability of each man to carry out the assignment given him. That means hours and hours of practice.

Jones marked everything from the ball. He placed the fullback exactly 4 yards directly behind the ball. The right halfback lined up

straddling the outside leg of the right tackle; the left halfback strad-
dled the outside leg of the left tackle. Each halfback placed himself
so his heels were on a line with the fullback's toes.

Because everyone began from a precise position, we could work
out exact timing. Each back knew exactly how many steps he would
take, what route he should follow. Every Monday the coaches would
review the defense of next Sunday's opponents and then prepare a
"short list" of plays against them, consisting of a dozen runs and a
dozen passes.

We would give the plays to the players on Tuesday morning.
Twice a day until Saturday, the team would go through the plays,
over and over and over until each play became almost automatic. At
night, each man would draw diagrams of the plays so each knew all
assignments.

During the game, the quarterback would intersperse the new
plays with others worked out for earlier games. If a play worked,
we'd repeat it several times. In a usual game a team has the ball about
seventy times. In the old days, the routine was pretty well frozen:
run on first and second, pass on third if more than a yard or two was
needed, punt on fourth. Using our modern T-Formation with man-
in-motion, we would pass on any down.

Blocking took on new dimensions. Hunk Anderson's reverse
body block gained new importance. We developed many ramifica-
tions of it. The blocker had to shoot off on the proper foot and pivot
at exactly the right time to give thrust to the body. If done correctly, this block would remove from play a man 50 pounds heavier.
If a defensive linebacker came in low, the blocker would shove him
down with a hip and then step over him. If he came in high, planning to wrestle, the blocker would throw a body block at his knees,
or lower, and flatten him.

Jones impressed on each player the need to watch his opposite
number closely and seek a clue which might give away the opponent's intentions. A linebacker about to blitz the quarterback might
place his feet in a different position. A receiver might wipe his hands

on his trousers. A back might look at the intended receiver as the team lined up.

Sometimes we found clues. Sometimes they proved useful. Sometimes we guessed wrong. It always added interest and, now and then, a score.

I told my boyhood friend, Charlie Pechous: "Charlie, we're five years ahead of everybody."

To make our T really work, we needed a powerful running back. For some time I had been hearing about a big strong man from the north woods who was good for 10 yards or so every time he carried the ball for Minnesota. The coach there, Doc Spears, said he had found his Hercules one day when driving through the woods along the Rainy River which separates Minnesota from Canada. He was seeking a boy he had heard about and saw a young man pushing a plow without aid of a horse. Doc said he stopped and asked the plowman the way to the house he was seeking.

"Right over there," the plowman said, picking up the plow and using it for a pointer. Doc said he forgot about the other boy and went for the plowman. His name was Bronko Nagurski. Bronk does not tell the story himself but he does not deny it. Doc finished with Bronk in 1929. I made sure the Bears got him.

Halfway through the 1930 season, Notre Dame expelled one of its more colorful players, Jumping Joe Savoldi, for offending a Notre Dame rule against marriage. The expulsion became a popular subject of discussion for press, radio and the public. I offered him a place on the Bears. He accepted quickly. I was well aware of the very solid rule the League had made, with my help, against teams signing players before their class was graduated but I told myself, and anyone who asked, that Jumping Joe was a special case. I was not taking him out of school. Notre Dame had put him out. He was no longer a collegian, by action of the college officials.

Before long Mr. Carr told me I was guilty of offending the League rule. I put my case. He said the expulsion did not change the rules. The rule said a player could not be signed until his class was graduated. He agreed the rule did not allow for the possibility of expulsion and, because of that, he would not impose a fine although he would declare me guilty. I said in that case, he must fine me. He did. I had to pay $1,000. Perhaps Savoldi was worth it.

Coach Jones, the T, Bronk and Red put us back onto the winning side. We ended the 1930 season with nine wins, four losses, one tie. We were on our way to becoming the Monsters of the Midway.

Billie Jean King

BILLIE JEAN

Along with Gloria Steinem and Betty Friedan, tennis great Billie Jean King epitomized the Women's Movement of the 60s and 70s, in part because of her efforts to create the women's tennis tour, but mostly for her televised match with Bobby Riggs in 1973. As well as establishing the strength of women's athletics by pitting a man head to head against a woman—a woman who happened to win—the match blew tennis out of the country clubs and made it a mainstream sport for the first time. Here, King tells the story of how the match came together, on and off the court.

On May 13, 1973—Mother's Day—Rosie Casals, Marilyn Barnett, my personal secretary, and I were on a flight from Tokyo to Los Angeles, returning from a tournament in Japan. All of us were keyed up. There was a match being played that Sunday afternoon near San Diego, California, and we were desperate to find out the score. We landed in Honolulu, a short layover, and literally ran into the airport terminal. They've got all those little television sets, right? So I put my little quarters in. Nothing. No tennis. Reruns of "Gunsmoke" or something. Turns out they delay everything in Hawaii a week. We just flipped. Rosie was running around, I was going crazy, kicking the TVs, and Marilyn was trying to calm us both down. Finally Marilyn remembered Rosie's super tape recorder-radio and turned it on. We just got the last part of a sports report:

"Bobby Riggs beat Margaret Court today, 6–2, 6–1." What can I say? I went bananas. None of us could believe it. No way. Right then and there I said, "That's it. I've got to play him." The moment I heard those scores. 6–2, 6–1, I knew I *had* to play Bobby Riggs. The door had been opened and things were out of my control. It was only a matter of time and place and money.

Until 1971 I'd never met Bobby Riggs or even seen him play, but everybody in tennis knew his record and reputation. Bobby never had a power game, but he was one of the best ball-control artists of all time and won Wimbledon once, in 1939, and Forest Hills twice, 1939 and 1941. He lost a lot of good years to World War II, turned professional, and like all professionals in those days, dropped out of sight. Riggs was a hustler from the beginning. Clyde Walker, my first coach, told me many stories about this little punk who used to come out to the courts around Los Angeles and hustle matches when he was thirteen. He was a compulsive gambler. In 1939 he bet £100 on himself to win the Wimbledon singles (betting's legal in England) and when he won that he let the money ride through the doubles and the mixed. He got the slam—and over $100,000. At country clubs he'd play handicap matches—give some local guy a few points a game or a few games a set—and usually win. And when he got tired of that he started in with the gimmicks. He'd play while walking a dog on a leash, or in an overcoat, or with chairs placed on his side of the court: "How many chairs you want?"

So when he came out with his first challenge, in 1971, I had a pretty good idea what he was up to. He wanted to play for $5,000 or something like that, winner take all, and he was already into his Male Chauvinist Pig thing. He claimed *any* man could beat *any* woman, that the women's game was dull compared to the men's, and that there was no reason for us to get equal prize money. I don't know how serious he was about all of that back then or even how serious he is now, but the hustler in him must have sensed the possibilities in a "Battle of the Sexes" match right from the beginning.

At Forest Hills that year I remember I was practicing on the Club-house court one day when he suddenly came out of nowhere, jumped over the little fence by the court, and kept saying to me, "You've got to play. How can you not want to play?"

I turned him down, cold. At that time my mind was only concerned with getting the Virginia Slims circuit on the road, nothing else. We were trying to prove that women could make it on their own and I didn't want to get anything started that might distract from that goal. I didn't think that any of us women needed to play against an older man, and even if we did, just what was it gonna prove? If we played and I won, so what? I beat somebody twenty-five years older than me. If I lost, Bobby would carry that MCP thing on forever—or at least until somebody did beat him.

The odds were lousy. Our circuit was struggling then, and if Bobby had won, just enough people might have believed his spiel to send our whole tour down the drain. It was that touchy.

He kept saying what a great hype our match would be for the women's tour, but I told him that if we couldn't make it on our own then we didn't deserve to make it at all. I more or less told him we didn't want him.

And so the whole thing died until February, 1973, when he issued another challenge through the newspapers. It was the same old stuff. "The women couldn't take more than one or two games a set from the good men's players . . . So why should they be paid the same as men? . . . The women are getting more money than they deserve, anyway. . . ." Etc., etc., etc.

I still didn't want to play him. Our tour was coming along pretty well by then, but still, what would it prove? So I turned him down again, even though Larry felt there was a good chance I could make somewhere between $35,000 and $50,000 from the match. But then the public got interested—got very demanding, in fact—and Jackie Barnett, Bobby's agent, got in touch with Larry. Before anything serious could happen, though, the first week in March, Margaret Court announced to a group of us in the dressing room at Cobo Hall in

Detroit that *she* was going to play—for a $5,000 guarantee and another $5,000 if she won.

Margaret was really excited. She felt that was a lot of money for just one day of tennis and I didn't say too much to discourage her because she was so happy. But I tried to warn her. "It's not just a one-day deal, Margaret," I said. "It's gonna be a six-week deal." I didn't think she understood how hectic things would get for her.

I was disappointed she was going to play him at all, and even more disappointed that the money was so little. She was literally putting her name and the reputation of women's tennis on the line—at least that's how I knew the public would look at it no matter how she or the rest of us felt personally—and all for a dinky $5,000, maybe $10,000. (She did eventually get the $10,000, even though she lost.)

I really wanted Margaret to win, for herself and for us, and I thought that she at least had a good chance. There were a handful of women who could have beaten him and she was definitely among them. But whatever happened, I wanted the match to be good, and entertaining. Unfortunately, it wasn't.

Although I didn't see the match myself, I caught a tape of it a week or so later at a television studio in Savannah and I almost got sick. Did she do a nerve job? Oh, yeah, without a doubt. The psych began when Riggs handed her those flowers before the match and never let up. I could tell after she hit two balls what was happening. It just killed me to see it. It kills me to see any athlete have that bad a day. I mean, you want to see both players play great and just whoever has the better day win. That kind of crackup happens to everybody one or two times in his or her career and it's just unfortunate that it hit her on that particular day. I felt sorry for her and I think there must have been great sympathy for her from everybody who watched the match. But it really made me sick, and it made me stop and think what I was getting myself into, which was good.

❖   ❖   ❖

I only talked with Margaret about the match once. That was in Nashville five weeks before I played Riggs. Even then I felt funny asking her about it. I knew it would be a sore point with her and I really didn't know whether she wanted me to win or not. She said she didn't remember a whole lot about the match, which I could understand, but one thing she did tell me was that Riggs couldn't hit through his backhand very well. That is, he couldn't hit over the ball with much power from that side and so had to rely on placement almost entirely.

That was useful information, because before he and I played I really knew very little about him. I'd never played him, of course, so there was no track record to go on, and his match with Margaret was so one-sided that even seeing the tapes didn't tell me much. It was obvious he hadn't played anywhere near his best, wherever that is.

Riggs's people got in touch with my people again almost immediately after the Court match and in late June, just before Wimbledon, we signed to play. We announced the match on July 11, and from that moment on, right up until the time we stepped on the court in the middle of the Houston Astrodome on the night of September 20, life was one big circus. The contract was unsettled from the beginning and in fact the final details weren't fixed until the very day before the match. I'll talk about that a little later, but the basic terms were these: $100,000 in prize money to the winner, plus about another $100,000 in guarantees and ancillary rights to be split evenly between us. Everything else that came along, before the match, was to be split fifty-fifty too. The endorsement offers started to pour in almost immediately, but Bobby and I said no to all of them except Sunbeam (for a hair drier television commercial) and Sugar Daddy. And basically that was it.

From the very first I wanted the match to be the best of five sets, and Bobby agreed. Most people thought a long match would work to my advantage (the Court match had been best of three), but at the time I have to admit I really didn't think it would. I'd been sick and injured a lot that year, and the longer the match, the better the odds were of something else happening to me. But I also didn't want there to be any loopholes for him if I won, none of this, "Well, it was only a three-set match and I could have taken her in five." One of the things Riggs kept egging me on about was how we women couldn't stand up physically to men in a long match, and I felt that if we played best-of-five it would be more convincing.

The hoopla began immediately and didn't let up for ten weeks. And I'd warned Margaret the whole thing would take six! What the media didn't generate, Riggs supplied himself with all that nonsense talk about his vitamin pill popping, his special diets, and with his entourage of honeys to keep up the MCP image. He made scores of public appearances, and the match was written about in almost every newspaper and magazine in the country, maybe the world. We both knew it was a one-shot deal, especially if I won, but, otherwise, each of us treated the match very differently. I was deadly serious about it; for him it was the ultimate ego trip, a vehicle for a super hustler to carry off (he hoped) the ultimate hustle. He knew it was a hustle, I knew it was a hustle, the media knew it was a hustle, and, no mistake, so did the 30,472 people who saw the match live in the Astrodome and the 40 million who saw it on television. In a way that's part of what made the thing so perfect, the thought that everybody else was having a ball and the idea that what we were doing was great for tennis, just great. Sure, it was a one-shot deal, but on that night, I think, the game of tennis finally got kicked out of the country clubs forever and into the world of real sports, where everybody could see it.

But still I tried to stay somewhat away from the show biz atmosphere that was building up. Two reasons. First, compared to other athletes, Bobby's pretty easy to figure out, to get into his mind and understand how he thinks, and I realized the one thing Bobby wanted me to do was get caught up in everything. He's a hustler, but in order to hustle you he's got to see you, know where you are, keep tabs on you. I felt if I hid from him, if I wasn't around physically, it would drive him nuts. And so I stayed out of sight, especially in the last two or three weeks. Second, I knew in the match itself I was going to expend more nervous energy than I ever had before, and using up nervous energy is a lot harder on you than just wearing yourself out physically. So I gave very few interviews and no autographs and tried to keep to myself and stick to my regular routine.

I wanted to be able to analyze the match strictly from an athlete's point of view. I felt if I got caught up in public opinion and all the whoopteedoo it would slant my feelings toward the match instead of letting me look at it as simply as I could—as a contest between him and me and that's all. I felt if I started to listen to every Tom, Dick, and Harry that came along I'd be so confused by the time I walked into the Astrodome I wouldn't have any idea what I was there for. In some respects the match was going to be the most important one in my career, and I wanted to keep that in mind right up to the last moment.

✤ ✤ ✤

At Hilton Head, a posh resort on the Carolina seacoast, the atmosphere was really great. It's a nice place to begin with, and I was able to isolate myself relatively easily from the press and anyone else I didn't want to see. The only people around were Larry, who flew in and out, Annalee Thurston, a secretary at King Enterprises, and Dick Butera, president of the Philadelphia Freedoms, who had become a very close friend in the short time I'd known him. That was all. We went out to dinner together, and to the movies, and listened a lot to the radio.

But mainly, when I wasn't playing tennis, we just sat around and talked about the match while Annalee answered the phone and told people I was busy. I was hyper the whole time, very intense. I lived in a condominium apartment by the golf course, and in the morning the first thing I'd do was get up and walk outside by myself, maybe hit a few golf balls, and try to think through exactly what the whole thing meant, to me, personally. And then I'd talk with Dick and Larry and Annalee some more. By then the television promo spots on ABC were coming hot and heavy and it was really sinking in how much of a happening the whole match was turning into. I remember watching the college game of the week (Stanford versus Penn State) the Saturday before the match when at half time the Stanford University band formed the letters "B J K" and played "I am Woman." I honest-to-God got teary-eyed.

Okay, the match was a spectacle, but in a sense it was also the culmination of the second phase of my career. The first had been the fight to become the Number One player in the world. I'd done that. The second was the fight for equality for the women's tour, and in the space of just a few weeks it seemed like that fight was being won. First, the Virginia Slims and USLTA women's pro circuits had just merged and we knew our tournaments would pay $50,000 each the next winter—same as the WCT men's tour. Second, Forest Hills had offered that equal prize money. Third, the television tournament at Hilton Head had paid $40,000 to the winner—Margaret Court—the largest top prize ever in women's tennis. And fourth—the Riggs match. He and a lot of other men are still talking about how much he did for women's tennis by playing Margaret and then me. But—and this is an important point—there's no way our match could have had the impact it did if I hadn't made a name for myself first, and the place I'd done that was on the women's tour—our tour. If we had played even three years before we did, our match wouldn't have made half the splash it did. It was only because women's tennis had come along so far. We gave old Bobby a vehicle with which to exploit himself; it was almost like a marriage situation. And I think that's being as fair as I can about the whole thing.

So it was important to me that the match be straight up and on the level, and that everything about it be exactly right. And because I felt that way it almost fell through—twice.

The original contract was with Jackie Barnett, the guy who'd handled the Riggs-Court match. Then Jerry Perenchio, another Los Angeles promoter who had helped put together the first Muhammad Ali-Joe Frazier fight, got interested and bought out Barnett.

So far so good, except one day in Hilton Head Marilyn Barnett called to say she'd heard from some of her Los Angeles friends that Riggs was getting a piece of the gate. I blew up. I was edgy anyway, maybe even subconsciously looking for a way out, and that was in clear violation of our agreement. I said, "That's it. The match is off. Bad vibes. Call Perenchio. I want to tell him."

Dick Butera said, "Billie, you can't cancel on a rumor. Let me talk to Jerry."

Perenchio was in Los Angeles and caught the next plane East. By the time he arrived I had about nine different reasons why we shouldn't play the match and I lit into him as soon as he got in the car at the airport and didn't let up until we'd finished dinner at a little restaurant in Sea Pines. Perenchio was cool. He told me the thing about Riggs and the gate just wasn't true and he had the right answers to all the other questions I asked him. That took care of that.

But the problems weren't really over yet. ABC had hired three announcers to do the match, Howard Cosell for play-by-play, Rosie Casals for women's color, and Jack Kramer for men's color. I'd told Roone Arledge, the head of ABC Sports, from the beginning that I would not play the match if Kramer was in the broadcasting booth that night. Kramer and I had been going at each other for years and not just because of my walkout at the Pacific Southwest tournament two years before. Kramer, I felt, just didn't like women's tennis, never had and never would, and I wasn't about to give him a national forum to spout off his views on the night of maybe the biggest match in my life.

Arledge knew how I felt three weeks before we ever got to Houston, but when we did, Kramer was still ABC's guy.

Tuesday night about 1 A.M.—two days before the match—Roone called me. I was asleep and Larry intercepted the call.

Roone said he couldn't fire Kramer. Larry went through my arguments again.

"Get Billie Jean up," Roone said. "I want to talk to her."

"I won't do it," said Larry, "but I warn you, she's not kidding around."

The next afternoon—Wednesday—a meeting was scheduled to firm up the special ground rules for our match. I said I wasn't going to go to it unless I knew Kramer was off the air, because if he wasn't, there was no point talking about rules and I didn't want to waste my time.

We agreed to meet in one of the Astrodome offices—Roone and his people, and me and mine.

I said, "Hi."

He said, "Hi."

I said, "Roone, you've known for at least three weeks how I feel about Kramer and I really would appreciate it if you would get him off. I don't want him there. No way."

"What do you mean, 'No way?' " Roone asked.

"I mean no way. I'm not gonna play."

"C'mon," he said. "You're gonna play."

"Roone, if he's in that TV booth when I walk out on the court I'm not gonna play. I've waited too long not to have things right now. This is my night and Bobby's night, not Jack Kramer's night."

All the time Roone was looking at me like, "God, this kid's crazy, letting a chance like this go by."

But finally he started to get the message. "Are you sure that's how you feel?" he asked.

"I'm positive."

"Okay, but we've got to make a public statement. If we don't, it'll embarrass Jack."

"You could have done this two weeks ago so quickly and so quietly nobody ever would have known."

"We'll have to announce that Kramer's being up there will hurt your performance."

"*Bullshit*. No way he's gonna hurt my performance. I don't care if the Queen of England's up there. That's not the point."

So we went on about that for awhile. In the end we agreed that Larry would read a statement at the beginning of the program explaining why Gene Scott was doing the color instead of Jack Kramer. That wasn't a totally satisfactory solution, but at least the matter was settled. By now the match was less than a day and a half away.

I'd begun preparing for Riggs seriously the day after I lost that TV match to Evert. At Hilton Head I got into a routine I always try to use when I'm playing night tennis. I forced myself to stay up late and sleep in until ten or eleven in the morning so that when the match came around my body would really be used to that time schedule, to having its high point from seven to ten o'clock at night, when I really feel the best. It seems like a small thing, but when I want to get psyched up I spend a lot of time on the details, to make sure everything's perfect.

I did a lot of lifting weights for my legs and knees. I did a lot of that and it really helped. My legs were so strong the night of the match I couldn't believe it. I took good care of myself and got a lot of rest. And I got my head together.

Pete Collins, the resident pro at Hilton Head, made himself available to me anytime I wanted to hit. He and I had two sessions a day of about an hour each. I didn't overdo it because I felt it was too late to start really training hard. Pete and I mainly just rallied a lot, and I tried to concentrate on each shot, each swing of the racket, to get a good rhythm going. Sometimes we hit just to see how long we could keep the ball in play, and I got very patient inside. When I get that way I can stay on the base line all day if I have to.

That was going to be my alternate strategy—the base-line game. I wanted to be able to mix it up—go in some, stay back a little—but what I wanted to do especially at the start was to go in and put away some volleys because I thought that would break Bobby down faster psychologically. I practiced a lot of volleying and a lot of lateral movement and up-and-back movement. I felt pretty sure he didn't realize how quick I was or how good a volley I had. He knew, of course, I had a good volley—for a girl. But I thought my volley was strong in anybody's department, men's or women's, and I was counting on him underestimating me in that respect.

I hit a lot of service returns and overheads, especially overheads because I knew he was going to throw up a lot of lobs and wait for me to miss a few. But I felt that if I could either run them down or put them away, he'd be done. Finished. Pete was fantastically patient. He must have hit two hundred lobs a day.

I didn't practice my service very much because I'd already decided I wouldn't serve very hard to him. He's at his best when he can counterpunch against his opponent's power, and so I'd decided not to give him any power at all. I did practice changing my service all the time, going from a hard, flat serve to a slice serve to a topspin to a twist. It's not easy to do with any consistency because it takes a real sense of touch and accuracy. So as far as my service went, I thought in these terms: keep changing it around and serve the ball into his body a lot. I felt that was going to be important: to serve into him, then go wide—make him go exceptionally wide—to always keep him off balance, because he's the type of player who relies on his own balance to keep the rally under control.

Finally, I worked on keeping my shots to his backhand side—his weak side—then hitting very sharply to his forehand. Again, the idea was to confuse him, run him around the court, keep him from getting control.

Marilyn Barnett, who'd come in from L.A. late in the week, Dick Butera, and I left Hilton Head for Houston on the Sunday night before the match—Larry was already there—and I swear, it was like we were all going off to war or something. It was very upbeat, but very eerie, too, like we were going someplace we might not return from. I really didn't know what to expect.

My parents arrived the next day and we all stayed together in a hotel about fifteen minutes from the Astrodome. I tried not to change my routine at all from what it had been in Hilton Head. The only real difference—except for a big press conference on Tuesday and that business with Roone Arledge on Wednesday—was that a practice court had been set up in the Astrodome parking lot under a plastic bubble and that's where we went to hit, for two hours a night, until the match.

The days went quickly, and then it was Thursday.

I got up around noon, had breakfast, and started eating candy. I ate candy all day. My parents stopped by, along with Larry, Dick, Marilyn Barnett, and Dennis Van der Meer, my coach from Berkeley, who was going to be my official "second" that night. Wednesday night Dennis, Pete Collins, and I had looked at the Court-Riggs tape again and had discussed my strategy—the kinds of things I've already mentioned—and we went over that some more. Then I got antsy. I left my room and went downstairs and around the corner to a supermarket, and shopped. Got some cheeses, apples, other snack stuff, and I'm sure it blew the minds of the other customers.

The rest of the day I just lay around the hotel room, mostly in my favorite position—on the floor with my feet up on the bed—talking to whoever happened to wander by. I listened to "Jesus Christ Superstar" on the radio, and read through some of the hundreds of telegrams that had been pouring in throughout the week.

About four in the afternoon, I went over to the Astrodome with Dick and Marilyn. It was only the second time I'd actually been on the field, and it's really important for me to get the feel of a place, the atmosphere—like I do at Wimbledon every year—by just walking around and absorbing the sense of where I am. I tried to let the Astrodome sink in really fast. Like, triple time. I went down to the court, which was laid out approximately where second base is, and looked up and thought, "This is it, man. You've got to get used to this place."

It was such a huge building that the feeling of space was weird, not like a tennis stadium at all. But the room around the court, between the court and the $100 ground-level seats, wasn't very much at all, especially behind the base lines. And straight up—there was this ring of lights hanging over the center of the court and I knew right away if a lob ever got up in there, forget it.

I had the Astrodome people take me into the locker room and show me where my brother, Randy, dresses when the San Francisco

106

Giants play in Houston. I had specifically asked for the visitors' dressing room for that reason. They showed me Randy's locker and it turned out the number, 22, was the same as my birth date. A good omen. It also turned out later it was the wrong locker.

I did an interview with Frank Gifford for ABC, and finally went out and hit two-on-one against Pete Collins and Dennis Van der Meer. Nothing fancy. I was just trying to get used to the court. This was the biggest problem both Bobby and I had. The court was the same one we'd played on in the bubble, but out there it was laid over asphalt and played very fast. Inside, it was stretched over a plywood basketball court and was really dead in spots, and slow all over. It took us both a while to adjust.

After I finished hitting, I had a shower and changed clothes, then had a real training-table pre-match meal of Gatorade and candy. By then the people were starting to come in, the band was playing, the lights were turned on bright for the television cameras—and the pressure of the whole thing finally got to me. It hit me in a very strange way. I had my usual pre-match tension, of course, but, beyond that, in the hour or so before the match I felt more utterly alone than I ever had in my life. I just got totally wrapped up in my own thoughts. I remembered all the hassles and the headaches of the early years of the Slims tour, and I thought about how far we'd come in such a short time. It really came home to me—hard—that if I lost to Riggs much of what we'd won for ourselves might go right out the window. I'd sensed it before, but now I knew this match was one of the big three in my life—the others were against Maria Bueno in the 1966 Wimbledon finals and against Chris Evert at Forest Hills in 1971—in each case where a defeat would just about erase everything that I'd done before. Everybody else in Houston was having a ball, but that hour before Bobby and I actually stepped on the court was probably the most agonizing one of my life.

✤ ✤ ✤

Then the extravaganza began. Bobby was wheeled out in that ridiculous rickshaw, and I was carried onto the court in one of those throne-like litters, a little item I'd checked out carefully beforehand. I'm terrified of heights, and wobbling around four feet off the ground is just about my limit. Then Bobby presented me with a gigantic Sugar Daddy—about the size of a tennis racket—and I reciprocated by giving him Larimore Hustle, a little Male Chauvinist Piglet brought in for the occasion. (Bobby's middle name is Larimore. In answer to many queries, Larimore Hustle got lost in the excitement after the match, was found late that night huddled in a corner of the Astrodome, and now lives on a farm in Oklahoma—assuming the price of pork hasn't dictated another fate.)

When we walked on the court to warm up, I couldn't believe the crowd. The Astrodome wasn't sold out, but I'll guarantee you nobody else could have gotten in and had a good seat for a tennis match. Now it really was like a circus, or a baseball game, or maybe even a heavyweight title fight. Balloons, bands, noise, the works. People were shouting, "Right on, Billie Jean," or, "Go, Bobby," from the moment we entered and even well into the match. I loved it. Just the way a tennis crowd ought to be, everywhere. No indifference. I doubt if there was a neutral person in the whole Astrodome.

But once the match started, everything was straight. No gamesmanship, no hustle, no nothing except tennis. At the rules meeting the day before, when we'd decided on things like the special ten-minute injury time out, I'd been emphatic about that. I told Bobby, "I don't care what you do before we walk on the court, but once that match starts you don't walk over to my table, you don't talk to me, you don't touch me. . . ."

"Aaaw, Billie Jean, you don't care if I . . ."

". . . Nothing. We're gonna play a match, straight tennis."

I didn't want there to be any doubts at all about the match. It had to be on the level, and it was. When we were warming up, he called me over for a chat and I waved him away. I knew that if the match started turning in my favor he'd try anything, and I wanted to shut him off before he could begin.

Just before the match began I told myself, "Okay, this is it. Take each point by itself and don't rush things." Geez, just thinking of that moment months later I still get nervous and start to sweat.

I served first and won the first game of the match, and I knew right away this wasn't going to be a repeat of the Margaret Court thing. I also couldn't believe how slow he was. I thought he was faking it. He had to be. At the change after the first game I asked Dennis, "He's putting me on, right?"

Dennis assured me I was seeing the real thing, but I think Riggs did coast the first three or four games, though, trying to figure me out and at the same time not give away all of his wonderful secrets.

He broke my service in the fifth game when I missed a backhand volley by two inches, and took a 3–2 lead. I thought the next game was the most crucial of the match. If he held he'd be up 4–2 and I'd have to win three of the next four games to get back even and deuce the set at 5–all. If I broke back right away it would help my confidence and also let him know he was in for a real fight. Up to that point I'd been trying to make my shots too good, but I realized I just didn't have to go for the lines every time. He was slow, he couldn't hit with a lot of pace, and I could take the net any time I wanted. I just didn't need to make that good a shot. And so I calmed down, broke his service immediately to even the first set at 3–3—and then really got into it.

I was kind of shocked because I thought he would be a lot better than he was. He didn't have a big service, and his spins—"The ones that always get the girls"—weren't that great either. And I was absolutely right about him not realizing how quick I was at the net or how well I could volley. Five of the first six times he tried to pass me off his backhand side I just ran the ball down and—bam— volleyed away a winner. Near the end of the first set there was a great point where he hit wide and deep to my forehand, then wide and deep to my backhand. I ran 'em both down, and on the second shot

I flopped up a base-line lob and got right back into the point. He didn't believe I could run down those kinds of shots.

I concentrated hard on winning that first set and when I did—on a double fault by Bobby—I knew he was in big trouble. That meant he'd have to play at least four tough sets to win the match, probably more hard competitive tennis than he'd played in years. I felt I was in pretty good shape, and that things were going my way.

✣ ✣ ✣

About midway through the second set, I knew that the match was mine if I could just keep up the pace. But I didn't let up because I'd gotten into trouble too many times before thinking I had a match won before it was over.

Everything that I thought would work before the match did work. I played conservatively those last two sets and always waited for the right shot before I came in. I thought he'd be running everything down and keep throwing up lobs the whole time, but he just didn't do it. His backhand never got any better, I missed just one overhead the entire three sets, and at the end I was playing with complete confidence.

On match point I threw my racket in the air and just when I looked down I saw him finish his jump over the net. He came over to congratulate me, and then he was really nice. He said, "You're too good," and that was it.

Up to that point I'd really had mixed feelings about Riggs. I always liked him personally but I had also resented a lot of the statements he had made, if only in jest, before the match. When it was over, though, I kind of felt sorry for him, and I put my arm around him. Then all hell broke loose.

I don't know what the Astrodome people thought. I guess they figured that because it was a tennis match the people would be dignified when it was over. They weren't. They were great. George Foreman, the world heavyweight champion, was supposed to make the presentations, but fat chance. I got bombed from all sides. Larry was trying to protect me. Marilyn was trying to protect me. Marilyn! She must weigh 100 pounds. She had bruises all over her body from the crush. So did Larry. So did I. Larry finally lifted me on a little table so I could show off the trophy. Then a security guard arrived and Foreman was able to give me the check. I remember looking down at the "$100,000" written on it and thinking that looked pretty funny. I'd never seen a check that big before—made out to me.

I got to the press conference first—I guess Bobby went to comb his hair forward in that funny way he does. I had a beer. I couldn't wait to have a beer. Then I sat there with my shoes off with all those microphones around and looking at all those faces and thinking about all the past things that had happened to get me to where I was that night. I was so relieved. I was just happy it was over.

That night Jerry Perenchio held a party at the Astroworld Hotel but I was whacked out. I did a five minute walk-through, then got out of there and went back to my hotel and ate ice cream with Larry and my parents, read some more telegrams, and went to bed. Ten weeks of getting psyched up for one night of tennis and then, boom, it was all over.

The match was tough, mentally and physically. I've played better matches, but under the circumstances I played as well as I possibly could, and so, I think, did Bobby. I'm sure a lot of players who watched the match are convinced they can beat Riggs too, so what's the big deal? Well, sure they can beat him—on Court 50 at their home club with three people watching. But let 'em try it before 40 million people and I think things would be different.

As far as the importance of the match, it proved just two things. First, that a woman *can* beat a man. Second, that tennis can be a big-time sport, and will, once it gets into the hands of the people who know how to promote it.

Jim Brosnan

THE LONG SEASON

The Long Season, pitcher Jim Brosnan's funny and revealing journal of his 1959 season playing for the St. Louis Cardinals and then the Cincinnati Reds, was the first sports memoir to lift the curtain and show us a glimpse of our heroes, warts and all—the one without which all the other memoirs which have followed, could not have been written. This excerpt begins with Brosnan meeting his new team, the Reds, at Chicago's Wrigley Field, Brosnan's former home park.

June 11
Chicago

The high-pitched, almost girlish, laughter of Yosh Kawano, the Cub's clubhouse man, greeted me when I arrived at Wrigley Field. I parked my car in the Cub parking lot (to the disgust of the police sergeant who takes his "clout" from fans who wish to park near the ball park. My station wagon takes up space for one and half cars, at a buck per car.) I tipped Eddie a large hello, and headed for the Waveland Street entrance and the long walk beneath the stands to the visiting club's dressing rooms. Kawano, rushing from the Cub clubhouse on one of his mysterious and urgent errands, spied me as I entered the gate, carrying a dusty Cardinal duffel bag.

"Finally got rid of Hemus, didn't you, Jim?" he said, as I clapped a hand on his shoulder. In my years with the Cubs Yosh Kawano and Al Scheuneman, the Cub trainer, were my closest friends on the club. Together, Yosh and Al could usually figure out most of my ballplayer's problems. Had I needed advice or consolation about my relations with Solly Hemus [the Cardinals' manager–ed.] I'd have gotten them from Kawano and Scheuneman. But, of course, having matured as a ballplayer, I did not need advice. I just got rid of Solly. And how mature can you get?

"Yosh, is everything all right?' I asked, as I usually do. "You tell Doc that I'll be up to see him tomorrow before the game. What time does Grumpy leave the clubhouse?"

"Scheffing won't mind your coming into the clubhouse," he said. "You're welcome any time up there. You oughta know that, Jim. Doc and I'll protect you. Yosh laughed at such a likelihood.

"Yosh," I said, "I gotta run. You and Doc are coming to supper, aren't you?"

As soon as you invite us," he said. "Good luck over there. Wish you were over here."

"Me, too," I lied. What the hell, I hadn't had time to become unhappy with the Reds, yet!

The Reds were half-dressed by the time I walked into the clubhouse. The half-dress uniform of the Cincinnati club is the same as that of every other club I ever played with. Except the Reds wear solid red stockings over their sanitary hose. The visiting clubhouse man stood at the door as I climbed the stairs.

"Joe," I said, "I'm back already. Where did you put me?"

"You're in Jeffcoat's locker," he said. "Next to Frank Thomas."

Clubhouse men try to put each player in the same locker every time he comes into town during the season. Since there are seven different men to each locker off and on during the year, the task of keeping the arrangement straight is painstaking, even for a clubhouse man. But why not make a man feel at home on the road? Provide comfort, earn a bigger tip.

The gloom of night prevails in the visitors' clubhouse at Wrigley Field, even with all the lights on. If I couldn't find my name (or

Jeffcoat's) above a locker I could always look for Thomas instead. I didn't have to.

"Oh no," he said. "There goes ten points off my batting average."

"Hello, Frank" I said, as he held out his hand. "You're really having a lousy year, aren't you?"

"Whaddya mean," he said.

"Well, we hadn't played you but once this season over at St. Louis. I know damn well you were counting on eight hits off me. What do you think you'd have hit last year if I hadn't pitched against you?"

"About what I'm hitting now, I guess." He smiled.

"That's nothing to laugh about, Thomas," said Frank Robinson, who shoved a huge hand at me.

Of all the reasons why I was glad to be traded to Cincinnati, being on the same team with Frank Thomas was most satisfying. In the three and a half years that I had been pitching against Thomas I hadn't gotten him out enough to remember. He had personally beaten me in three games, and had one streak of nine straight base hits, six of them for extra bases. Though he was now having a bad year at the plate so far, all he probably needed was to see me wind up on the mound and it would all come back to him.

I set my bag down on the chair and walked around the room to say hello, good to see you, glad to be here, etc. My tour of the clubhouse wound up at the manager's cubbyhole. Mayo Smith looked up from the lineup card he had filled out in triplicate. "Jimmy," he said, "glad you're here. Now, I want to talk to you in a few minutes. When did you pitch last? Never mind. You're ready to go now, aren't you? Right. Get dressed, then, and well have a little chat."

In Jeffcoat's locker I found a pile of red sweatshirts, a uniform, a dirty cap, and a wool-and-nylon windbreaker, all the property of the Cincinnati ball club. The shirts were too big for me, the cap too small, and the sleeveless uniform awkwardly ill-fitting. No sleeve on the uniform shirt means more freedom for the arms, I suppose. It didn't feel right to me.

Just after we started batting practice rain fell, chasing fans under the stands and ballplayers into the dugout. Mayo Smith cornered me there. "I have a proposition for you," he said. "What would you rather do, start or relieve? Now, I like to think of you as a relief pitcher. What I saw of you over at Philadelphia last year makes me think so. You seem to get tired about the seventh when you start a game. Right?"

I started to say, "Who doesn't?" One of the indelible blots on my pitching career has been my inability to go nine innings. Since only 20 per cent of all starting pitchers in the majors *do* go nine innings, I feel less ashamed than I should be, perhaps. Smith who had managed Hemus at Philadelphia in 1958 had seen me lose a two-run lead twice in the late innings. In both games I had breezed for seven, then blown my victory.

"Yes, sir," I said, "whatever you think I can do for you I'll try my best. I feel that I can pitch in the majors, both as a starter and a reliever. I've done both, and had fair success most of the time. But, whatever you say."

"Well, now," he said, "which would you rather do?"

"It makes no difference to me," I said.

"I want you to be happy out there, doing what you think you'd like to do," he said.

"It's up to you," I said. The rain fell, the humidity rose, and I wondered if we'd ever get to the point. Mayo had already stated his opinion—I couldn't start. The only thing I had left to be happy with was relief.

"Here's my reason for talking to like this," he said. "I'm desperate for a good relief pitcher, somebody who can come in and stop them for an inning or two. We score runs. I've got no complaint about that. But did you know that seventeen times this year we've had a lead in the eighth and ninth innings, and fourteen times the pitchers have blown it?"

I shook my head. "That's baseball," I thought, facetiously.

"If we had won just half those games," Smith went on, "we'd be right up there with the Braves right now instead of in sixth place. I need a relief pitcher and I think you can be the man. Now, what do you say?"

"Like I said before, Mayo, you're the boss. I get just as much kick out of saving games as I do out of winning them. I know I can pitch better than I have so far this season. I never did get myself straightened out over at St. Louis."

"You're a better pitcher than that, we know," he assured me.

June 12
Chicago

"Just what kind of pitcher are you, do you think?"

Clyde King, the Reds' pitching coach, has a reputation for erudition. An anomaly among pitching coaches, he wants to know WHY instead of WHO, WHAT instead of WHEN. His analysis of a pitcher's style is subjective rather than objective. He had startled me with his approach.

"I really don't know what to say," I said. "What kind of pitcher do these guys say I am?"

"You're answering my question with a question," he chided me. "We won't get anywhere that way. Now, I haven't seen you pitch, so I don't know what kind of pitcher you are, myself. I've talked to the hitters on this club. They say you've got a lot of good stuff, but you're inconsistent with it. One time you'll throw a real good fast ball, the next fast ball might be straight, nothing on it. What would *you* say is your best pitch?"

"The one I rely on?" I asked. He nodded his head. "Well, I'd have to say I throw my slider when I'm in a jam."

"Don't you think those hitters know that by now?" he said. His attitude was that of a pedantic teacher who already knew the answers and asked the questions to see if *I* knew them. Which is all right with me, as long as he had the answers to *my* questions, too. "What's wrong with your fast ball?" he asked.

I fingered the baseball he had handed me as we sat down in the bullpen. "There's nothing wrong with either one of my fast balls, I guess. I just prefer to use them to set up a hitter for the slider or change or curve, whichever is working best for me."

He gave me, a quizzical look. "You have two fast balls, you say? Which is the better of the two?"

I shrugged my shoulders. Neither one of them appealed to me at times. Once in a while they both moved pretty well. "I prefer to use the one that sails away from a right-handed batter. It's better to pitch away, if possible. But that gives me three pitches that move the same way, the curve, the slider, and the sailer. And that's not too good."

"Yes"' he said, "and—"

"But," I interrupted, "my sailer hasn't been moving this year. I have to let it go at a certain angle—about three-quarters instead of overhand. My other fast ball has to come directly overhand, and I've been getting the two mixed up. When I come in between, neither of them works much."

"Let's get a catcher. I want to look at what you're talking about." He called Pete Whisenant out from the bench. "Mayo might want to use you for an inning today. But a little throwing now won't hurt you."

King stood behind me as I warmed up. Discounting my last short term in a Cardinal uniform, I hadn't pitched in ten days. My arm felt strong, almost heavy, and the ball moved well. For ten minutes I threw as King directed me, mixing my two fast balls with curves and change-ups. ("We know you can throw the slider," he said.) Whisenant, another former roommate of mine (on the Cubs in 1956), shouted exuberant commands. "Give it to me right here, now. Put a little something on it. Atta boy, big man. Wow, has this guy got great stuff, Clyde. You oughta win twenty, you big stiff!"

King called a halt, took the ball, and led me back to the bench. "Pete" he asked Whisenant, "if you were hitting against Brosnan what would you look for?"

"Bross?" he said. "Well, he'd get me out on his slider a couple times, maybe, but eventually he'd hang one and I'd cream it. Bross thinks too much. And he doesn't give the hitter credit for doing some thinking, too."

"What the hell do you think I'm thinking about on the mound,

Whiz?" I protested. "I'm thinking: what are you guys thinking? You oughta give me credit for respecting you, too."

"Jim" said King, "I really think you should forget about that 'sailer,' as you call it, and concentrate on your other fast ball. It rides in to a right-hander pretty well and much more consistently. Another thing. Move over on the mound. Pitch from the right-hand corner of the rubber. Bend your back leg as you start your motion home. That'll make your arm and back follow through better and keep you from being high with all your pitches. And please, start to throw that fast ball more often. You got a better fast ball than I thought you had. You got a better one than you think you have, too."

King's advice was specific, personal, and easy to understand. I should have realized, myself, that my trouble with high pitches had stemmed from a lazy back leg. (In order to keep his pitches consistently low, a pitcher as tall as I am has to dip his back knee in order to lower the line of the projected trajectory of his pitch. Especially when he throws the slider and fast ball as often during the game as I do.)

"But if these guys think my slider's my best pitch, and the catchers at St. Louis and Chicago think so, too, why should I argue with them and throw fast balls?" I wasn't going to give up my simple style of pitching without an argument.

"Don't be simple, Bross," said Whisenant.

"You just try those things, Jim," said King. "You want to improve yourself, don't you? Wouldn't you like to make it easier on yourself out there?"

One thing all pitchers share in common is a desire to make the job easier. At last I had heard some specific directions that had come from direct observations. If King and I weren't on the right track, we were at least headed somewhere.

"Bross," said Whisenant, "you just listen to me and Clyde, and everything's gonna be all right."

"Did you hear where Grissom quit?" I asked.

"Yes, sir. That's too bad," said King. "He had a very sore back, I understand."

Grissom's decision to retire had come just ten days after he'd returned to the active list. He made two torturous trips to the mound in that time and had been treated as painfully as he must have felt. The vision of Uncle Marv shambling determinedly to the mound like a great St. Bernard bringing relief to a floundering pitcher would haunt us no more. He'd always been on the other side until this year, so I could hardly remember his pitching with pleasure. Admiration, perhaps; respect, certainly. Yet, Grissom's presence lingers in my memory. His was a pleasant, patient personality. He made me feel like someday I might learn to be a pitcher. Marv had class. He was a true Old Pro.

June 13
St. Louis

. . .My check was in my locker along with two bills from the Cardinals and a fan letter from Florissant, Missouri, that said Devine was a louse, Hemus was a bum, and I was still all right. I had not finished dressing in uniform when the meeting started. Smith called me over to his locker and said, "We have played this team only once all year so far. Is there anything that any of these guys are doing that I ought to know about?"

I looked at the score-card lineup. "Blasingame has had a lot of success hitting to left field, but I think you can still jam him and curve him. Keep the ball down, I'd say. He and Cimoli love to hit-and-run. Cimoli's been hitting mostly to right. He's hit that screen a lot this season. It's just the right distance for him, I guess. He hates to be knocked down, I know, and he complains about being jammed a lot. I guess that's the best way to pitch him. He's a long way from the plate, but it's hard to get a ball by him on the outside corner, unless he's been set up pretty well."

"How about Bill White?" asked Smith. "He never looked like a .300 hitter when he was at New York."

"Bill's a pretty smart boy. He was supposed to be a low-ball power hitter, and everybody pitched him up high at the start of the season. Then he went to punching the ball, and now I'd say he's a better high-ball hitter. At least he's a good one. He's been hot, recently, I know. He's got quick hands. You can't change up on him much. The rest of these guys you know. Oliver's playing left field, I see. I didn't see enough of him this spring to say how he hits, and they brought him up just before I was traded so I don't remember too much about him. He strikes out a lot, I know. Probably has trouble with breaking stuff. He's got a lot of power."

"What's wrong with Musial?" he asked.

"I thought last year that Stan started to have trouble getting around on the ball. He's not as quick with his wrists as he used to be. But don't make a mistake! When he's feeling all right he's still a sweet hitter."

Musial stood at the batting cage with Cunningham as we trooped onto the field after the meeting. I slapped a hand on Stan's shoulder.

"You think we'll get fined for fraternizing if Secory sees us talking here, Stash?"

"Why, James, where you been?" he said. "I've been looking all over to find somebody to talk to during the game."

"Why don't you buy Hemus's contract and ship him out, Stan? Then you could play whenever you wanted."

Cunningham poked me with his bat. "Secory's waving at you, Prof. Let's not get us fined now. Stan and I can't afford it. Right, Stanley?"

Musial tossed the heavy bat aside and walked into the cage to hit. His first three swings sent balls into the right field screen. What a sweet swing!

The night air turned warm, the mosquitoes buzzed busily, and the score stood at 1–1 as we took the field in the tenth. My new roomie, Tom Acker, was the pitcher. White singled, Boyer beat out a ground ball, and Acker wild-pitched them to second and third. Cunningham took two high pitches for balls, and Mayo called time to take Acker out and bring me in. The fans, yelling for the kill, greeted me with more-than-gracious applause. Harry Caray booed, probably, but some fanatics are incorrigibly ill-spirited. It is not unusual for a ballplayer to be unpopular one day, only to change uniforms and be welcomed a week later. Fans reserve their loudest criticism for the home team.

Dotterer, the Reds' catcher, and Smith both asked me how I was going to pitch to George Crowe, who was obviously going to pinch-hit for Flood.

"I'll have to jam him, and hope he pops it up," I said. "He takes the first pitch a lot. We'll give him one good fast ball for a strike and then throw him breaking stuff on his hands."

They both nodded. I walked Cunningham purposely to load the bases, poured the fast ball into Crowe for a called strike, then threw the slider. Crowe popped it up, but into right field. Bell came in three steps, caught the ball, and threw to the plate as White raced home from third. I cut in front of White to back up the plate. The throw was true. Dotterer reached for the ball as White did for the plate. Suddenly the ball took a last-minute hop. Dotterer, one eye on the ball, the other on White's leg, didn't time the hop of the ball and it bounced off the edge of his glove into my bare hand as I stood a few feet behind the plate. It might have been a close play.

"You made the right pitch" said Mayo in the clubhouse. "Do you think you can start on Sunday?"

"Why not?"

June 15
St. Louis

One of the first decisions a pitcher must make when he knows he's to pitch the second game of a Sunday double-header is what time to eat breakfast. Some managers allow the second-game starter to report to the park after the first game has started. He then eats normally four hours before his game is most likely to begin. However, rain or extra innings may prolong the start of the second game. If the pitcher eats four hours before the first game he may feel starved by the time the second game begins. Mayo declined to permit me a late arrival. "You can rest at the park just as well as at the hotel," he said.

"When will I eat, then?" I said, dismayed. It's just an old superstition, of course, but starting pitchers love to be given special handling.

My second decision of the day involved whether or not I should chew tobacco during batting practice and during the first game. I was too nervous not to. My spitting area had just turned brown when Harry Caray came down the steps into the dugout. "Here's my wife's chance," I thought. He said, "Hi ya, Jimmy boy." I aimed at his shoes, subconsciously wishing him ill. But my head turned at the last second and the tobacco splashed on the dugout steps. "I'll just ignore him," I decided. "Two-faced old. . ."

Caray sat next to Mayo Smith, wheedling opinions from him. "And what do you think of Solly taking himself off the active list? He says he can think better if he doesn't worry about keeping in shape," said Caray.

Ah, so! Hemus nct going to play, eh. Not going to take a chance. Well, it's just coincidence that I'm starting today. He *knows* I wouldn't throw at him, even if I got a chance. I wouldn't think of giving him a low slider right on the knee. Nah!

We lost the first game to make it three losses in a row. As King handed me the warm-up ball for the second game, he said, "We have to have this game. Go as far as you can, now, and we'll bring you help if you need it."

I needed it in the first inning. After Ricketts, a Cardinal rookie pitcher, had walked home one run in our half of the first I told myself, "Just hold them, now. We're gonna bust loose and score ten runs." I walked Blasingame to start the inning, and walked Musial five hitters later to force in the tying run. Smith came out to talk to me.

"Just settle down, now," he said. "Clyde says for you to bend your knee. Everything's high. Now, I know you can get out of this. You got good stuff."

Hal Smith bounced a slider back to me and we were out of the inning, but I couldn't help brooding on the bench. "Nothing's going where it should. I *know* how to pitch these guys but I can't seem to do it."

The innings and hours rocked by, bumpily. I was in trouble every inning. Most of the time I pitched from a stretch, knowing that the hit-and-run or steal was on, and hoping Dotterer could throw somebody out. If I didn't make a bad pitch, I made a wild pitch and walked the batter. When I did make a bad pitch with runners in scoring position, however, the batter lined into a double play. I gave up trying to pitch and tried to throw my best stuff every time, hoping it came close to the strike zone.

By the end of the seventh inning I had thrown 150 pitches and the third finger of my right hand was bleeding from a punctured blister. The temptation to beg off pitching any more tormented me. Deservedly, over the years of my career, I had gotten the reputation of a late-inning Blister-Finger. At the end of six innings, my pitching hand inevitably developed a blister, I lost my stuff, and had to be relieved. "Blisters" was my nickname on any opponent's bench in the Pacific Coast League, 1955. Although I won seventeen games that year I needed a lot of help, and my reputation as a pitcher was slightly soiled. In the spring of '58 I finally decided, "I'm never going to be taken out of a game because of a blister again. It just isn't going to bother me any more." It's amazing what self-hypnosis can do.

Frustration ate at my pride as I sat on the Busch Stadium bench. I *had* to ignore the irritation of my bleeding finger. "It hurts when I throw breaking stuff but I can't control that anyway. So, forget it," I told Smith. Mayo, nevertheless, signaled to the bullpen to warm somebody up, and we promptly scored two runs to take a 3-1 lead.

As I trudged out to the mound in the eighth inning I had an additional frustration plaguing my conscience. "Goddamn it, I don't want to blow this, now. For Christ's sake, let me have an easy inning." Boyer lined a double off the left field wall and out came Smith waving for help. Pena came in and retired the side. I ran across the field, through the Cardinal dugout, up the stairs, into our clubhouse. As the ninth began I was at the mirror shaving and praying that Pena could hold them one more inning. He did. The radio sighed, tearfully. "Well, we won one game, anyway," cried Harry Caray. "We shoulda won that second one, too. Ricketts pitched a fine game in his first start for the Cards. It's too bad. The winner for Cincinnati was that fellow we traded. He needed help, though, in the eighth. But he still gets credit for the win."

"Shut that bum off," I said, happily.

June 18

En route to San Francisco

"What are you figuring out, Broz? Your batting average?"

I looked up from the writing table that had been inserted into my plane seat. The roar of the DC-7 motors outside my left ear was stupefying. Willard Schmidt stood in the aisle, stretching and shaking himself to relieve the stiffness of our day-long flight. Willard pointed to the paper on my table.

"No, no, Will," I said, "this is just one of my more morbid pastimes. I've been working out how much I'm worth dead. If all four motors of this plane stop, the nose turns over, and we land head-first in the Grand Canyon down there I'd be worth five times as much as I will if we land safe in Frisco."

"Yeah" he nodded. "But what good would it do ya?"

"Don't be so matter-of-fact, Willard. With all the insurance the ball club takes out on you, and double-indemnity clauses, doesn't it give you a feeling of affluence to make this trip to the Coast?"

"Feeling of what?" he asked. "Could you break that down into smaller words. I'm working a crossword puzzle."

"No, I can't, Will" I said. "When I'm talking about millions I gotta use hundred-dollar words."

"Save a couple bills for tips, there, man," said Frank Robinson. He walked by us, yelling to Pinson in the plane's galley. "Two milks and a coffee!"

Robinson returned with a tray of food, swept my money-fantasy papers onto the floor, and said, "Here ya go, man. Suck it up."

"You and Pinson always serve the food on these plane trips, Frank?" I asked.

"That's right. We feature quick courteous service from our sparkling clean kitchens. You got any complaints?"

"Where's the beer? The Cardinals always had a couple of cases aboard for these long flights."

"The beer was all gone five minutes after we left the ground. We got some serious drinkers on this club, man."

"You got any champagne? Or, like that?"

"Next stop for that jazz," he said.

The next stop was the International Airport in San Francisco. Hiding my chagrin at losing all that insurance money again, I rushed into the lobby, and headed for the telephone booth. We were scheduled for three games. That gave us two free nights. Arrangements had to be made to free-load two dinners. That is not difficult on the West Coast. One of the principal economic motivations in California is reciprocal free-loading. "You get me two tickets for the ball game and I'll buy you a drink, feed you a meal, get you a date, etc." Five phone calls later I was set for two suppers and a lunch.

"Who are you with now?" asked the Free-loaders.

"I'm with you, dad, of course," I said. "Let's have dinner at your place and I'll bring you up to date."

It's easy.

Newcombe won the first game of the series, 2-1, under the lights. We lost the second game, under the sun. Ever since I'd joined the club, we'd played .500 ball on the road. The Book says that a ball club that breaks even away from home should be a pennant contender. The Book is a rich fund of bad logic. Why aim to break even? Why be half-ambitious? Win 'em all, or lose 'em all. Be great champs or big bums.

"That big bum can't get anybody out. Why don't your manager get him outa there?" yelled a free-loading fan behind the bullpen. In the sixth inning of the third game of the series we trailed 6-3.

Nuxhall stood helplessly on the mound, muttering to himself as Giant base hits fell safely all over the ball park. Of the thirteen Giant hits, nine had been bloops, squibs, or Texas League singles. The wind, blowing in erratic gusts, had dropped two pop fly balls into right field instead of in Robinson's first-base glove. Temple, the second baseman, had booted three ground balls to add to Nuxhall's frustration.

"Tomorrow's paper will say Nuxhall was *blasted* for thirteen hits. Watch and see," I said.

"Joe's had this kind of luck all year long. I never saw anything like it," said Lawrence.

"What are you doing down here, Brooks?" I asked him. "You're a starting pitcher aren't you?"

"On this club, who knows?" said Lawrence. "Mayo hasn't made up his mind, yet. But then, the season's only half over. We oughta get straightened out during the All-Star break."

"Don't be bitter, Brooksie," I said. "Maybe Mayo won't even be around. I heard today that rumors are flying. Some gamblers got Smith fired already." . . .

❖   ❖   ❖

June 24
Cincinnati
Back home again in Cincinnati.

"How many tickets do you want?" I said into the phone. . . "That's a lotta box seats. . . . I guess I can get 'em. The way we been going I don't think we're gonna pack Crosley Field. . . . Mom coming with you tonight? . . . She's never seen me pitch at a major league ball park, has she? . . . Well, tell her to get there early. You sometimes can't see the starting pitcher if you're ten minutes late."

The threat of rain ended when I started to warm up. Through the grandstand I could see blue sky on the horizon. The thunderclouds rolled away and the wind that had been blowing hard from the southwest (the worst direction) died down. I noticed the flag flapping limply against the pole in left center, and I breathed a sigh of relief. First good omen of the day. My blister finger popped open even before I completed my warm-up throwing.

"You think you can make it?" asked Smith.

"Why not?" I said. "I'll give it a try. It bothers my breaking stuff mostly. I'll lay off the curve and use my slider."

As "The Star-Spangled Banner" boomed from the Crosley Field organ I said to myself, "Big boy, your job tonight is to concentrate. Have an idea on every pitch and make every pitch count."

Tony Taylor hit first for the Cubs. "He's been hitting pretty well lately," I said to myself. "Keep the sinker down and in. Make him hit something into the ground. He uppercuts the ball slightly." Taylor reached for a slider away from him and lofted the ball over shortstop for a single. Great start!

"You little Cuban Hot Dog," I said to myself as I looked at Taylor standing on first. "Dark's gonna hit-and-run probably. He hits the ball in on him better to right field than the ball away. Make him hit the slider." Dark swung at a belt-high slider on the outside of the plate, and popped it up. "Pretty good stuff on that pitch."

Walls came to the plate. "My old roomie! Last time at St. Louis he hit a good slider right on the nose. He must be looking for it. I'll make him hit the sinker." Walls wouldn't bite on two inside fast balls and I eventually walked him. With Banks up, and only one out I was already in trouble.

"Wonder if Mother is here, yet," I thought. "I can't take a chance throwing Banks a breaking ball away and down. That's a good double-play pitch but if I make a slight mistake I'm behind three runs." I shook off Bailey's signal for the curve; shook again on the slider; and again on the slider when he returned to that sign. He obviously didn't want the old hummer. Why not? It ain't hummin' tonight? I stepped back off the mound to rub some ideas into the ball. Bailey must like my slide ball. Maybe it's better than it feels when it leaves my fingers. (Most of the pitcher's control on breaking balls lies in his fingers. I had a bad finger. I must have poor breaking stuff. Q.E.D. Well, Bailey probably never heard of Q.E.D., so why not give him what he wants?)

Banks went for the slider, up and away from him. Not a classic pitch, but he was late with his bat and popped it up. Two high sliders and two pop-ups. I had either a good slider or a lot of luck.

Long was next. "Try to jam him with a fast ball or a slider," I said to myself. Long hit the slider on a line to left field. "Don't fall down, Lynch," I said as I ran to back up home plate. Lynch didn't move till the ball landed in his glove.

"That's your bad inning, Jimmy," said Mayo. "Keep that back leg bent now. Your fast ball's alive."

I'd only thrown one. The slider must look like a fast ball from the dugout. That's good. That's the way the slider should look. "Doc," I said to the trainer. "Let's go to work. This finger's bleeding. You got any collodion we can put on it?"

Anderson fished through his satchel and pulled out a bottle. "This'll do the trick, my boy. Just let old Doc take care of your finger. You take care of the batters. You can't use a Band-Aid, I guess, huh?"

"No, Doc," I said "Not only is it illegal but I lose my grip on the baseball."

"Okay, swell. Let's try this stuff, then. Put a coat over the sore. There. Now, see if that sticks on there when you throw. Stings a little, doesn't it? That just proves you're alive, my boy."

Lynch, Robinson, Bell, and Bailey scored within a dozen pitches and by the time I returned to the mound I felt like a new man. Nothing like a four-run lead to give a pitcher courage. "They'll have to drag me off this mound before the sixth inning now," I said to myself.

Thomson hit sixth for the Cubs. "Why waste a slider? Jam him with the sinker right away. That's what I'll throw at him eventually anyway." He hit it to Kasko at shortstop for one out.

Moryn. "Keep the ball in on him, and fast. No slow stuff." Moose swung and missed three high sliders. Damn! That's a pretty good pitch tonight.

Sam Taylor. "Same as Moryn. Nothing out over the plate." Sammy fanned on the same three pitches. Eight quick throws in four fast minutes and I felt like a pitcher again.

Twice more I went through the Cub lineup. Walls hit a 3-2 fast ball ("Don't walk him," I said. "Make him hit it to get on.") for a single to center. In the next inning Thomson reached for a slider that I meant to waste and hit it past me on the ground into center. Noren ("How do I pitch him?") hit a line drive over short for a single. ("Better keep it in on him next time.") But for the most part my arm worked like a well-oiled machine. The batter came to the plate. My experience classified him. My mind told my arm what to do. And it did it. It seldom happens precisely that way.

With a shutout in reach as I started the ninth, I told Anderson to pour on the collodion. He had covered the finger each inning but it soon wore off. Blood-marks dotted the baseball after each sinker pitch; But as a psychological prop the collodion kept me together for nine innings.

Walls took a slider for strike three to begin the ninth. Banks, as he stood at the plate, crouched a little deeper in the box. I had jammed him the last two times up. "I better go away with the slide ball this time," I decided. I didn't get the slider far enough away and Banks whipped the fat part of his bat against it. "Uh-oh!" I thought. "There she goes." The ball took off for the center field fence, but the wind caught it and blew it toward right field. Pinson chased it, running like a greyhound after the rabbit. "Good Lord! What a catch!"

Long took two straight strikes. "Why not experiment a little?" I thought. "Think I'll throw him a change-of-pace. Defy the Book." Long grunted as he saw the expected fast ball change speed. He swung at the ball anyway and bounced it to Robinson who tagged first and stuck the ball into his back pocket.

"Oh, no, Robby," I said. "That one's mine."

June 28

Cincinnati

Life in the Cincinnati clubhouse in midsummer is lived in the raw. Pregame uniform is jock strap and shower clogs. The thought of putting on a flannel uniform over woolen socks and undershirt starts the sweat rolling.

"How many electric fans you got in here, Chesty?" I asked the clubhouse man.

"Not enough" he said. "It's too hot already, isn't it? I don't envy you guys goin' onto that field today."

"I'm not going, myself," I said. "It may get to be a hundred on the mound like it did yesterday and I'm staying right in that air-conditioned dugout."

Willard Schmidt walked into the clubhouse, with his sport shirt already unbuttoned. "Pitchers hitting today, Jim?"

"No, Willard," I said. "You know pitchers never hit on Sunday."

"Good," he said. "It's too hot to swing a bat."

"You got an air-conditioned house, Will?" I asked.

"No. Why?"

"How do you sleep at night in this heat?"

"On my back," he said. "Don't get personal. You got your family living in a hotel?"

"Yeah," I said, "but I don't know whether it's good to have an air-conditioned room to sleep in or not. This heat knocks you over when you come outside."

"Better to have a frigid wife to keep the bed cold," he said.

"I don't like 'em."

The trainer's room filled rapidly. The trainer keeps a large jug of salt pills next to the vitamin tablet bottle and players reach for a handful whether they intend to sweat or not. Big Don Newcombe lay on the table, Doc Anderson kneading Newk's mountainous torso, rubbing oil into his big arm. Frank Robinson sat on the other massage table staring at his bandaged wrist.

"Everything all right, Robby?" I asked.

He rose from the table, gave me a dirty look because I'm a pitcher, and walked out of the room.

"Guess he can't play, huh, Doc?" I said.

"Guess not," said Anderson. "What kind of guy is that Anderson over at Chicago? The pitcher?"

"He's a nice kid," I said. "I don't think he was throwing at Robby. Consciously, that is. But when a guy is hitting pitchers the way Robinson was hitting the Cubs, you gotta expect him to be knocked down. He must have had ten for fifteen off the Cubs in the last six games."

"Well, Anderson got him good, I'll say that for him," said Schmidt.

"Robby was probably hanging in there looking for Anderson's curve ball," I said. "You know, two years ago when I was with the Cubs, Anderson didn't even have a curve. He sure has improved."

"Hey," said someone in the other room, "Doc, tell the Whale to get off the table so us regulars can rest a little bit."

Newcombe grunted, unpoetically.

As we started out of the clubhouse to the field, Schmidt said to me, "How about coming down to the bullpen, Brosnan? Your wound still bothering you?"

"This terrible heat might cause it to start bleeding again, Willard," I said. "No, it's all right. I think I could go a couple . . . hitters"

I walked under the grandstand to the ramp leading onto the field, bumping into Broglio at the gate.

"Everything all right Ern?" I asked. "How much weight did you lose yesterday?"

Broglio grinned, then groaned, "God, musta been ten, twelve pounds anyway. I didn't think I was going to make it."

"You just wanted an excuse to shave your beard, is all," I said, punching him in the arm as he walked out into the sun. Broglio had vowed, just before I left the Cardinals, not to shave till he won a ball game. He had lost his first five games. Since then he'd won two in a row. You never know what will work for some pitchers.

By the end of the first inning I wished I was in the bullpen, just to get away from the suffering. The Cardinals scored seven runs in the first inning on four hits and three errors. Mayo moaned audibly, biting his lips, mussing his silver-streaked hair till he no longer looked like a successful, retired Florida rancher, but more like a man in the last throes of bankruptcy. "What are you gonna do?" he mumbled half to himself.

If he didn't know, neither did any of us. The Cardinals spent thirty minutes batting in the first inning. It looked like we might not get home till eight o'clock. Dipping a sponge into ammonia-treated water, the grumbling hitters squeezed some life onto the backs of their necks and battled back. They got as close as 8-6 in the fifth, then pooped out.

After an ill-tasting lunch of crackers and cheese, ice cream and grape soda, we went back out for another try. The Cardinals, by winning the first game, had moved ahead of us into sixth place. (Here I had thought I was moving up in the league when I was traded.)

"Jim," said Clyde King, "you come down with us to the bullpen. Mayo says we have to win this game. He's going to use both you and Purkey in the late innings if he has to."

("If he hadn't botched up his pitching staff all year using starters in relief he might not be in such a position," I thought. Ballplayers ought to know where they stand.)

"Why did Burkhart throw Thomas out in the ninth?" asked King.

"Frank had to get in the last word. He thought the pitch hit him, and Burkhart didn't. It looked from the dugout like it was all settled, then Thomas stepped back out of the batter's box and said something else. You know the Donkey. He never knows when to stop," I said.

The Cards scored nine runs before we could get one in the second game, and the fans, full of beer and indignation, booed each move that Mayo made.

"They're gonna run him outa town just like they did Tebbetts," said Purkey.

As the sun sank behind the grandstand in the seventh, we scored. Ricketts, the Cardinal pitcher, retired two men but had to leave the game when a line drive bounced off his knee. Jeffcoat relieved, gave up three straight hits, and left the mound without getting a man out. McDaniel relieved Jeffcoat, and gave up two more hits, the second a double by Newcombe. Pendleton tried to score from first, but the heat, fatigue, and the ball caught up with him at the plate to retire the side. Eight runs!

"Now, that's the way this club should look," I said. The incredible excitement of a succession of line drives can stir the most cynical baseball fan. "It's hard to believe, isn't it? Eight line drives!"

"Yes," said King. "If only this club could score those runs before the other team. We get a lot of runs but they don't seem to make the job any easier on our pitchers. If the pitching's good, the hitting's off. And vice-versa."

"Jeffcoat's mad at you, Bross," said Whisenant. "You're making the trade look bad."

"If I'd only known *he* was going to look so bad!" I said, facetiously. "Poor guy. Caray will rip *him*, now."

Eight runs was one run short. That's the way it stayed.

July 5
Philadelphia
Willie Jones joined us in Philadelphia. I associated Jones with trouble; on two May nights he had started rallies for the Phils while I was pitching for St. Louis. Apparently the Phil management didn't consider that of much value, for they traded Willie to Cleveland. The Indians used him for a week, then looked around for a buyer. The way he hits me, I'd buy him any time, just to keep him out of my hair. He shook hands with me regretfully; another pitcher he could no longer hit.

The Philadelphia fans who had booed Jones with all the mighty fervor of an outraged mob (typical of Philadelphia fans) greeted him in a Cincinnati uniform as if he were the Prodigal Son. They gave him a standing ovation which reduced him to tears at the plate. Even the Phillies' ballplayers, embarrassed by their own unprofessional sentiment, applauded Jones from the steps of their dugout. What makes a ballplayer look better in an opponent's uniform?

Even without Jones in their lineup the Philly batters treated me as badly as their fans. I started the game, and in the third inning Freese hit a grand-slam home run to knock me out of the box. I never did recover from the blow; I still think about it. Freese just isn't that good a hitter, and it just wasn't that bad a pitch. The rest of our club, however, recovered enough to win the second game of the twi-night double-header, and also the Friday night game. These two wins kept Philadelphia from climbing over us into seventh. With the first half of the season coming to a close our momentary escape from the cellar was greeted like a reprieve . . . for the club if not for the manager. Mayo Smith said to a sportswriter before the double-header, "Last year I was in the first division, closer to first place than I am now. And I still got fired. So what are you gonna do?"

Clutching a two-game winning streak to our hearts we headed west to Pittsburgh, regarding the Fourth of July hopefully. Not only did we have virtually an off-day (to play only one game on a holiday reduces work to leisure), but we seemed to have a better-than-average chance to win a third straight game. Bob Friend was scheduled to pitch for the Pirates. In past years this prospect was a chilling one; the pitcher scheduled to work opposite Friend would say, pessimistically, "Why in hell do I have to draw the best in the league every time!" The season 1959, however, had deflated Friend's reputation. He looked like just another pitcher, proficient but beatable. "He's not quite as fast as he was," said the hitters, "and he's not getting his breaking stuff over when he has to. He's always been around the plate with his pitches but he gives you more to hit now."

Our hitters got ten hits and a couple of walks but could squeeze just three runs out of the traffic. The Pirates scored four times, the last run coming after the third out had been apparently called. Bailey tagged Groat sliding home with an inside-the-park home run. Bailey then dropped the ball, which rolled an inch and a half toward the Pirate dugout before Bailey could snatch it up again. Umpire Delmore in a dramatic gesture signaled Groat out and failed to see the fumble. The second base umpire, however, detected the error from his position 182 feet away in center field. His piercing vision, unerringly centered on the play though three ballplayers and a dust cloud hindered his duty, is a tribute to the aggressive-ness and hog-headedness of some National League umpires. Protest by Smith, Nuxhall (the pitcher), and Bailey, though colorful and worth while recording, was unavailing.

So, what are you gonna do?

Acker pitched four shutout innings after Groat was called safe. He bought the early edition of the Sunday paper to read about the game.

"Rooms," I said to him, "you're making your salary drive a little early, aren't you? That's about four good games in a row."

"Don't worry about me, mother," he said. "I see where you're starting the second game tomorrow."

"Who says?" I asked.

"The paper's got you scheduled. You and Purkey."

"Somebody oughta tell me, don't you think?"

Jeez, here I had three starts in three months. Now I get two more in three days.

"Who's working for them?" I asked.

"Guess you'll get Kline," he said.

"That figures," I moaned. Leaving Acker to watch the Saturday night Westerns on TV I went across the street to Danny's.

"You are pitching tomorrow, Jimmy?" Danny asked "Then I will come to see you. But first I will fix you a meal so that you will be strong and pitch a good game. Maybe I still want the Pirates to win but it should be a good game. I will go to the kitchen and pick the roast beef myself for you."

Like fatting up the calf for slaughter. Danny didn't even smile,

During the first game on Sunday rain fell in thunderous large drops, but it quickly stopped. The Pirate ground crew had trouble starting their new motor-driven infield cover. By the time the tarpaulin reached the outfield grass the rain had ceased. Then the motor wouldn't work and the ground crew couldn't get the field uncovered. While the fans hooted impatiently the players on our bench relaxed, and I scanned the western sky to see if more rain was coming to cancel my game.

"Joe Brown paid forty thousand dollars for that damn thing," said Purkey, "and the first time they try it, it falls apart."

"Another bonus beauty flops," I said "General managers have nothing but bad luck when they spend money in big chunks like that. That's why they're stingy when it comes time to talk contract."

Using a crowbar, the crew foreman finally jammed the cover back into its hole, and we proceeded to lose the game 7-5. Drizzle fell briefly as I warmed, up for the second game. "Piss or get off the pot," I said to the clouds. The game started.

In, the second inning I had the bases loaded with two out, and Kline was the next Pirate hitter. Kline is not a good hitter, even for a pitcher. "For Christ's sake, don't walk him!" is the usual pregame strategy. A lousy hitter, however, presents a special psychological problem for me. "What do I throw him?" I don't dare just lay the ball in there for him to hit it, but I don't dare to start working on him, either. What if I walked him?

Bailey asked for the slider and I threw it. Kline lunged at it and hit a ground hall to my left. On a normal infield Robinson would have charged in from first base to field the ball. The Forbes Field turf, however, has the consistency of a hardwood floor. Kline's grounder moved right along toward right field. "Come on, Temple, where in hell are you?" I prayed. Temple never got to the ball, which rolled into right field to drive home two runs.

Virdon hit next. "This guy hits me like he owns me," I said to myself. "That's why he's got such a big smile when he says hello. I better load one up. He's never seen me throw one, yet." The pitch didn't move much but Virdon popped it up to right, anyway.

The bases remained practically untrodden for the next six innings. Having hit against Kline twice I didn't think he had too much stuff, and he had a hit off me so I couldn't have been too impressive. Mayo greeted me as I came to the dugout after the seventh.

"Let's let Whitey hit for you, Jim. Nice game."

"Yeah," I mumbled. "Great." Lockman grounded out for me and I ran over to the clubhouse, feeling a bit depressed. Is it better to get shelled as I did in Philly, or frustrated in a 2-0 game? Sometimes I think it's better to be bombed. You know where you stand . . . or stood. The black mark on your record is no smaller when you pitch well enough to win but still get beat.

"Brosnan, who usually doesn't pitch too well against the Pirates," said the Pirate radio broadcaster, "pitched well enough to win this game."

"Go to hell," I said. "You got any beer, Tommy?"

The first rule I'd heard about when I joined the Reds was "No Beer in the Clubhouse." But clubhouse men usually can find some when absolutely necessary.

"It's Sunday, Broz," the clubhouse man said. Pennsylvania has blue laws, too.

"Yeah, I know. You got any beer?"

"How many you want? Couple of your guys ordered some for the bus trip to the airport."

"They aren't hitting today anyway. To hell with 'em. Can you let me have six? I'll drink a couple now, and take the rest with me. I've got a three-hour wait for my plane to Chicago."

"Goin' home during the All-Star game, huh?" he said.

I took my shower, standing near the doorway, trying to distinguish between the noise of the water and the noise of the crowd in the stands. Maybe we could tie it up. Only two runs to get if they don't get any more off Pena.

"Three days off. I'm not even going to watch the All-Star game," I said to myself. "Damn game"

As I dressed, Tommy handed me a bag of beer and a can opener.

"Man on first, Bell the batter," said the radio. "Come on, Ronnie, get old Ding-Dong out of there. . . . Here's the pitch. . . . Oh, my, that one's gone. Upper deck. She's all tied up"

I tossed my shoe up in the air. That's the way. Gussie! Pulls me right off the hook. I punched a hole in the beer can. "Now that tastes good, like a beer should," I said.

July 8
Morton Grove

The phone rang at seven-thirty. We were still in bed. I reached up for the receiver.

"Who in the world would dare call us this early?" my wife said.

"What do you say, Donald? Is everything all right?" I said into the phone. "It's Don Studt," I whispered to my wife. . . ."Nice of you to call so early, Don. What's new? . . . What d'ya mean 'who's gonna be the new manager?' . . . Sure I like Mayo. Why not? He's treated me fine. Lets me pitch when I want to, never gets on anybody. Just like Solly Hemus. You know what I mean? . . . Phooey! I didn't care whether Hemus lost his job or not. What do I care if he starves . . . . Yeah, I'm leaving in about an hour for Cincy. We got a workout at eleven o'clock. . . . What the hell, if I make it, I make it . . . . No, I didn't watch the All-Star game. We all went to Brookfield zoo, instead. . . . Don't make bad jokes. We went on a picnic. . . . You should try it. Fresh air, sunshine, it'll kill you. . . . So the Cardinals are ahead of us, so what?. . . I'm happy, I'm happy. I'd rather be with Cincinnati than any other club in the league. . . .No, I haven't read the paper. I'm still in bed. . . . With my wife, yeah. . . Oh, just as good as ever. What's in the paper? . . . Oh. . . . Great. . . . What I mean is GREAT! I like him. . . . Yeah. . . . Thanks for calling, Don. Say hello to Gwen. . . . See ya. . . . Let's get together next time the Reds are in town. . . . 'By.

"That was Donald E. Studt. We've got a new manager," I said.

"Who?" she said.

"Hutch," I said.

"Oh, God, there goes your starting job!"

✤   ✤   ✤

from THE LONG SEASON

July 11

Cincinnati

Our first home stand under Hutch was scheduled for just five days. My wife stayed in Morton Grove rather than commute to Cincinnati for such a short time. I moved into the Brosnan family mansion on Price Hill. Free-loading on one's family is so much more satisfying to one's conscience. In fact, I got a better room than I'd had as a mere member of the family.

"Your wife says you won't be starting any more because Hutch is manager. Is that right?" asked my brother Mike. Unaccountably he had risen from bed before noon and had shown up in time for breakfast.

"What you doing up so early?" I asked. "And when did Anne Stewart say that?"

"I've got a game this afternoon," he said. Mike pitched American Legion ball. "And she mentioned it the last time she was down here. That's when the papers were talking about who would be the new manager. Doesn't she like Hutchinson?"

"She wouldn't dare not like him!" I said. "And so far she's wrong. I'm starting this afternoon against Antonelli."

"I hope I do better than you will," he said, laughing like a brother.

"Well, you go play your itty-bitty game and let me worry about the Giants," I said. "I would draw Antonelli, though. Even in the Army I never beat him. He was at Fort Myer when I was at Fort Meade and we hooked up a couple times. He used to strike out eighteen of our guys a game."

"Even you?" he said, in phony amazement.

"You're trying to get on me, kid," I said. "Don't play with fire."

"Would you rather be a starter if Hutch would let you?" he asked.

"I don't know," I said, thinking about it. "I'd say he's better than most managers in handling starting pitchers. He lets his starter go a long way. If you're rested and ready and he says you're his best for the day, you have to prove it to him that you're not. Which is good for a pitcher's morale in the long run."

"The way the Reds score runs, a starting pitcher has a chance to win a lot of games, doesn't he?" said Mike.

"Well, we score runs just like any other team in the second division," I said. "You read too many sportswriters. They think they can prove our pitching staff is lousy because the Reds score more runs than anybody else. That's the most misleading statistic in baseball."

"Why?" he asked.

"Most of the time a potentially high-scoring team will run up a potful of runs in one or two games, then may score once or twice a game for a week. The pitchers depend on the hitters to bail them out; the opponent's pitchers think they have to bear down extra hard; managers tend to play for the big inning too often rather than take a run any way they can get it; and everybody gets hitter-conscious instead of correlating hitting, pitching, running, and defense. You follow me?"

"No," he said.

"Well, you better stick to your own brand of baseball, and stop trying to run mine. Okay?"

"I'm not trying to run anything," he protested. "I get my opinions from the papers. Lou Smith always writes, 'Competent Observers Say Such and Such Is True.' I have to assume he's right, don't I?"

"I don't know whether you're trying to be sarcastic or not," I said. "By 'Competent Observer' Lou Smith means himself, and the 'Competent' means he's not legally insane."

"You're just bitter 'cause he never mentions your name," said Mike.

"He quoted me twice, just after I was traded," I said. "What I was supposed to have said I never would have said even if he had asked me which he hadn't since I'd never even met the man yet."

"Okay, okay," Mike said. "If Hutch lets his starters go so long, how come he used you so much in relief last year at St. Louis?"

"First of all, I was going good. Secondly, St. Louis is a hellhole in the summer and a pitcher can't be expected to go nine innings without getting pretty tired. Why not bring a fresh pitcher in if he's going good? Then, there are plenty of other reasons that all managers nowadays operate with."

"Like what?" he asked.

I ticked them off on my fingers. "The lively ball, bigger players, and better bats. They make every hitter a potential Babe Ruth. . . . You can't afford to make any mistakes on the mound so the tension gets to you, especially in low-score games. The tension gets to you *and* the manager. Also, the ball parks are all small in this league except for Milwaukee and Pittsburgh so that adds more pressure on the pitcher. The umpires don't make it any easier on us, either. They've shrunk the plate and the strike zone so much. There are just two umpires in the league who consistently give you a strike on the outside corner. And where the strike zone used to be from the shoulders to the knees, it's now from below the letters to above the knees. Some of those bubbleheads interpret that rule to mean the strike zone is between the lowest button of the shirt to the top button of the pants crotch. So the pitcher has to come in with the ball if his first two pitches just miss and—Boom! . . . the ball goes out of the ballpark and you go out of the game."

Mike nodded his head. "They're using relief pitchers this year it seems even when they don't have to."

"The relief pitcher used to be second-rate; now he's usually as good as anybody on the staff," I said. "Some managers tend to panic when the starter gives up a hit in the late innings. So they drag in a fresh man. Then, too, the percentage of right-handed pitcher against right-handed hitter and lefty against lefty is used blindly. It's supposed to be a percentage move. A lot of guys think percentage always means one hundred, I guess. It's all a part of personal panic and overmanaging. The trouble with it is the manager seldom lets his players in on the reasons why he does some of those things, and the player ends up thinking instead of doing."

"You think too much yourself, Lou Smith says," said Mike.

"Go lose yourself a ball game," I said. "I gotta go to the park."

Antonelli had pitched two consecutive shutouts, and he started out on another. For six innings we made just two hits, and no runs. The Giants! Spencer hit a ball past my left shoe for a single to start the fourth. I should have caught it. Brandt bunted him over. Landrith took two balls and a strike. "I'll throw one fast ball past him," I thought, "and strike him out with a curve." He hit the fast ball through my legs to drive in a run. Bressoud hit the next pitch against the center field wall. It landed just six inches above Pinson's glove although I gave it all the body English I could to bring it back far enough for the catch. Antonelli bounced my best curve ball over my head and Landrith scored as Kasko threw Antonelli out at first. One foot lower and I catch the ball on the bounce. . . . no run scores.

Bressoud hit a double in the fifth on another slider. In the seventh I tried to jam him with a fast ball and he hit it over the left-field wall. The wind blowing out to left didn't hurt the drive any. It landed just behind the fence. Davenport doubled and Kirkland singled for the fourth run before Hutch started to warm up another pitcher. I was ready to collapse from the heat and fatigue, but I hadn't walked a batter so Hutch must have thought I was just being dramatic about the sweat that soaked my uniform. Even my cap was wet. The temperature on the field was ninety-nine degrees and I'd thrown 125 pitches. Mays and Cepeda were the next hitters, and I could feel my strength ebbing. But Willie struck out on a 3-2 curve and Cepeda took three strikes while looking for an inside fast ball that he could hit out of the park. I staggered off the mound figuring that I was through for the day. Hutch said, "Let's see you go one more." I swallowed two more salt pills, the sweat having virtually stopped. There was no more in me. I made it through the eighth, somehow, but we lost the game. I lost thirteen pounds, also, for a completely wasted day.

"How could you get Mays and Cepeda out and let Bressoud beat you?" asked Mike when I got home.

"Go stuff your head, kid. How would you have pitched him?"

"Bressoud's hitting .214 and you let him get two doubles and a home run," said my other brother, Pat, when he arrived for dinner.

"Good God in the foothills! Let's forget it."

"You should never have lost that game," said my dad.

"How can you let a guy like Bressoud beat you?"

"If I wasn't so damn tired," I said, "I'd leave home."

✠ ✠ ✠

August 4

Cincinnati

. . .Ellis "Cot" Deal met us in Los Angeles.

"I hope you still got a sore arm, Cot," I greeted him. "Clyde ran us so much he couldn't comb his hair his arm was so tired."

"My arm is in good shape, James. How are you?"

"Everything's going to be all right," I said. "How did you get your arm to come around?"

"I've got some exercises I do with an iron ball. I'll have to show them to you. Your arm sore?"

"Hell, no," I said. "I only pitch once a week or so. What was all the shooting about in Cuba? I hear you nearly got killed."

He shook his head and whistled. "I tell you, I never felt so lucky in my life. You read about it, of course. I'd been thrown out of the game against Havana and Frank Verdi took over for me coaching at third base, see. These Cuban soldiers were shooting off their rifles in the stands! And a stray bullet knocked Verdi over and hit the Havana third baseman. Well, that was enough for us. We packed up and came back to the States. But, think of it. I could have been standing at third instead of Verdi, and I'm an inch or two taller than Frank. The bullet went through his cap and bounced off the helmet liner he wears inside it. Had I been there the bullet probably would have gone through my ear.

"I believe your hair's turned gray there around your temples," I said. "Glad you're still with us. How's Green doing?"

"Gene was a little disappointed when he came down from the Cardinals, and he stayed red-assed for about a week. But pretty soon he came around and started hitting real well for us. How did Solly look while you were over there?"

"Solly and I didn't see eye-to-eye on much of anything, you know. I probably couldn't criticize him objectively if I tried. But I will, anyway. Hemus tried hard, I'll say that for him. Maybe he tried too hard. He tends to overmanage and he gets panicky for no good reason at all. You'll see. We play 'em a couple more times this year."

"The hardest lesson a first-year manager has to learn," said Deal, "is not to overmanage. You can't help yourself, sometimes. The panic gets to you."

"Yeah, but that goes for any manager. The good ones seem to control themselves. You know Hutch, of course. He's got a fist of iron . . . I mean a will of iron."

Deal laughed at the slip of my tongue.

"Would you rather manage than coach, Cot?" I asked.

"I'm happy to be here," he said, smiling.

"Great. We're happy to have you. And I'll never ask you again."

❖ ❖ ❖

August 13

Cincinnati

Our chances of overtaking Pittsburgh and finishing in the first division were no less difficult than the pennant chances of the three top contenders. We had to win all six remaining games we had with the Pirates. Since it was absolutely necessary we saw no reason why we wouldn't do it. The schedule presented a greater problem. We had to play (said the revamped National League schedule) nine games in six days, five of them on the August 14-16 weekend, and the other four with Milwaukee.

Gabe Paul recalled Bobby Henrich, a shortstop, from Savannah, Georgia, and Henrich reported in time to warm up pitchers in the bullpen during the Milwaukee series.

"Why in hell didn't Gabe bring up a pitcher, Cot?" I asked.

"He didn't consult me, Jim," Deal said soothingly. "Besides, Henrich's a seasoned traveler and Gabe knew he wouldn't panic when the notice came. Right, Bob?"

"I wish they'd pay me by the mile for this season," said Henrich. "I left L.A. in the spring to train in Florida, was optioned to Savannah, came back here in June when McMillan was hurt, was sent to Seattle when Mac got back in the lineup, went back down to Savannah from there, and now I'm back in Cincinnati because McMillan is hurt again. If I'd gone straight up in the air on March 1 I'd be at the moon by now."

Neither Purkey nor Acker showed up at the hall park. The news that both had the flu made everyone in the bullpen sick. "Who's going to comb my hair for me after this weekend?" I asked Deal.

"Don't worry about it. Incidentally, if Purkey can't pitch Thursday, you're nominated."

"Well, isn't that just too sweet," said Schmidt. "That means he won't be in the pen all week."

"Oh, no, it doesn't," said Deal. "Hutch says you guys will just have to double up."

"I've got a cramp in my arm already, Ellis," I said.

When the fifth inning started on Thursday night I also had an eight-run lead. Pinch-hitter Lee Maye led off for the Braves. I had never pitched to Maye before. "He'll be taking one strike anyway," I thought. "Then I'll try to jam him with the slider. It's working well for me." I laid the first pitch right over the heart of the plate.

Maye hit it into center field and I turned around to look at the Milwaukee bench. How could Haney let him hit the first pitch when he's eight runs behind? It just isn't done. Avila bunted, a move that I expected even less than Maye's first-pitch single. I waited for Bailey to come out from behind the plate and field the ball, and he waited for me to come off the mound. Avila got a base hit. Mathews took three sliders just inside, fouled two others off, and then walked as I missed with a curve just outside. Five good pitches in a row and I, still couldn't get him out. The fans started to grumble and Hutchinson called the bullpen.

I knew I'd be out of there if I didn't get Aaron. He had already hit two sliders right on the nose in his first two times up. He was also hitting .385 or something like that. "I'd better waste one slider and gamble on him leaning into a hummer: If I can jam him good on one pitch I'll be able to go back to the slider which is my best pitch." Aaron tommy-hawked the high inside fast hall and bounced it right back to me. Bailey took my throw to the plate and doubled Aaron at first. The entire grandstand breathed a sigh of relief. "Hutch has gotta let me, stay in here now," I thought.

Covington fouled-off four sliders just like Mathews had, and I tried to outthink him. "He can't be looking for a change now, I'll slip it right by him." He hit it over the center field fence to make the score 8-3. "There goes my shutout," I thought.

The tensions of the inning plus the heat and humidity undermined whatever strength I had left after throwing eighty-seven pitches, many of them frustratingly good ones. In any given game a pitcher expects 80 per cent of his good pitches to result in outs. (In Crosley Field *bad* pitches are frequently called gopher balls in the next morning papers.) The Braves, however, were either taking my good pitches or fouling them off, neither action pleasing me. Some good pitches must be "set up," that is, certain sliders are no good unless the batter is guarding against the jamming fast ball or the low sinker. And a good breaking-ball hitter must be given a peek at a close slider or curve before he's susceptible to a hummer on the hands. One "good pitch" may involve two other pitches. I was tired.

Pinson homered in our fifth but I had to go back to the mound all too quickly. Before the inning was over I could feel myself "pushing" the ball, and hoping for a mediocre swing. Torre popped up a high curve that he should have "creamed" and he cursed so loud he woke my brother Mike who was watching the game on television. Avila singled sharply on my next pitch, a crackling noise that brought Hutchinson to the mound. He said, "It's a hot night. I'm bringing in Pena."

I showered and poured a bottle of rubbing alcohol over me to stop the nervous sweating. Pena held a five-run lead through the seventh, by which time I was driving home to watch the end of the game on TV. With a cold beer in one hand and a burning cigar in the other I waited impatiently to celebrate my sixth win.

"Come on, Orlando, you bean bandit," I yelled at the TV screen, "get 'em out one more time."

Aaron, Adcock, and Logan singled to knock Pena out in the ninth. Nuxhall got Crandall but gave up a single to Lopata and a double to Pafko. Avila walked to load the bases and the score was 9-8. I spilled my beer, cursed the day I ever got into baseball, and shocked my mother, who said, "You ought to be ashamed of yourself. A grown man crying about baseball. It's only a game."

Lawrence relieved Nuxhall and went to a 3-2 on Mathews while I urged him in a hoarse whisper, "Don't walk him, Brooksie. Don't let 'em tie it up. Make him hit the ball." Mathews popped up to make it seem just like a game instead of a moment of truth.

✢   ✢   ✢

August 25
Cincinnati
Among the folksy traditions of the Cincinnati baseball season is Family Night at Crosley Field. Wives and children of the Redleg ballplayers are led onto the playing field to receive varying degrees of applause, depending upon the size of each domestic group. Gus Bell, a hunk of potent virility the likes of which has seldom been seen in organized baseball, had seven Bells ring around him. The applause was deafening.

My wife had her usual complaint three hours before the gala event. "What am I going to wear, Meat? I haven't got a thing."

"Wear a maternity dress so it looks like we mean to belong to the club," I suggested. "Most of these guys have three kids or more, or have their wives pregnant."

"Do you know that your father wants Timmy to wear a little baseball uniform?" she said.

"A nauseating suggestion if I ever heard one. The suit's cute but it's out. Timmy can wear Bermudas and a polo shirt. One comic figure to each family on the ball field."

"You do look awful in your uniform, Meat," she said. "For some reason or other you've got the wrong shape. I guess you just weren't cut out to be a ballplayer." She laughed at my sorry mistake.

"Listen, love, baseball is feeding you pretty well even if you haven't got anything to wear."

Jay Hook was introduced to the crowd after us, and he came out of the dugout cheered by the approving fans behind home plate. Only twenty-two and married just two years, he carried a baby and led his pregnant wife carefully by the hand. They picked up fishing rods and a check from the management, then lined up next to us.

"Gee, that's a lovely dress, Mrs. Brosnan," said Mrs. Hook. "I sure hope I'll get to wear one like that again." She smiled wryly at her husband.

Hook joined us later in the bullpen as the game began.

"Good boy, Jay-bird," I said to him. "You never know when you may pick up some useless information down here. Brooks, show Hook how to fire a rocket. He's an engineering student. Maybe he can help us reach the scoreboard from here."

Lawrence peeled the foil from a pack of Wrigley's Spearmint gum ("We use the best materials in our rockets, Hook") and wrapped it carefully around the head of an unlit match. "Hand me the launching pad, Broz," said Lawrence. I gave him the broom which we use to sweep cigarette stubs and candy bar wrappers from the bullpen. Setting the "rocket" upright in the broom, and pointing it toward the field, Lawrence lit the foil-covered head. Five seconds passed as the flame gradually heated the foil. Then, streaming smoke, the match arched over the railing of the bullpen into the grass beyond the left field line. "Tracking stations please measure the shot," Lawrence said.

"Dr. Wernher von Lawrence, you've done it again," said Deal. "Now let's watch Purkey slip the green weenie past Banks."

"Slip the what past Banks?" I asked, my ears twitching. "Where in the world did you pick up an expression like that, Ellis?"

"That's an old baseball terrm," he said. "I've been using it for years."

"Sure, but what does it mean?"

"Oh, I don't know," he said. "I guess it means give the batter something he doesn't like."

"You guys come up with the damnedest expressions," I said. "Brooks made one last week. We were talking about sex and he comes out with, 'Say you're trying to make a home in some other town.' Now I never heard of any phrase like that. It's a definition for pursuit of happiness on the road, isn't it, Brooksie?"

"Why do you always ask for definitions, Brosnan?" Lawrence said. "Where did that word come from? What does that word mean?' What's with you? You writin' a book or something?"

"Nope, I'm just trying to learn the language."

Deal let go with several familiar terms.

"What happened, Cot?" said Lawrence.

"Purkey just hung a slider and Neeman hit it out of the park. Willard, you better put that book down and loosen up. What in the world are you reading, anyway? You haven't said a word all night."

"*Lady Chatterly's Lover*," said Schmidt. "It's Brosnan's book. He said it would improve my mind. Who gets it next?"

Powers reached for the book and handed Schmidt the warm-up ball. "Dutch will catch you, Willard," he said. "It's my turn on the book."

Every pitcher in the bullpen but Lawrence eventually got into the game. I told Deal that I didn't think I could go very far because my wrist still hurt from last week's tumble, but Hutchinson left me in for three scoreless innings . . . to test it, I guess. I could have sworn I wouldn't be able to throw my slider.

We lost the game 8–5, but we'd just won three in a row. "You can't win 'em all. Losing gracefully is gallant and sportsmanlike," I said to myself philosophically as we climbed the ramp into the clubhouse. The door to Hutchinson's room slammed shut, and the sound of falling chairs and upset tables reverberated throughout the clubhouse. Hutch disjoints furniture instead of dismembering his failing athletes. Which is his only mark of restraint when he loses a ball game.

He makes it difficult to be complacent.

✤ ✤ ✤

September 20

Pittsburgh

. . .The light of our first-division dreams flickered on Saturday as the Pirates won in twelve innings, 4-3. The season then ended, practically, at two o'clock the next day.

I started the Sunday game. Every other pitcher on the club went to the bullpen except Newcombe, who had pitched the day before. Most of them got into the game. To start with I struck out the first Pirate batter. Superstition has it that it is bad for a pitcher to retire the first hitter on a strikeout. That's ridiculous, of course. It's not the first out but the last out that you should worry about. I didn't have to worry about the last out. I never even saw it. Two walks and four singles sent Pirate runners circling the bases around me. . . .

"There goes my winning streak," I thought as Hutch silently took the baseball from me and gave it to Willard Schmidt.

"There goes my E.R.A.," I said to myself in the showers. From below 3.00 it soared to 3.47 in fifteen minutes.

"There goes my salary drive," I thought as I dressed and left the ball park

"That's enough for one year," I hoped. It had been a long season.

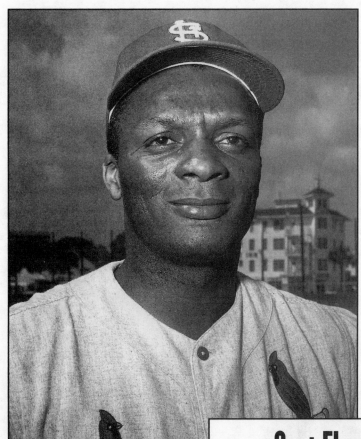

Curt Flood

THE WAY IT IS

St. Louis Cardinal outfielder Curt Flood (1938–1997) forever changed sports when he challenged major league baseball's reserve rule and, for better or worse, sacrificed his career to help bring about free agency. In these chapters from The Way It Is, *Flood tells what it was like being in the eye of this self-created hurricane.*

The tensest episodes of the 1969 season occurred toward its end. We still had a mathematical chance of winning in our division, but the front office had already given up on us. As the saying goes, they had decided to "build for the future." They ordered Red Schoendienst to begin using a couple of promising but raw youngsters as regulars. Joe Hague began playing first base and batting third. Ted Simmons, a catcher, batted fifth. I liked the kids but hated what was happening. With Hague batting third, Lou Brock and I—the first two batters in the order—would not see any decent pitches. The other teams would pitch around us—walk us, if necessary—to get at the kid. They then could pitch around the fourth man to get at the other kid. Since both Lou and I were struggling to get our averages up to .300, and had not yet abandoned all hope of winning the divisional title, I concluded that the front office was sabotaging us.

"They've already sold a million-and-a-half tickets this season," I ranted, "so they can well afford to prevent us from having good years. Wait and see how they rub it in at contract time next winter."

I went to Red Schoendienst and demanded, "If you insist on playing those goddamned kids, at least don't put them in the heart of your lineup."

Bland as ever, and as cooperative, he shrugged and replied, "Okay. If you feel that way about it."

Red seemed relieved to have an excuse for changing the batting order. I knew in my bones that the experiment had been suggested by the front office, and now the feeling was confirmed. Angrier than before, I confided to Jack Herman, a reporter for the *Globe-Democrat*, that the top management had tossed in the towel for 1969. I went on at some length.

The next day, he published my views, attributing them to an unnamed veteran. Bing Devine, our general manager, responded with a crusher. "The only reason the regulars are complaining," he said, "is that they are afraid of losing their jobs."

I think I had known it for months without admitting it to myself. Now I said to me, "Brother Flood, you are going to be traded. You have had it."

To which I answered, "They would not dare!"

"Wanna bet?" I replied.

On October 8, I was sitting in my apartment, waiting for my nervous system to come down to earth. The season was over. I had finished with a batting average of .285, which was below my usual standard. On the other hand, only nineteen full-time players in the league had managed higher averages. I had hit safely 173 times—eleventh in the league. If only nine more batted balls had dropped in, I'd have hit .300. Reveries of a baseball player. No wonder so many of us drink during the off-season. No wonder so many of us drink all year round.

In three days I would leave for Copenhagen, where I could unwind in blissful anonymity. Europe enthralled me, and Copenhagen was my favorite place. An all-night town, Copenhagen, marvelous for its uncomplicated directness. The Danes have never heard of baseball. A black face might intrigue them, but it neither alarms nor dismays them. Copenhagen was a poultice for my bruised, battered and self-pitying soul. Johnny and Marian Jorgensen had told me often that I would love the place. I had been there and they had been right.

The telephone sounded.

"Hello, Curt?"

"Yes."

"Jim Toomey, Curt."

A chill entered my belly. Toomey was assistant to Bing Devine in the front office.

"Curt, you've been traded to Philadelphia."

Silence.

"You, McCarver, Hoerner and Byron Browne. For Richie Allen, Cookie Rojas and Jerry Johnson."

Silence.

"Good luck, Curt."

"Thanks. Thanks a lot."

Twelve years of my life. I spent the rest of the day in the chair right next to the telephone, answering none of the calls. *Twelve years of my life.*

I said to Marian, "There ain't no way I'm going to pack up and move twelve years of my life away from here. No way at all."

If I had taken inventory before the front office called, I would have compiled a formidable list. Expensive athlete. Painter of oil portraits as negotiable as any currency. Student of the human condition. Impervious to shock. Subdivision: black. Belief in the American dream: lapsed.

Wrong. The dream dies hard. It lay deep within me, dormant but not destroyed. Just as stress can arouse a latent virus, one miserable telephone call released the poison of self-pity. The hard-boiled realist who answered the telephone was a weeping child when he set the receiver down.

The lightning had struck. The dream lay shattered. It was a bad scene. Feverishly, I harped on my twelve years of service, my place among the all-time stars of the Cardinals. My batting average of .285 had not been bad for a losing year. If I had been a foot-shuffling porter, they might have at least given me a pocket watch. But all I got was a call from a middle-echelon coffee drinker in the front office. Was I not entitled to a gesture from the general manager himself?

The formality materialized the next day: A printed form on which filled-in blanks officially advised Mr. Curtis Charles Flood that his contract had been assigned to the Philadelphia Club of the National League. Signed by Vaughn P. Devine. Bing's personal bye-bye.

I was an expert on baseball's spurious paternalism. I was a connoisseur of its grossness. I had known that I was out of phase with management. I therefore had known that I might be traded. Yet now, when the industry was merely doing its thing, I took it personally. I felt unjustly cast out. Days passed before I began to see the problem whole.

Philadelphia. The nation's northernmost southern city. Scene of Richie Allen's ordeals. Home of a ball club rivaled only by the Pirates as the least cheerful organization in the league. When the proud Cardinals were riding a chartered jet, the Phils were still lumbering through the air in propeller jobs, arriving on the Coast too late to get proper rest before submitting to murder by the Giants and Dodgers. I did not want to succeed Richie Allen in the affections of that organization, its press and its catcalling, missile hurling audience.

"I have only two choices," I told Marian, after treating her to another outburst of my inexhaustible anger and hurt. "I can go to Philadelphia or I can quit baseball altogether. I will not go to Philadelphia." The words of a typical baseball player, prostrated by the unchallengable rules of the industry.

I telephoned Bing Devine and told him that I would retire.

"That's entirely up to you, Curt. Good luck."

I told the reporters that I would retire. Nobody believed me. Traded players are forever threatening to pack it in. Few can afford to.

I wanted to cancel my Copenhagen trip, but Marian persuaded me to go. A change of scene would do me good.

She saw me off. We sat in the airport bar and she listened to me fume.

"I'm not going to let them do this to me," I announced. "They say that if I don't play in Philadelphia, I don't play at all. Right there, they shoot down my rights. They shoot me down as a man. I won't stand for it"

"Why not sue?" she asked.

I could have listed several reasons why not. The enormous cost, for one. The invulnerability of baseball, for another. The idea was impractical. I pushed it to the back of my mind. And there it grew.

Copenhagen was enchantment. If baseball was gone from my life, why not spend part of my time in Copenhagen? I wondered if I could open an American-style cocktail lounge, featuring the kind of rock musicians the Danes seldom heard except on records. I met Claire, a beautiful black Dane who spoke several languages fluently and knew the restaurant business. Yes, she would run such a place for me. Yes, she would help me find a location. Yes, she would be able to come to the States for a week or two and see how Americans operate. Her husband endorsed the idea. I would return home, try to put my baseball affairs in order, come back to Denmark. And, if all was still well, bring Claire to America for her instructional tour.

John Quinn, general manager of the Phillies, had been trying to reach me. He was in St. Louis on business.

"Mr. Quinn, you're wasting your time. I've made my decision."

"Can't you spare a few minutes for a chat?"

I met him at a hotel and was impressed. He was warm and understanding. He told me that the Philadelphia operation was being overhauled. Good new players were coming. A new ball park was in construction. Money was there for me. I agreed to see him again.

I no longer was bothered about Philadelphia, as such. I was thinking more clearly. The problem was no particular city but was the reserve clause, which afflicted all players equally no matter where.

I dropped in on Allan H. Zerman, a young lawyer who counseled the operators of the photography business that bore my name. I liked him. He was the only man who had ever refused to take free World Series tickets from me. He had helped my brother Carl. I told him my story in fairly clear perspective. I no longer was bleeding. The issue was not me alone but the reserve system. Like thousands of players before me, I had been caught in its machinery. Before being ground to bits, I'd get out.

"St. Louis is my home," I said. "I'm known and liked here. I have business possibilities here. What the hell is there for me in Philadelphia? Screw 'em. I'm quitting."

"There's one other alternative," said Zerman.

"Are you talking about suing baseball?"

"Have you considered the idea?" he parried.

It had been germinating in me for weeks. Sooner or later, someone would challenge baseball's right to treat human beings like used cars. If this lawyer had not ruled out the possibility of a suit, why should I?

I telephoned Marvin Miller for an appointment and flew to New York to pick his brains.

"I want to sue baseball on constitutional grounds," I told him. His eyebrows rose. "I want to give the courts a chance to outlaw the reserve system. I want to go out like a man instead of disappearing like a bottle cap."

Marvin looked at me hard.

"How much thought have you given this?"

"Plenty. I should be able to negotiate for myself in an open market and see just how much money this little body is worth. I shouldn't be confronted with an either-or proposition like the one now facing me. Somebody needs to go up against the system. I'm ready."

"A lawsuit might take two or three years," said Marvin. "It would cost a fortune. And you could lose, you know. Others have."

"I could also win."

Marvin wouldn't let me off the hook.

"If you have any idea about becoming the first black manager, you can forget it after suing. You can also forget jobs as a coach or scout."

"I never had a chance anyway."

"Your present salary is around ninety thousand, right? You're only thirty-one. Think of the money you'd lose by staying out of the game during the next two or three seasons."

"You're not telling me anything I don't know."

"Is there anything in your personal life that they could smear you with? They would."

"You haven't begun to scare me yet. Let's sue."

He took a deep breath.

"Not yet, please," he insisted. "I won't raise a finger to help you until I'm sure that you've given enough thought to all the possibilities. Go back to St. Louis and think. When you're done thinking, start all over again. Don't commit yourself to this until you have covered every detail and are sure that the positive outweighs the negative. Please."

I promised.

While in New York, I spent four hours over drinks and dinner with John Quinn. A lady at an adjoining table leaned over and said, "I know you from somewhere. Don't tell me. Lou Brock!"

In situations like that, you get up and introduce yourself before they have a chance to call you Jackie Robinson, Satchel Paige and every other black ball player they can name. We all look alike.

"I'm Curt Flood," I said, "and this is John Quinn, general manager of the Phillies. I'm with them now."

Technically, it was true. In my haste to appease and silence the woman, I had omitted the details. The flat assertion may have signified more to Quinn than it did to me. It may have accounted for his perplexity when I filed suit. He had thought that I looked upon myself as a Phillie. He blamed Marvin Miller for changing my mind. This was untrue, and as unfair to Marvin as to me.

That evening, Quinn offered me a combination of salary and reimbursement for spring training expenses that would have raised my 1970 earnings above $100,000. When somebody talks that kind of money one does not respond with a flat no. Marvin Miller had advised me to think. Quinn's proposition would give me more to think about.

"How can you pay me all that expense money?" I asked.

"Don't worry about it. Let us handle it."

I told him that I would let him know.

I holed up in my St. Louis apartment and followed Marvin's instructions. The more deeply I explored myself, the more determined I became to take baseball to court. I was in luck. Until me, no player had been able to do himself the honor of committing so fundamental an act in behalf of his profession. Danny Gardella, a Giant outfielder blacklisted for playing in the Mexican League, had sued the owners and had won in the Circuit Court of Appeals. But he had been persuaded to settle for cash.

I would not settle out of court for any amount, unless the bargain included employer-employee relations of a kind acceptable to me and the Major League Baseball Players Association. I had little money, but I was fortified by what I am not ashamed to call spiritual resources. I had spent good years with Johnny Jorgensen. I would do us both proud by trying to improve my own corner of society before moving on. Win or lose, the baseball industry would never be the same. I would leave my mark.

"Marvin, I'm going ahead with it Can you help?"

"It's possible. Come to our Executive Board meeting in San Juan on December 13 and talk to the player reps."

I went. I spoke for at least half an hour. I told the players that I was going to proceed with the suit whether I got Association help or not, but that I needed all the backing I could get. I explained my beliefs about the reserve system and the unreasonable powers it gave to the club owners. I spoke of the affronts to human dignity of a system that indentured one man to another. I pointed out that fair bargaining and real professionalism would remain distant hopes in base-ball unless I fought my fight.

The men questioned me closely. Many wanted to make sure that I was not engaged in a classic ploy—threatening suit in hope that the Phillies would raise the ante. Others wondered how I would react if baseball offered to settle a few hundred thousand dollars on me, out of court.

"I can't be bought," I said.

Tom Haller asked the good question . . . about a possible link between my suit and black militance. The discussion was thought-ful, serious and heartening.

Nobody trotted out the threadbare and entirely insupportable argument—heard for so many years in so many locker rooms—that modification of the reserve system would ruin baseball. The Association had grown up.

The board excused me from the meeting and then voted (25-0) to support my case. It authorized the Association office to retain the best possible counsel for me.

Time was precious. Marvin Miller wasted none. He called Mr. Justice Arthur J. Goldberg, his former colleague in the steelworkers union, and asked him to consider taking my case. Mr. Goldberg already understood the basic issues, having been involved years before in a similar case that did not get to court. He invited me to meet him in his office.

Mr. Goldberg is a well-turned-out man with unmussed white hair and an unmussed mind. I was nervous about meeting him, partly because I was a stranger to conferences in the private offices of for-mer Supreme Court justices, and partly because I sensed that my future might depend on the impression I made. He put me at ease by getting right to the facts, discussing the subject I knew best. Just as Marvin Miller had done, he played devil's advocate, reviewing all the dire possibilities to make sure that I had overlooked none.

"I just won't be treated as if I were an IBM card," I said.

"All right," he answered. "Let's go."

Ho-lee cow! Little old Curt Flood had him the most famous lawyer in the world.

On December 24, I fired the opening shot, a letter to Bowie Kuhn, the Commissioner of Baseball, with copies to John Quinn, Marvin Miller and the press. The letter said:

Dear Mr. Kuhn:

After twelve years in the major leagues, I do not feel that I am a piece of property to be bought and sold irrespective of my wishes. I believe that any system which produces that result violates my basic rights as a citizen and is inconsistent with the laws of the United States and of the several States.

It is my desire to play baseball in 1970, and I am capable of playing. I have received a contract offer from the Philadelphia club, but I believe I have the right to consider offers from other clubs before making any decisions. I, therefore, request that you make known to all Major League clubs my feelings in this matter, and advise them of my availability for the 1970 season.

The reporters swarmed. Was I going to sue? Was Arthur Goldberg actually going to represent me? Did I really think I could defeat baseball? Could baseball survive without the reserve clause? I refused all comment, pending the Commissioner's reply. It came under a December 30 dateline, and started promisingly.

"I certainly agree with you," wrote Kuhn, "that you, as a human being, are not a piece of property to be bought and sold. That is fundamental to our society and I think obvious. However," he veered, "I cannot see its applicability to the situation at hand.

"You have entered into a current playing contract with the St. Louis club, which has the same assignment provisions as those in your annual Major League contracts since 1956. Your present contract has been assigned in accordance with its provisions by the St. Louis club to the Philadelphia club. . . ."

He also pointed out that the reserve system was embodied in the

163

basic agreements negotiated by the owners and the Association. This was not true. The Association has never agreed to the reserve system and has always questioned its legality. On the other hand, Kuhn did not mention that the owners had been refusing to negotiate changes in the reserve system. In case I had doubted it before, I now saw that we faced a long and punishing fight.

Mr. Goldberg's first step was to ask for an injunction under the Sherman and Clayton Antitrust Laws, plus applicable state laws. The goal was to invalidate the trade, make me a free agent and, most important, end the reserve system as a violation of the antitrust laws.

Robin Roberts told the press that "going to court is the wrong way." He still believed that some day sweet reason would persuade the owners to relent. Carl Yastrzemski complained that the Association's executive board should not have supported the suit. He demanded a referendum of all players. (The Association's collective bargaining proposals for revision of the reserve system had been drafted after a survey of the players.) Willie Mays allowed that he would not object to being traded, so long as the paychecks were large enough. Joe Cronin and Warren Giles warned about the ruination of the game and deplored my departure from the path of collective bargaining between the Association and the owners.

Eddie Kranepool described Yastrzemski as a yo-yo for the owners. Jackie Robinson, Bob Gibson, Dal Maxvill, Lou Brock, Rich Allen and dozens of others came flat out in behalf of the principle I was trying to advance.

Robinson said, "I think Curt is doing a service to all players in the leagues, especially for the younger players coming up who are not superstars. All he is asking for is the right to negotiate. It doesn't surprise me that he had the courage to do it. He's a very sensitive man concerned about the rights of everybody. We need men of integrity like Curt Flood and Bill Russell who are involved in the area of civil rights and who are not willing to sit back and let Mr. Charlie dictate their needs and wants for them. . . ."

A bit flattering in spots, but balm for my spirit.

Justice Goldberg informed me that during preliminary conferences, baseball's representatives rejected his attempts to avoid litigation. He had pointed out to the eminent Paul Porter that the problems could be arbitrated, or could be resolved by negotiation with the Players Association.

"Not practical," replied Porter.

Commissioner Bowie Kuhn was upset because I had made it plain that I would remain out of baseball while the issue was being contested. Goldberg told him at one conference that he had advised me that to play baseball while suing would hurt my case and might even cause its removal from the docket. Federal courts do not accept a case unless it is plainly a legitimate dispute. For me to play might make the whole issue hypothetical—what lawyers call "moot."

Kuhn reacted to this with great self-assurance, as though playing cat-and-mouse with the average witness. He was picking on the wrong man and should have known it.

Said Kuhn, "You mean, Mr. Justice, that you are advising Mr. Flood not to play?"

Goldberg jumped on him. "If you want to do any quoting," he said, "you had better be accurate in what you quote. The decision about whether Mr. Flood will play will be made by Mr. Flood. I have given him legal advice as to the impact of his decision. The decision is his. The only quotations you are authorized to make are (a) Mr. Flood will make the decision and (b) as to his reasons for not playing, he does not wish to be considered a piece of property and he considers the reserve rules both immoral and illegal. That is all you may quote."

Later, Kuhn asked with apparent dismay, "Is it true that negotiations are out—that the suit will proceed regardless?" Again Goldberg took him apart. "You have a terrible habit of misquoting," he said. "It is my understanding that if appropriate modifications can be made through negotiation, they would satisfy Curt Flood. Therefore, if you want to carry out your legal right to negotiate, please do so."

Comparatively few newspaper, radio and television journalists seemed able to understand what I was doing. That a ball player would pass up a $100,000 year was unthinkable. The player's contention that he was trying to serve a human cause was somehow unbelievable. Who had ever heard of anyone giving up $100,000 for a principle? For them, the only plausible explanation was derangement. Or perhaps I was a dupe of Marvin Miller. And, in any case, I would surely show up in time for spring training. I wasn't that crazy. As a matter of fact, more than one newsman nudged my ribs with his elbow and winked conspiratorially about the money he thought I might blackmail from the Phillies with this suit. I began to wonder if the whole goddamned country wasn't infected with moral corruption. Some of the same people who criticized me for threatening the Good of the Game made it clear enough that they would respect my acumen if I abandoned the Players Association, disavowed honor and signed for a higher salary than the Phillies had previously offered.

For the record, and to be as fair as possible about the press, the myopia was not universal. The syndicated columnists Red Smith and Jim Murray knew what was afoot and said so. Leonard Koppett reported the case and its background with entire accuracy in *The New York Times*, whose sports columnist, Robert Lipsyte, also understood. Gene Ward of New York's *Daily News* and Howard Cosell and Kyle Rote of television were others who seemed neither confused, cynical nor enraged. *Sports Illustrated* and *Sport* also presented the facts without hysteria. No doubt many others played it straight. But I do not subscribe to a clipping service, nor spend my life glued to the radio and television sets. I can say with conviction that the preponderance of material I read and heard was distressingly cynical and ill-informed. Nothing I said in interviews got through to such people. These guys evidently felt that responsibility to principle was the hallucination of a nut.

Upset as I was by the zeal with which so many commentators were supporting the position of Bowie Kuhn, I was happy to take a telephone call from David Oliphant, a Connecticut businessman who wanted to talk to me about a book. It turned out that Dave himself had been harpooned by a phase of the reserve system neglected in these pages but immensely important. A phenomenal pitcher as a New York high school boy, he signed with the New York Yankees for a $3,000 bonus and spent two-and-a-half seasons shunting around the team's lesser farm clubs. The treatment he got was similar to mine during the two seasons with the Cincinnati Reds. Oliphant is Jewish. So they sent him to a club whose manager, a rabid anti-Semite, ostracized him—except when threatening to get rid of "that Jewboy." Concluding that the Yankees really did not want him, Dave asked for his release, hoping to connect with another organization.

After considerable haggling, the Yankees actually sold Dave's contract to his father for $2,000! Dave then caught on with the Dodgers, who were rich in pitching talent. He almost made the big club, but not quite. His record indicated that he could pitch for other major-league teams, but the terms of the reserve system condemned him to years in bushes, hoping that Don Newcombe or Carl Erskine or Don Drysdale or Preacher Roe might wear out. He finally left baseball. At one point, his anguished father made such a stink—and seemed so ready to expose the Yankees—that they refunded $1,000 of the money they had gouged from the Oliphants for the kid's release!

Dave loved baseball, just as most of the rest of us do. He loved to play the game. He loved the camaraderie. But he detested the industry's barbarism, its indifference to human dignity. For years, he had been waiting for a whack at the reserve system. He was thrilled at what I was doing. He thought that I should write a book. I could tell my story without interruption or modification by anybody. I agreed. Dave introduced me to Herbert M. Alexander, publisher of Trident Press. Herb recommended the writer, Richard Carter.

Carter arrived in St. Louis at the end of February, while I was on pins and needles awaiting the decision on our plea for a Federal injunction. Judge Irving Ben Cooper, of the U.S. District Court for the Southern District of New York, had heard the legal arguments with great enjoyment. Instead of calling a brief recess, he beamed that it was time for "a seventh-inning stretch." At the end of the arguments, he said, "Now you have thrown the ball to me and I hope I don't muff it." I think I must have been the grimmest person in the courtroom. My sense of humor was on the injury list. I wanted the issues resolved quickly so that I could play baseball in 1970.

Nobody really believed that Judge Cooper would rule on the legality of the reserve system. Every precedent indicated that this was a job for the U.S. Supreme Court. Nevertheless, it was theoretically possible that he might liberate me to play ball while the broader issues were being tried. He declared that the law forbade it. On March 4, 1970, when my body was aching for the exertions of baseball, he denied the injunction and recommended that the merits of the reserve system be dealt with in a full-dress trial.

The press descended. Marian was ready with a prepared statement from me. "The failure to obtain a restraining order means that I have lost my one chance to play ball this year. I can only hope that after a full hearing on the merits that my position will have been vindicated and that my career will not have been ended by the time lost in pursuing what I believe to be right."

It was not enough. The networks and newspapers demanded interviews. I told Marian to stall them for a while.

"I don't want to see those guys," I told Carter. "I don't want to see them and put on a brave front. I don't want to tell them that the money is inconsequential to me because I can paint and get rich in private enterprise and do anything I want. It's a lot of bullshit. I'm a baseball player and I'm supposed to play out my string. I'm supposed to be in Florida now, romping around and hitting the ball and cussing with Gibson and banging the chicks."

I had never ducked reality, yet had never confronted it in such quantity, and had never enjoyed it less. I had declared myself ready to make sacrifices for a principle, and now I was getting the bill. Baseball, the thing I did best in this world, was finished. Very likely, I was through. The photography business, in which I had had such hope, was foundering. I had not been able to pick up a paintbrush in weeks.

The Copenhagen venture was in its death throes, sex having caused complications which neither Claire nor I could handle.

"All right," I said to Marian. "Set up a press conference for tomorrow afternoon. If I can't stand the heat, I'm supposed to get out of the kitchen. I don't know whether I can take it, but I'm staying in the goddamned kitchen."

At noon, I took Claire to the airport for what both of us knew was a last good-bye. I primed my pump at the airport bar and then proceeded to Allan Zerman's office, every room of which was filled with television equipment, tape recorders and interrogators. I had my largest and darkest glasses on, hoping that nobody could see the despair in my face.

I went through my usual spiel. Nothing had changed, I said. I would proceed step by step until a conclusion was reached. I assumed that our next move would be a trial, but I had not yet consulted Mr. Justice Goldberg. Yes, I supposed that my career was over, although I was ready to resume at any time possible. No, I was not trying to ruin the national pastime. Yes, a principle was worth more than $100,000 a year. Yes, a peon remains a peon no matter how much money you give him. It reminded me of who I was and what I was about. I could scarcely walk when I left the place, yet I felt better. I had been upchucking for two days, but now it stopped.

The strain got to Marian. She came down with a nasal hemorrhage in the middle of the night. Nothing we did stopped the bleeding. At the hospital she caused consternation by insisting that her next of kin was Curt Flood. After winning that battle, she submitted to treatment. She had lost a great deal of blood. But we had caught it in time. I cried for her and for myself and for the road we had come together. She stayed in bed for a couple of days on doctor's orders and then, defiantly, resumed charge of me.

"Get to bed, Babe, for God's sake," I commanded.

"I'm too busy."

"Get to bed."

"What are you going to do about Jim Lefebvre? He called again about the portraits of his family. He's such a nice man."

169

"Jim Lefebvre, Jim Lefebvre. That's all I hear from you! I'm tired of this constant talk about men! It's sick, I tell you! Sick!"

The banter had returned to normal.

Dave Oliphant came to St. Louis to see how the book was going. He conceded that Judge Cooper's decision and other events beyond our control might well have deflected Dick Carter and me from our work. He commended to our attention that vodka was not the best fuel for the kind of vehicle we were trying to assemble. He dragged me outside for a game of catch. It was just the right therapy. First catch of the 1970 season. I was as limber as ever. My arm felt great.

"I could be ready to play in a couple of weeks," I said.

"Keep your chin up," said Dave. "They're going to settle this thing out of court. Wait and see."

The trial was to be held in New York before Judge Cooper. Shortly before it started, Monte Irvin telephoned. Monte had been a great player in the old Negro leagues. In 1949, at the age of thirty, he had come up with the Giants and starred for them. And now he was working in the office of Commissioner Bowie Kuhn. He told Marian that the Commissioner wanted to have a chat with me. A private heart-to-heart. She said that she would relay the message.

Two days later Monte telephoned again and got me. The Commissioner had cleared the whole thing with Justice Goldberg's office. Would I meet him in Los Angeles? For a strictly informal chat?

"Damnit, Monte, the last guy who saw the Commissioner for an informal chat wound up getting a boot in the ass." I was thinking of Denny McLain.

"He'd have been in worse trouble if he hadn't come in," said Monte. This sounded to me like a threat.

Then came a third call from Monte. I was not at home.

"The Commissioner definitely wants to talk to Curt," he told Marian. "He's willing to pay Curt's expenses to Los Angeles."

"What on earth does he want to talk about?" she asked.

"The Commissioner has worked out a deal. Curt can play for any National League club of his choice without jeopardizing the litigation."

"Oh, come on, Monte!" laughed Marian. "You know very well that the Commissioner can't change the rules of the Federal judiciary. If Curt plays ball, his case becomes moot. Now tell me what the Commissioner really wants."

"He's a very compassionate man," said Monte. "He wants everybody to be happy."

"Oh?" said Marian.

"This is the last door open," threatened Monte. "If I don't hear from you by tomorrow, I'll know that you've closed the door."

"Thank you, Monte."

A few days later, I got a telegram from Bowie Kuhn:

AM DISAPPOINTED YOU DECLINED MY INVITATION FOR A PERSONAL CONFERENCE IN LOS ANGELES ON FRIDAY. I DESIRED AN OPPORTUNITY TO DISCUSS WITH YOU PERSONALLY YOUR BASEBALL CAREER WITHOUT PREJUDICE TO THE BASIC ISSUES INVOLVED IN THE PENDING LITIGATION. MY COUNSEL HAS ASCERTAINED FROM YOUR COUNSEL THAT THE LATTER HAD NO OBJECTIONS TO SUCH A CONFERENCE WITH THE EXPLICIT CONDITION THAT HE WAS NOT RECOMMENDING THAT YOU ASSENT OR DECLINE. THIS IS TO ADVISE YOU THAT IF YOU RECONSIDER I WILL CONTINUE TO BE AVAILABLE.

I now knew that someday the owners of baseball would instruct Kuhn to issue a similar invitation to Marvin Miller and the leadership of the Major League Baseball Players Association and me, to discuss revisions in the reserve clause. Life was brightening.

But the trial was dull. The points at issue were matters of constitutional and legal scholarship. Testimony was less significant than the arguments contained in the briefs. So we got a parade of testimonials from witnesses who opined that the reserve system was bad or unnecessary or both after which the defense produced testimonials from witnesses who contended that the system was vital to the perpetuation of the game. The proceedings held little interest for me after I caught their drift. One high spot was the arrival in court of Jackie Robinson, who came directly to me, shook my hand and congratulated me on my stand. His praise choked me up. The defense provided a certain sad amusement by its repeated assertion that modification of the reserve rules would ruin "baseball as we know it."

What they meant was that the change might reduce their profits. The term "baseball as we know it" denoted a national pastime immutable in form, because any change might displease or confuse the beloved fan. I was deeply grateful and rousingly entertained when Leonard Koppett wrote on June 14, 1970 in *The New York Times*:

As for 'baseball as we know it'—as who knows it? And when?

Is baseball as 'we' know it sixteen teams playing 154-game schedules, twenty teams playing 162-game schedules, or twenty-four teams playing in four divisions with playoffs to decide pennant winners?

Is it independent minor-league teams and free competition for new players, or subsidized minors with a free-agent draft?

Is it unlimited control of hundreds of players by any one farm system, or an 'unrestricted draft' that limits certain control to the forty-man roster?

Is it a half-century of immovable franchises crammed into eleven cities in the northeast quadrant of the country, or sixteen changes in the major-league map in the last seventeen years?

Is it a game played on natural grass or on a synthetic surface? Is it one in which starting pitchers complete 75 percent of the game or 25 percent? Is it a game where men who hit .400 fail to win a batting title or one in which a man with .301 does? Is it a lively ball or a dead ball, symmetrical stadia or old ball parks, big gloves or little gloves, 400 major-league players or 600 major-league players, with a legal spitball or without, with two umpires on the field or four, under lights or all in the daytime?

The reserve clause has been 100 percent effective since 1915, when the Federal League folded. All the above changes have come about since then. The only aspect 'preserved' by the reserve system is the reserve system itself.

Frederick Douglass was a Maryland slave who taught himself to read. "If there is no struggle," he once said, 'there is no progress. Those who profess to favor freedom, and yet deprecate agitation, are men who want crops without plowing up the ground.... Power concedes nothing without a demand. It never did and never will."

To see the Curt Flood case in that light is to see its entire meaning. I have asked the Federal courts to affirm that national policy requires reasonably equitable relations between employers and employees, and that baseball is no exception. I have promised to pursue the matter to the Supreme Court of the United States, if necessary. I have no choice. The owners left me none. Their refusal to stop violating the antitrust laws meant that I could obtain my rights only through litigation. After the courts rule that the present reserve system is unlawful, the employers will be obligated to do what they should have done years ago. They will sit down with the players and negotiate reasonable conditions of employment.

✣ ✣ ✣

I spent most of the summer of 1970 bedding and boozing and waiting for Judge Irving Ben Cooper to shunt my case toward the U.S. Supreme Court where it belonged. Apart from the lawsuit and occasional sessions with Larry Albert of The Aunts and Uncles, I was involved in nothing useful. I lacked the patience to paint. I refused employment in the photography businesses that used my name. Illogically—even superstitiously—I avoided gainful pursuits, as if they might indicate that I was trying to start a new career in expectation of losing my case. So I marked time. And I slowly went to seed.

In August, Marian managed to get my concentrated attention for the first time in weeks. I found myself focusing on some unpleasant truths.

"The Curt Flood corporations are on the rocks," she was saying. "They're about to go under. You simply cannot go on like this."

"Don't curdle my vodka. It's a great big beautiful world. Love conquers all."

"Things are past the joking stage, dear. Try to listen to me."

"I'm as clear as a bell. The Curt Flood corporations are in deep trouble. Maybe I should put some money into them."

"Dear, you don't have enough and none is coming in. At the rate you're going, you'll be lucky to get through the year."

I had been whistling in the dark. I actually had believed that the businesses would keep me alive if the need arose. Their prosperity had been what I had in mind when I assured everyone that my commercial interests meant that suing posed no financial hardship for me. Failure of the corporations would be a crushing embarrassment.

"I'll be ashamed to show my goddamned face in St. Louis after playing bigshot all this time," I grieved. "I might as well clear out now, before the stuff hits the fan. I'm through in St. Louis baseball and I'm through in the town itself. Time to go, baby."

Marian looked stricken.

"I'll go to Copenhagen," I announced. "Nobody knows me. I can stretch a dollar further there. Maybe I can find a bar or restaurant to buy into. Best of all, I can sweat out the federal courts without having to worry about my image all the time. It will be a real vacation."

Marian finally agreed. I suppose she was in favor of anything that might stir me out of my vegetative stupor. I wondered whether she also felt, as I did, that my departure would be her liberation. She could now go back to Oakland and lead a genteel existence instead of cleaning up after me. I had been exploiting her terribly.

Brief inquiry confirmed that the businesses were indeed on their way to hell, and that I could do nothing to salvage them. I packed my bags. Marian and I agreed that this was not a permanent good-bye. Just another bump in the road, this. I then flew away. She disposed of the apartment and drove to the Coast.

I found a pleasant room overlooking a yacht basin near Copenhagen. I bought a sketch pad and beret and grew a goatee. I played artist on street corners and in the happy hunting grounds known as Tivoli Gardens. "Little do these beautiful Danish pastries realize," I mused, "that the aesthetic black in the beret and goatee is actually Curt Flood, the famous St. Louis business tycoon and athlete, vacationing between triumphs."

I began negotiating to buy a restaurant, after finding someone able to help me run a business of that kind. I learned by mail that Judge Cooper had ruled, as expected, that the issues in my case could not be resolved at his level. American servicemen on leave from Germany told me that Bob Gibson was having a great year although the Cardinals were terrible. And then I discovered that my supposed vacation was not at all what I had planned.

Technically, but entirely without design, I was on the lam. The collapse of the photography businesses had hurt some people badly. They had struck back. A lawsuit or two was being filed against me. It was conceivable that neither the corporate nature of the businesses nor my own abstention from their affairs would free me of all legal responsibility.

All of a sudden, Copenhagen was no longer a vacation resort but a jail. To run away from social discomfort—as I surely had—was no worse than self-indulgent and silly. But to find that my flight had rescued me from more serious embarrassment was downright awful. Was the black champion of players' rights supposed to end like this—hiding from creditors in a Danish hotel room? And what a splendid combination of lawsuits to be involved in! One case majestically on its way to the Supreme Court and history. The others before some lowly tribunal concerned with unpaid bills.

While awaiting the arrival of more details, so that I'd know how best to proceed, I got a telephone call from a reporter on the *Washington Post*.

"What do you think of the deal?" he began.

"Deal?"

"Don't you know that the Washington Senators have acquired the rights to negotiate with you?"

It seemed that Robert E. Short, owner of the Washington club, had agreed to give Philadelphia a player just for the right to talk to me. A few minutes later, while I was pondering this strange development, Short telephoned.

"What's the possibility of us getting together?" he inquired, as if he were downstairs in the lobby instead of an ocean away.

"You know how I feel about the reserve clause, Mr. Short. And you know that the whole thing is in court. You know that I must talk to people in New York before I can even consider talking to you."

"Curt, you've already made your point in court. You've stayed out for a whole year. The rest is up to the Circuit Court of Appeals or the Supreme Court itself. You've got nothing more to gain by staying out of baseball."

"Maybe so, maybe not. The last I heard, I could not play without harming our case. If anything has changed, I'd love to know it."

"Come to New York as my guest," urged Short. "Talk to your lawyers. Then let's get together. I'm sure we can work something out that won't hurt your case but will put a lot of money into your pocket and help my ball club."

It all sounded unrealistic to me, but I could not resist a free trip to New York. I cabled Marvin Miller and took off. At worst, I'd learn at closer hand about the present status of the lawsuit. And about the real situation in St. Louis. God, I wanted to play baseball again. Could it possibly happen?

As usual, Marvin Miller addressed me with supreme objectivity. Just as he had not influenced me to file suit, he now refused to tell me whether or not to negotiate with Bob Short. It was entirely up to me.

"But would my playing in 1971 hurt our chances in the higher courts? Can a case be dismissed as moot *after* it has been tried and has entered the appeals process? Might not our situation be different now that the actual trial is over with?"

"That's a question for Arthur Goldberg," replied Marvin.

It was late October. Goldberg was in the thick of his campaign as Democratic candidate for governor of New York. Yet he took time to meet with Marvin, Dick Moss and me. He knew about my business reverses. He told me what I wanted to hear:

"By remaining out of baseball and giving up more than a hundred thousand dollars in income last season, you suffered real damages which go to the heart of your dispute with the reserve system. I therefore think that you could play in 1971 without hurting the case in the higher courts."

When he, Miller, Moss, Max Gitter (a Goldberg associate), and I met with Bob Short, we handed him a list of written proposals. In effect, these suggested that he give me a contract from which the key provisions of the reserve clause were eliminated. We asked him to agree (a) not to trade me without my consent, (b) to pay me the full year's salary even if I were cut from the team before the end of the season, and (c) to release me unconditionally if he and I were unable to agree on terms for a 1972 renewal of the contract. We also demanded agreement that the owners would not argue in court that my presence on the playing field invalidated my suit.

Bob Short has been around. He is a lawyer and a trucking and hotel magnate who developed the almost bankrupt Los Angeles Lakers basketball franchise into a multi-million dollar bonanza. He reviewed our demands without turning a hair. He agreed to them all. Goldberg and Gitter returned to their offices to draw up a memorandum embodying this agreement. Short and I were about to sign the first equitable player's contract in the history of major-league baseball! The precedent would be tremendously impor-tant—the first huge step toward industry-wide modification of the reserve system.

Three hours later, we reconvened. Short is usually a bluff, out-going man but he was now curiously subdued. He explained that

177

he was obliged to offer some second thoughts. For example, he no longer could agree to modify the standard reserve provisions in my contract.

"Commissioner Kuhn will not permit it," he said, sheepishly.

This meant that Short's fellow owners—his colleagues in the payment of Kuhn's salary and in the establishment of Kuhn's policy—had issued orders to restrain Bob Short.

Short had been given the word in a telephone conversation with Alexander (Sandy) Hadden, former counsel to the American League and now counsel to Kuhn. Hadden was still on the line. Shore consulted him frequently while talking to us. The owner of the Senators was empowered to agree that the contract could contain a covenant in which both parties stipulated that my playing was not prejudicial to the issues under dispute in court. And, if I insisted, the contract also could grant me veto power over one kind of trade.

"If you want, I can agree not to trade you to Philadelphia without your consent," he said.

By then we were all so shocked and angered by Short's retreat that we did not even laugh at the Philadelphia ploy. We simply rejected it.

And there we sat. The decision was up to me. I said that I needed time to think.

Short was in a hurry. He said that he would pay me "around a hundred thousand" for the season. Justice Goldberg suggested $110,000. Short grabbed it.

He then promised to help me straighten out my financial affairs. He also spoke of giving me a job during the off season. And, finally, he indicated he would not let the other owners force him to renege on his word to me.

"I made good-faith assurances," he said, "and I'll keep them."

This was better. But was it good enough?

I returned to my room and took stock. On the positive side:

1. Nobody—including myself—could justly accuse me of selling out my principles for money. I was not dropping my case against the owners. I would continue to pursue it until a resolution was reached

either by court order or through negotiation with the Major League Baseball Players Association.

2. Apparently my playing would not prejudice higher courts against our appeal. I had Justice Goldberg's assurances on that score, and would get the owners' promise in writing not to try to defeat our suit on grounds that my playing undermined my arguments.

3. The $110,000 salary would help me get back on an even keel.

4. Short had offered me a job in the Florida Instructional League beginning in November. I could get into decent shape before spring training began. I could expect every opportunity to re-establish myself as a first-rate outfielder.

On the other hand:

1. Many fans would surely suppose that I had sold out or, at the very least, had been pressured into abandoning the fight. In 1970 I had called myself a $90,000-a-year slave and now I would be playing quietly for $110,000. This would tend to reaffirm public belief in the invincible power of the baseball establishment. Worse, it would encourage cynicism about the durability of principles—not only mine but everyone else's.

2. Many baseball players would be bitterly disappointed. Some might be hostile. They would wonder if I had used the Major League Baseball Players Association for the sole purpose of getting myself a $20,000 raise. That the Association had been supporting not Curt Flood himself but a suit against the hated reserve system would take much explaining. Months or years might pass, furthermore, until anyone could be absolutely certain that my return to uniform had not weakened our position. Meanwhile, I could expect a rough time. I would be baited as the self-styled man of principle who ran out of principle in one season. I would be ripped as the successful businessman who kept saying that "some things are more important than money" until his businesses disappeared and he signed with Washington. For money.

Too bad. Too bad for me. Too bad for those who might misunderstand or misrepresent me. Too bad that I had sacrificed only $100,000 or so in salary and only one year of my waning athletic career. I would have preferred enough wealth to pass up $100,000 a year for as long as it took the courts to rule on our principle. I would have preferred such wealth not only for its own green sake but because my public position would then have been uncomplicated. Too bad.

And too bad that I now was only a hop and a skip from bankruptcy. I called Marvin Miller and Dick Moss and Arthur Goldberg and told them that I would sign. I then called Short and signed. I went to Copenhagen for my clothes, and to explain why the restaurant deal would have to wait until the fall of 1971.

I then returned to the United States to get ready to do my thing.

Jim Bouton

BALL FOUR

When Ball Four *was published in 1970 it was called "an authentic revolutionary manifesto" by the Boston Globe. Thirty years later, this hilarious and revealing account of playing in the big leagues is not only still in print, but was recently named one of the "Books of The Century" by the New York Public Library. And while it played an historic role in helping to change the balance of power between players and owners,* Ball Four's *enduring strength lies in the human stories it tells—and the way Bouton tells them.*

Fall, 1968

Wyckoff, NJ

signed my contract today to play for the Seattle Pilots at a salary of $22,000 and it was a letdown because I didn't have to bargain. There was no struggle, none of the give and take that I look forward to every year. Most players don't like to haggle. They just want to get it over with. Not me. With me signing a contract has been a yearly adventure.

The reason for no adventure this year is the way I pitched last year. It ranged from awful to terrible to pretty good. When it was terrible, and I had a record of 0 and 7, or 2 and 7 maybe, I had to do some serious thinking about whether it was all over for me. I was pitching for the Seattle Angels of the Pacific Coast League. The next

year, 1969, under expansion, the club would become the Seattle
Pilots of the American League. The New York Yankees had sold me to
Seattle for $20,000 and were so eager to get rid of me they paid
$8,000 of my $22,000 salary. This means I was actually sold for
$12,000, less than half the waiver price. Makes a man think.

✤ ✤ ✤

February, 1969

Tempe, AZ

Reported to spring camp in Tempe, Arizona, today, six days late. I
was on strike. I'm not sure anybody knew it, but I was.

I had signed my contract before I knew there was going to be a
players' strike and I was obligated to report on time. I found that out
at the big meeting the players had with Marvin Miller, the players'
representative, at the Biltmore in New York earlier this month. I'm
much in sympathy with what Miller is doing and I think, given the
circumstances, he won a great victory. I think the owners understand now that we're going to stick together—even the big stars,
who don't have that much at stake. Still, I was going to live up to my
contract and report on time. What made me change my mind was a
phone call I made to Lou Piniella, a twenty-six-year-old rookie who'd
been in the Baltimore and Cleveland organizations.

Since the Pilots were not a team yet we had no player representative, so the three or four Pilots at the meeting in the Biltmore were
asked to call four or five teammates each to tell them what happened.
I reached Lou in Florida and he said that his impulse was to report,
that he was scared it would count against him if he didn't, that he
was just a rookie looking to make the big leagues and didn't want
anybody to get angry at him. But also that he'd thought it over carefully and decided he should support the other players and the strike.
So he was not reporting.

That impressed the hell out of me. Here's a kid with a lot more at stake than I, a kid risking a once-in-a-lifetime shot. And suddenly I felt a moral obligation to the players. I decided not to go down.

The reason nobody knew I was on strike, though, was that I'd asked the Pilots to find a place for me and my family in Tempe. They couldn't. So I said that as long as there were no accommodations I couldn't report. I sort of took it both ways. You take your edges where you can. I learned that playing baseball.

As soon as I got to the park I went right over to Marvin Milkes' office and we shook hands and he asked me if I had a nice flight. He also said, "There's been a lot of things said about the strike and I know you've said some things about it, but we're going to forget all that and start fresh. We have a new team and everybody starts with a clean slate. I'm giving some people a new opportunity. I've got a man in the organization who is a former alcoholic. I've even got a moral degenerate that I know of. But as far as I'm concerned we're going to let bygones be bygones and whatever has been said in the past—and I know you've said a lot of things—we'll forget all about it and start fresh."

I said thanks. I also wondered where, on a scale of one to ten, a guy who talks too much falls between a former alcoholic and a moral degenerate.

✤   ✤   ✤

When I started out in 1959 I was ready to love the baseball establishment. In fact I thought big business had all the answers to any question I could ask. As far as I was concerned clubowners were benevolent old men who wanted to hang around the locker room and were willing to pay a price for it, so there would never be any problem about getting paid decently. I suppose I got that way reading Arthur Daley in *The New York Times*. And reading about those big salaries. I read that Ted Williams was making $125,000 and figured that Billy Goodman made $60,000. That was, of course, a mistake.

I signed my first major-league contract at Yankee Stadium fifteen minutes before they played "The Star-Spangled Banner" on opening day, 1962. That's because my making the team was a surprise. But I'd had a hell of a spring. Just before the game was about to start Roy Hamey, the general manager, came into the clubhouse and shoved a contract under my nose. "Here's your contract," he said. "Sign it. Everybody gets $7,000 their first year."

Hamey had a voice like B. S. Pully's, only louder. I signed. It wasn't a bad contract. I'd gotten $3,000 for playing all summer in Amarillo, Texas, the year before.

I finished the season with a 7–7 record and we won the pennant and the World Series, so I collected another $10,000, which was nice. I was much better toward the end of the season than at the beginning. Like I was 4–7 early but then won three in a row, and Ralph Houk, the manager, listed me as one of his six pitchers for the stretch pennant race and the Series.

All winter I thought about what I should ask for and finally decided to demand $12,000 and settle for $11,000. This seemed to me an eminently reasonable figure. When I reported to spring training in Ft. Lauderdale—a bit late because I'd spent six months in the army—Dan Topping, Jr., son of the owner, and the guy who was supposed to sign all the lower-echelon players like me, handed me a contract and said, "Just sign here, on the bottom line."

I unfolded the contract and it was for $9,000—if I made the team. I'd get $7,000 if I didn't.

If I made the team?

"Don't forget you get a World Series share," Topping said. He had a boarding-school accent that always made me feel like my fly was open or something. "You can always count on that."

"Fine," I said. "I'll sign a contract that guarantees me $10,000 more at the end of the season if we don't win the pennant."

He was shocked. "Oh, we can't do that."

"Then what advantage is it to me to take less money?"

"That's what we're offering."

"I can't sign it."

"Then you'll have to go home."

"All right, I'll go home."

"Well, give me a call in the morning, before you leave."

I called him the next morning and he said to come over and see him. "I'll tell you what we're going to do," he said. "We don't usually do this, but we'll make a big concession. I talked with my dad, with Hamey, and we've decided to eliminate the contingency clause—you get $9,000 whether you make the club or not."

"Wow!" I said. Then I said no.

"That's our final offer, take it or leave it. You know, people don't usually do this. You're the first holdout we've had in I don't know how many years."

I said I was sorry. I hated to mess up Yankee tradition, but I wasn't going to sign for a $2,000 raise. And I got up to go.

"Before you go, let me call Hamey," Topping said. He told Hamey I was going home and Hamey said he wanted to talk to me. I held the phone four inches from my ear. If you were within a mile of him, Hamey really didn't need a telephone.

"Lookit, son," he yelled. "You better sign that contract, that's all there's gonna be. That's it. You don't sign that contract you're making the biggest mistake of your life."

I was twenty-four years old. And scared. Also stubborn. I said I wouldn't sign and hung up.

"All right," Topping said, "how much do you want?"

"I was thinking about $12,000," I said, but not with much conviction.

"Out of the question," Topping said. "Tell you what. We'll give you $10,000."

My heart jumped. "Make it ten-five," I said.

"All right," he said. "Ten-five."

The bastards really fight you.

✣ ✣ ✣

from BALL FOUR

March

Joe Schultz stopped by again today to say a kind word. I noticed he was making it his business to say something each day to most of the guys. He may look like Nikita Khrushchev, but it means a lot anyway. I'm sure most of us here feel like leftovers and outcasts and marginal players and it doesn't hurt when the manager massages your ego a bit.

I was moved up from last to next-to-last, and then to second, for my five minutes of batting practice, and I've decided there's no significance to the position. My arm feels good; no pain, no problems. Every once in a while I let a fastball fly and it comes out of my hand real easy and seems like it took no effort. I can almost hear a voice in the back of my mind whispering, "You can go back to it, you can find it, you can find your old fastball and you'll be great again." Of course, I've heard that siren song in my head before and I've won a total of fourteen games in the last four years. So I'm going to stick with my knuckleball. I'll probably throw it 90 percent of the time, and if my other stuff comes around for me, I'll probably cut it down to about 40 or 50 percent. But I've got to remember that if it wasn't for my knuckleball I'd probably be back in New Jersey, raising chickens or something. Remember, stupid, remember!

✢   ✢   ✢

For my ten-five in 1963 I won 21 games and lost only 7. I had a 2.53 earned-run average. I couldn't wait to see my next contract.

By contract time Yogi Berra was the manager and Houk had been promoted to general manager. I decided to let Houk off easy. I'd ask for $25,000 and settle for $20,000, and I'd be worth every nickel of it. Houk offered me $15,500. Houk can look as sincere as hell with those big blue eyes of his and when he calls you "podner" it's hard to argue with him. He said the reason he was willing to give me such a big raise right off was that he didn't want to haggle, he just wanted to give me a top salary, more than any second-year pitcher had ever made with the Yankees, and forget about it.

"How many guys have you had who won 21 games in their second year?" I asked him.

He said he didn't know. And, despite all the "podners," I didn't sign.

This was around January 15. I didn't hear from Houk again until two weeks before spring training, when he came up another thousand, to $16,500. This was definitely final. He'd talked to Topping, called him on his boat, ship to shore. Very definitely final.

I said it wasn't final for me, I wanted $20,000.

"Well, you can't make twenty," Houk said. "We never double contracts. It's a rule.". . .

The day before spring training began he went up another two thousand to $18,500. After all-night consultations with Topping, of course. "Ralph," I said, real friendly, "under ordinary circumstances I might have signed this contract. If you had come with it sooner, and if I hadn't had the problem I had last year trying to get $3,000 out of Dan Topping, Jr. But I can't, because it's become a matter of principle."

He has his rules, I have my principles.

Now I'm a holdout again. Two weeks into spring training and I was enjoying every minute of it. The phone never stopped ringing and I was having a good time. Of course, the Yankees weren't too happy. One reason is that they knew they were being unfair and they didn't want anybody to know it. But I was giving out straight figures, telling everybody exactly what I'd made and what they were offering and the trouble I'd had with Dan Topping, Jr.

One time Houk called and said, "Why are you telling everybody what you're making?"

"If I don't tell them, Ralph," I said, "maybe they'll think I'm asking for ridiculous figures. They might even think I asked for $15,000 last year and that I'm asking for thirty now. I just want them to know I'm being reasonable."

And Houk said something that sounded like: "*Rowrorrowrowrr.*"
You ever hear a lion grumble?. . .

. . .On March 8, my birthday, Houk called me and said he was
going to deduct $100 a day from his offer for every day I held out
beyond March 10. It amounted to a fine for not signing, no matter
what Houk said. What he said was, "Oh no, it's not a fine. I don't
believe in fining people." And I'm sure it never occurred to him just
how unfair a tactic this was. Baseball people are so used to having
their own way and not getting any argument that they just don't
think they *can* be unfair. When I called Joe Cronin, president of the
league, to ask if Houk could, legally, fine me, he said, "Walk around
the block, then go back in and talk some more."

After walking around the block and talking it over with my dad,
I chickened out. Sorry about that. I called Houk and said "Okay, you
win. I'm on my way down." I salved my wounds with the thought
that if I had any kind of a year this time I'd really sock it to him.

Still, if I knew then what I know now, I wouldn't have signed. I'd
have called him back and said, "Okay, Ralph, I'm having a press conference of my own to announce that for every day you don't meet my
demand of $25,000 it will cost you $500 a day. Think that one over."

Maybe I wouldn't have gotten $25,000, but I bet I would've got-
ten more than eighteen-five. I could tell from the negative reaction
Ralph got in the press. And I got a lot of letters from distinguished
citizens and season-ticket holders, all of them expressing outrage at
Houk. That's when I realized I should have held out. It was also
when Ralph Houk, I think, started to hate me.

✢ ✢ ✢

Decided to get a haircut today. My hair was quite long and the sideburns were thick and heavy. I didn't want to have a longhair image,
so I got a really short haircut and look like a stormtrooper. It's terrible, but it won't hurt me. You never can tell how spring training is
going to go. I could be one of those borderline cases and the differ-

ence between making the club and not making it might be the length of my hair.

I wore a mustache all winter and thought I looked pretty good. Cut it off before I came down. Richie Allen can wear those porkchop sideburns of his if he wants because he hits all those home runs. What's standing between me and *my* mustache is about twenty wins.

When I walked into the clubhouse with *my* new haircut, Sheldon said, "Now you look like the old Bulldog." Bulldog! That's what they called me when I was a big winner with the Yankees. Bulldog. *Gruff!* This is the impression I wanted to create all along. Maybe they'll think because my hair is short I got my fastball back. You got to use all your weapons.

One thing you *don't* do is what Steve Hovley did. He's an outfielder I played with in Seattle last year, twenty-four years old, intellectual type. He told Milkes that he wouldn't report until March 22 because he wanted to finish up some college classes. Milkes told him he'd never make the team if he waited that long and Steve said, well, he'd looked at the roster and didn't think he could make it anyway. Besides, he thought he could use another year or two in Triple-A.

That's a big mistake. No matter what the truth of it is, Milkes will now always think that Steve doesn't have enough desire to be a major leaguer. There are times you have to show hustle, even if it's false.

Baseball players' words to a beautifully tender song (Actually Overheard in the Clubhouse Division): "Summertime, and your mother is easy."

Steve Hovley was dancing to a tune on the radio and somebody yelled, "Hove, dancing is just not your thing."

"Do you mind if I decide what my thing is?" Hovley said.

So I asked him what his thing was. "I like sensual things," he said. "Eating, sleeping. I like showers and I like flowers and I like riding my bike."

"You have a bike with you?"

"Certainly. I rent one. And I ride past a field of sheep on the way to the park every day and a field of alfalfa, and sometimes I get off my bike and lie down in it. A field of alfalfa is a great place to lie down and look up at the sky."

I sure wish Hovley would make the team.

Uniform-measuring day. This is always a waste. They measure everybody carefully and the uniforms arrive three sizes too big. Part of the reason is that everybody is wearing tight-fitting uniforms these days. Pepitone refuses to take the field if his uniform isn't skintight. Phil Linz used to say that he didn't know why, but he could run faster in tight pants. And I understand that Dick Stuart, old Dr. Strangeglove, would smooth his uniform carefully, adjust his cap, tighten his belt and say, "I add 20 points to my average if I know I look bitchin' out there."

Bob Lasko is in camp. I was glad to see him. He's a pitcher, righthanded, and we broke in together in the Rookie League in Kearny, Nebraska, in 1959. He's thirty years old, too, and he's never pitched a game in the major leagues. He's a real big guy and I remember he had a tremendous fastball and a great overhand curve. I used to try to model my motion after his. I always seemed to be better when he was around. We roomed together in Amarillo in 1961 and became close friends. His trouble was that the Yankees tried to hide him. He pitched in about sixty innings all season at Kearny. One time he got in a ballgame, struck out the side for three innings and they took him out of the game and put another pitcher in. The rule at the time was that if you didn't get drafted your first year the organization could keep you for three years without moving you up to a major-league roster. Since he pitched so few innings, no one drafted him.

Bob told me today that he'd once complained about it. "I talked to one of the Yankee coaches," he said. "I told him I didn't think the Yankees had been fair to me and his neck started to get all red and he started to holler and damn, we almost had a fight, right there."

I asked him who the coach was.

"Ralph Houk," he said.

Steve Hovley sidled over to me in the outfield today and whispered into my ear, "Billy Graham is a cracker."

Okay, boys and girls, tomorrow is my birthday and I'll be thirty years old. I don't feel like thirty. I look like I'm in my early twenties and I feel like I'm in my early twenties. My arm, however, is over a hundred years old.

After the game Bobbie and I were at a party with Gary Bell and his wife and Steve Barber and his. Gary's wife, Nan, said she'd been anxious to meet me since she'd read in the Pilot spring guidebook that some of my hobbies were water coloring, mimicry and jewelry-making. "Everyone else has hunting and fishing, so I figured you must be a real beauty. I mean, jewelry-making?" said Nan. "Make me some earrings, you sweet thing."

Then we got to talking about some of the crazy things ballplayers do. Nan told a story of the time she called him on the road to check on a flight she was supposed to catch. She called Gary at 4:30 A.M., his time, and his roommate, Woody Held, answered the phone and said, without batting an eyelash, that Gary was out playing golf. And Gary's wife shrugged and said, "Maybe he was."

My wife and I burst out laughing when Gary asked me if I'd ever been on the roof of the Shoreham Hotel in Washington. The Shoreham is the beaver-shooting capital of the world, and I once told Bobbie that you could win a pennant with the guys who've been on that roof. "Pennant, hell," Bell said. "You could stock a whole league."

I better explain about beaver-shooting. A beaver-shooter is, at bottom, a Peeping Tom. It can be anything from peering over the top of the dugout to look up dresses to hanging from the fire escape on the twentieth floor of some hotel to look into a window. I've seen guys chin themselves on transoms, drill holes in doors, even shove a mirror under a door. . . .

Now, some people might look down on this sort of activity. But in baseball if you shoot a particularly good beaver you are a highly respected person, one might even say a folk hero of sorts. Indeed, if you are caught out late at night and tell the manager you've had a good run of beaver shooting he'd probably let you off with a light fine.

The roof of the Shoreham is important beaver-shooting country because of the way the hotel is shaped—a series of L-shaped wings that make the windows particularly vulnerable from certain spots on the roof. The Yankees would go up there in squads of fifteen or so, often led by Mickey Mantle himself. You needed a lot of guys to do the spotting. Then someone would whistle from two or three wings away, "*Psst!* Hey! Beaver shot. Section D. Five o'clock." And there'd be a mad scramble of guys climbing over skylights, tripping over each other and trying not to fall off the roof. One of the first big thrills I had with the Yankees was joining about half the club on the roof of the Shoreham at two-thirty in the morning. I remember saying to myself, "So this is the big leagues."

Mike Marshall was in the Tiger organization for a while and he says that, like the Yankees, they frown on players telling reporters the truth. A reporter asked Mike what he was being paid and he said he didn't feel he could say, but it was less than the minimum. The reporter printed it and asked how the hell the Tigers could be paying their No. 1 reliever less than the minimum. So Mike got called in by Jim Campbell, the general manager. Campbell wasn't angry that Mike was making less than the minimum, but that he told.

I asked Mike if he'd ever talked to Johnny Sain about contracts and he said he hadn't. Sain gives you good advice on how to get money out of a ballclub. John's a quiet guy and follows most of the baseball rules about keeping your mouth shut, but he's not afraid to ask for money if he thinks he deserves it. He was with the Boston Braves in 1948, the year they won the pennant. It was Spahn and

Sain and then, dear Lord, two days of rain. Warren Spahn and Sain were the staff and Sain really put it to John Quinn, who was the general manager. Sain had had a big argument in the spring about his contract and signed for less than he wanted. Now they were just home from a western trip and fighting for the pennant and Sain went to Quinn and said, "I'd like to talk about my contract."

"We'll talk about your contract next winter, when it comes up," Quinn said.

"No, I'd like to talk about it now," John said.

"What the hell," Quinn said. "You signed a contract and we're going to stick by it. We can't renegotiate a contract during the season."

"Well, you're going to renegotiate this one," John said.

"What the hell do you mean by *that*?" Quinn said.

"I'm supposed to pitch Thursday," Sain said. "But unless you pay me what I wanted in the beginning I'm not pitching."

That meant it would be Spahn and rain and pray for a hurricane, and then maybe a flood. So Quinn tore up his contract and gave him a new one, and John won 24 games. He used to say to me, "Now, don't be afraid to climb those golden stairs. Go in there and get what you're worth."

Those golden stairs.

Arm felt pretty good today after pitching yesterday and I don't know whether to attribute it to the aspirin or the bottle of beaujolais I polished off at dinner. Or maybe it was the ice I put on my elbow.

Batting practice is the time to stand around in the outfield and tell each other stories. At first we all sort of felt each other out, standing fifteen feet apart and doing the job the way it's supposed to be done. By now, though, we're standing in clumps of five or ten and take turns catching whatever fly balls happen to come our way.

It was Dick Stuart-story day today, and this one was about the time Johnny Pesky was managing the Red Sox and Stuart was playing for him and showing up late for a lot of things. For some reason this upset Pesky, so he called a meeting to talk about MORALE. Stuart was late for it. In fact he didn't show up until about half an hour before the game (three is considered about right) and he walked right into the middle of the meeting. All eyes were on him as he opened the door to the clubhouse and, without missing a beat, opened his doublebreasted jacket, paraded to the center of the room with his hips swinging, did a pirouette and said, "And here he is nattily attired in a black suede jacket by Stanley Blacker, with blue velvetine pants and shoes by Florsheim. The handkerchief is by Christian Dior." Everybody went nuts. Even Pesky had to laugh.

Stuart's a beauty. I remember a game we played against him in Boston with Earl Wilson (then with the Red Sox) pitching. On the first pitch of the game somebody hit a foul pop fly between the catcher and first base and Earl ran over to call who was supposed to catch the ball, and he made a tragic mistake. He called Stuart. The ball dropped to the ground in front of him with a sickening thud.

Earl picked up the ball and stormed back to the mound. The next pitch was another pop fly, this one in fair territory. Earl ran over screaming at the top of his lungs, "I got it! I got it!" He wasn't taking any chances. At the last second guess who ran into him and spiked him. Dick Stuart. The ball went flying and the runner got two bases.

Now Wilson's got a spiked left foot and a man on second and he's steaming mad. The next pitch is a ground ball on the first-base line and Earl runs over, picks it up, whirls to throw to first and Stuart isn't on the bag. First and third.

Wilson slammed his glove down and walked toward the dugout like he was quitting right there, but he thought better of it and came back to the game. And Stuart? Stuart was his usual jovial self. He knew he had bad hands and there was nothing he could do about it.

Curt Blefary is another guy with classically bad hands. When he was with Baltimore Frank Robinson nicknamed him "Clank," after the robot. Once the team bus was riding by a junkyard and Robinson yelled for the driver to stop so Blefary could pick out a new glove.

(If you're going to shake hands with a guy who has bad hands you are supposed to say, "Give me some steel, baby.")

Now that the cut-down season is here we'll soon be talking of deaths in the family. At least that's what we did with the Yankees. When a guy got cut we'd say he died. Fritz Peterson would come over to me and say, "Guess who died today." And he'd look very downcast and in the tones of an undertaker read the roll of the dead.

A player who wasn't going well was said to be sick, very sick, in a coma or on his deathbed, depending on how bad he was going. Last year when I was sent to Seattle, Fritz asked me what happened and I said I died.

"You can't die," Fritz said. "You're too good to die."

Like Mae West once said, goodness has nothing to do with it.

On the Yankees the Grim Reaper was Big Pete. Once he whispered in your ear that the manager wanted to see you, you were clinically dead. I remember toward the end of one spring training Don Lock, an outfielder with a pretty good sense of humor (he needed it, having spent a lot of years in the Yankee chain trying to break into an outfield of Tom Tresh, Mantle and Maris), barricaded his locker. He hung sweatshirts across the top, crossed out his name, piled up his gloves and shoes in front to form a barrier, then snuggled inside the locker holding a bat like it was a rifle, and fired it at anybody who came near. It was good for a few laughs, but in the end the Grim Reaper got him anyway.

Another way Big Pete would let you know you had died was by not packing your equipment bag for a road trip. There would be a packed bag in front of every locker except yours. Rest in peace. It's kind of like, "All those who are going to New York City, please step forward. Not so fast, Johnson."

✛ ✛ ✛

Yuma, AZ

Our first big road trip today to Yuma, Arizona, and we did what

196

ballplayers do at the start of every trip—stand around the airport, inspect the threads and make funny comments. . . .

You can start fights if you get on a guy about something meaningful, like race or religion. But you can kid a guy about his clothes, or about the way he looks. We couldn't decide, for example, whether Sal Maglie looked more like an Indian chief or Mafia enforcer. But we didn't tell him.

Me: "If you're a customs official would you check Maglie's bag?"

Bell: "I'd strip him to his shorts."

Holtville, CA

Today, while we were sitting in the bullpen, Eddie O'Brien, the All-American coach, said, just after one of our pitchers walked somebody in the ballgame: "The secret to pitching, boys, is throwing strikes."

Gee, Eddie! Thanks.

Wayne Comer got into an argument with an umpire, and they were jawing back and forth. The last thing said was, "All right, Comer. You'll be sorry you said that."

And he probably will. Umpires do get even with people, even good umpires. I remember when George Scott first came up to Boston. He must have irritated Ed Runge somehow because the word came out from Elston Howard that when Runge was behind the plate and Scott was hitting the strikes wouldn't have to be too good.

The first pitch I threw to Scott was about six inches off the plate. Strike one. The second pitch was eight inches outside. Strike two. The third pitch was a curve in the dirt. Scott swung and missed. He never had a chance.

Runge is one of the more powerful umpires in the league, mostly, I suppose, because he's a real good one. He's been wearing these long, gray sideburns that look just great against his tan. He is a striking figure out there. I asked him if he thought he could get by wearing the burns during the season and he said he didn't know, that Joe Cronin, the league president, hadn't seen them yet. But I'm betting on Runge. He's got power.

There was the time, for example, when Steve Whitaker was with the Yankees and bitched to him on a couple of calls and Runge told Mickey Mantle, "You better straighten that boy out."

That night Mantle and Whitaker ran into Runge at a restaurant and Mantle told Whitaker he'd better go over and apologize. Whitaker said the hell he would. But after Mantle explained to him what it might mean to his batting average he succumbed. Just call him *Mr.* Runge. . . .

❖   ❖   ❖

April

Wayne Comer says that Mayo Smith, the Tiger manager, once said to him, "Wayne, I think you're going to hit .290 this year—but you're going to be doing it in Montgomery, Alabama."

There was a notice on the bulletin board asking guys to sign up to have their cars driven to Seattle. Price $150. The drivers are college kids. I think I'd prefer Bonnie and Clyde. I say this because I remember college and how I drove an automobile in those days and I would not have hired me to drive my car. Still, a lot of guys put their names on the list—very tentatively.

❖   ❖   ❖

Opening Day

Anaheim, CA
Naturally we won our first game. Beat the Angels 4–3. Mike Hegan hit the first home run for the Pilots and Joe Schultz, jumping up and down in the dugout, clapped his hands and actually yelled, "Hurray for our team."

from BALL FOUR

When we came into the clubhouse, all of us yelling and screaming like a bunch of high-school kids, Joe Schultz said, "Stomp on 'em. Thataway to stomp on 'em. Kick 'em when they're down. Shitfuck. Stomp them. Stomp them good."

✤ ✤ ✤

This afternoon Gary Bell and I went to Pershing Square (in Los Angeles) to listen to some of the old ladies in sneakers tell us to be prepared to meet our maker. I confess I enjoy rapping with them and usually wind up assured that eternal salvation is beyond my reach.

Later on we came across a group that was into the Indian thing and they were chanting *Hari Krishna Rama Rama*, etc., and I got to talking to one of them, who said that their religion simply was to reaffirm love of God regardless of the particular religion and I thought that was fair enough and we hung around enjoying the chanting and sitar music.

Then a priest, probably about fifty-five years old, happened by and got into conversation with one of the group. When he left I asked what it was about. "He said this was a religion that didn't belong in this country," the young man said. "He said we already had enough religions in this country and that we should go back to India or wherever it was we came from."

Seattle, WA
I died tonight.

I got sent to Vancouver.

My first reaction: outrage.

Second reaction: Omigod! How am I going to tell Bobbie? The *problems*. Where to live? How to get rid of the place we'd already signed a lease on in Seattle? What would happen to the $650 deposit? Moving again. *Again*. And we just got here.

But mostly outrage.

We'd lost a 2-1 game to Kansas City when Sal came over and said "Joe wants to see you in his office."

My heart started racing. I mean Joe never wants to see me anywhere. So I knew. At the same time I thought, "Nah. It's too early. I've really only pitched the once. How can they tell anything from that? Maybe it's a trade? Or maybe he's just sore at something I've done. Let's see, what have I done lately?"

It takes a lot longer to tell it than to think it. As soon as I got into his office Joe Schultz said, "I hate to tell you a thing like this after such a close loss."

I almost laughed in his face. As though I'd be so brokenhearted over losing a lousy ballgame that I couldn't bear anything more, even a small thing like being sent to the minors.

Then Joe said he had to send me to Vancouver, and I thought, "What the hell, I'll go out with some class." I told him I would have done anything to help the club and that I really felt bad about having to leave it.

"I know," Joe Schultz said. "You work hard and you do all your running and you did everything we asked of you. We just didn't think your knuckleball did that much in Arizona and we wanted to see what it looked like when it got out of the light air, and it didn't look like it was coming around like we thought it should. We need pitching bad."

So I said, "Well, if I do real good down there, I'd like to come back."

I expected him to say, "Of course. You do good down there and we'll yank you right back here, stick you in and you'll win the goddam pennant for us." Or something reassuring like that. Instead Joe Schultz said, "Well, if you do good down there, there's a lot of teams that need pitchers."

Good grief. If I ever heard a see you later, that was it.

So I said thanks a lot and left.

I went back to my locker and there was a Coke sitting there that I'd opened. I gave it to Mike Marshall and opened a beer. This was not a night for Cokes. I threw my half-eaten corned-beef sandwich in the wastebasket and went over and told Gary Bell what had happened. He was kind of shocked, but as I started throwing stuff into my bag I could feel a wall, invisible but real, forming around me. I was suddenly an outsider, a different person, someone to be shunned, a leper.

. . . I stopped by to see Marvin Milkes, and he wasn't any help either. I told him I was running into some big and sudden expenses and could he do anything about it, and he said—and this was beautiful—"Well, you didn't show us much all spring" (10 games, 19 innings, 16 hits, 11 walks, 5 strikeouts, 3.25 ERA). If I *had* shown much more I wouldn't be getting sent down. I felt like kicking him in the shins, but I said, "Hell, I had a better spring than four or five guys. In fact, I'm healthy, which is more than you can say for at least two of the guys." What I didn't say, but what I thought, was: "What about Steve Barber? He hasn't been able to pick up a baseball. He had a brutal spring. What's this love affair with Barber? Why can't he go on the disabled list?" Ah, the hell with it.

One of the worst things about getting sent down is the feeling you get that you've broken faith with so many people. I know my mother and father were rooting real hard for me, and all my friends back home, and they'll all feel bad—not for themselves, but for me.

Quitting altogether crosses my mind. But I won't. I *can't*. I'm convinced I can still get out big-league hitters with my knuckleball. I *know* I can. I know this is crazy, but I can see the end of the season and I've just won a pennant for some team, just won the final game, and everybody is clamoring around and I tell them, "Everybody have a seat. It's a long story."

Tacoma, WA

There's nothing like walking into a minor-league clubhouse to remind you what the minors are like. You have a tendency to block it. It was cold and rainy in Tacoma when I went there to meet the Vancouver club and the locker room was shudderingly damp, small and smelly. There's no tarpaulin on the field, so everything is wet and muddy and the dirt crunches underfoot on the cement. The locker stalls are made of chicken wire and you hang your stuff on rusty nails. There's no rubbing table in the tiny trainer's room, just a wooden bench, and there are no magazines to read and no carpet on the floor and no boxes of candy bars. The head is filthy and the toilet paper is institutional-thin. There's no batrack, so the bats, symbolically enough, are stored in a garbage can. There's no air-conditioning and no heat, and the paint on the walls is peeling off in flaky chunks and you look at all of that and you realize that the biggest jump in baseball is between the majors and Triple-A. The minor leagues are all very minor.

There's no end to the humiliation. The kid in the clubhouse asked me what position I played.

Honolulu, HI

There are compensations to being in the minors. Like Hawaii. Arrived here today and it's beautiful. On the airplane, if you're Leo Marentette you play gin rummy. Leo used to be in the Tiger organization and the first thing he asked me was "How's Moon Man?" which is what the Tigers called Mike Marshall, the way the Pilots called Steve Hovley "Orbit." Leo took $70 meal money from Darrell Brandon and the word is that he bought rights to Jerry Stephenson, a gin-rummy mark, for the five-hour plane ride.

On the plane I discovered that Greg Goossen is afraid to fly. On the takeoff he wrapped himself around his seatbelt in the fetal position, his hands over his eyes. Then, as we were landing, he went into frenzied activity, switching the overhead light on and off, turning the air blower on and off, right and left, opening and closing his ashtray and giving instructions into a paper cup: "A little more flap, give me some more stick, all right, just a little bit, okay now, level out."

I asked him, "What's the routine?"

"I always feel better when I land them myself," Goose explained.

Meal money in Triple-A is $7.50 a day. In the big leagues it's $15. I don't know if they mean to have you eat half as much or half as well.

Pitched again today and did not have another bad inning. It was my third appearance in three days, and the dear knuckler has been jumping. One pop-up, one groundout, one strikeout. I know this is the kind of work I need, but I'm wondering why they're pitching me so often. They have fourteen pitchers on the staff. Could it be that somebody in Seattle thinks I need the work? Or maybe they want a last look before they release me? *Release me*? Good grief. . . .

It's great to be young and in Hawaii. Not only did I pitch in my seventh-straight game and get my third save, but I had a smashing bowl of siamin, corn on the cob and teriyaki out in the bullpen. Major league bullpen.

We get up around ten in the morning, put on our bathing suits, go down to the beach for three or four hours, come back to have a nice home-cooked meal (we all have kitchenettes and share the cooking), do some shopping and get out to the ballpark at around five. Sheldon brings a radio down to the bullpen and always asks if we want to listen to a ballgame or music. Sheldon, you must be kidding. . . .

I was on a radio show after the ballgame last night and today the guys were kidding me about the gift. In the majors it's usually something worth $25 or $50, but in the minors it's a choice: you can have a "best wishes for the rest of the year" or an "everybody's rooting for your comeback."

My great roomie, Bob Lasko, has led me down the trail of sin and perdition and gotten me smashed on *mai tais* (pronounced "my ties"). This is a Hawaiian drink brewed by the evil gods of the volcanoes and no fit potion for a clean-cut American boy like me. I could barely make it back to my room and turn on the tape recorder. (Can you sing a book?)

The reason I suffer from *mai tai* poisoning so often is that the other guys can drink them with no effect at all while I get drunk. They insist I come along so that they can, as they say, put the hurt on my body. Then in the morning they invite me for breakfast so they can observe the havoc they have wrought. While they gorge themselves on the veranda I bathe my eyes with Murine.

All of which decided us on two things about playing baseball in Hawaii: that in addition to the $7.50 meal money there ought to be a beverage allowance; and that if a guy's home team was Hawaii and he was called up to the big leagues he might well decide he didn't want to go.

Hello again.

The news came this morning. "*Hrrrmph*," Marvin Milkes said, or words to that effect. I was back with the Seattle Pilots. Not only that, but I had an hour-and-a-half to get my ass to the clubhouse and into uniform. Not only that, right after the game we're going on a road trip, first stop Minneapolis. Not only that, my suitcase has gone on ahead to Vancouver. Not only that, my hang-up suit bag is up there too and doesn't even have my name on it. Not only that, I'm inordinately happy.

May

Seattle, WA
Two trades today. We sent outfielder Jose Vidal to the Yankees for outfielder Dick Simpson. We also traded Aker for my old friend Fred Talbot. This is a little disturbing because Talbot and I didn't care too much for each other over there in New York. We're exact opposites. He's country and I'm city, and I always felt uncomfortable around him.

It's interesting, though, to see the Yankees trade Talbot, the guy they decided to keep instead of me . . . And they traded him for a guy who is, or at least should be, below me on the pitching totem pole over here. I believe Seattle would have wanted more than Talbot for me in a trade. . . .

. . .Last spring Fred Talbot said to me, "When I'm out there pitching, are you rooting for me, Bouton?"

"Yeah, Fred."

"Do you really hope I do well?"

"Yeah, Fred. But not at my expense."

What I should have said was, "Yeah, Fred, I hope you do well. I hope you have a helluva year down there in Triple-A." It ended up I landed in Triple-A and he stayed in the big leagues. When I was sent down I had a record of 1–0. Talbot was 1–8. I still think about that.

Emmett Ashford was behind the plate tonight and did an especially good job calling the knuckleball. A couple of times I threw it knee-high and the ball seemed to drop into the dirt. But it was only after it had crossed the plate, so he called both of them strikes. Some umpires call the pitch where the catcher catches it, not where it crosses the plate. If he catches it as a ball, it's a ball. But Ashford was great.

He missed one pitch. It was when a guy was stealing second and McNertney came out of his crouch to get the ball. This blocked Ashford's view and he called it a ball. I yelled at him. "But Emmett, it was a perfect strike." That's all I said, and it was true, but I felt guilty about having said anything at all. I try to be especially nice to Ashford because everybody else harasses hell out of him. He's not exactly the best umpire, but he is far from being terrible. He doesn't miss that many calls, and when he does he misses them on both sides, like any good umpire. But other umpires talk behind his back. Sometimes they'll let him run out on the field himself and the other three who are holding back in the dugout will snigger. I hate that kind of stuff. I mean, I don't mind it when it's pulled on a ballplayer. But Ashford, for goodness sakes.

And, of course, the players pick it right up. As soon as he makes
a bad call they start yelling, "Oh, that hot dog son of a bitch." Sure
he's a flashy umpire and sure he does a lot of showboating. That's
what got him into the big leagues in the first place. It's his bread and
butter. Instead of bitching the players ought to give him credit for
hustling. He hustles every minute he's out there, which is more than
you can say for some umpires.

It's not hard to understand why he's resented, though. They feel
he doesn't belong in the big leagues with his way of umpiring.
Besides, he's a Negro and they believe he's here just *because* of that.

It must be terrible for Ashford. When you're an umpire and travel
around the big leagues in a group of four and three of them are white
and the kind of guys who let you run on the field by yourself—well,
it can make for a very lonely summer.

I know about lonely summers. In my last years with the Yankees I
had a few of them. You stand in a hotel lobby talking with guys at
dinnertime and they drift away, and some other guys come along and
pretty soon they're gone and you're all alone and no one has asked
you what you're doing about dinner. So you eat alone. It must happen to Ashford a lot. And it's one of the reasons I can't bring myself
to argue with him. . . .

Brought a copy of the *Berkeley Barb* back to the clubhouse and
several of the guys were crowding around to read it when John
Kennedy said, "Bouton, I bet you bought that paper." I told him I
had. "Now, how did I know it was you bought that paper?" he said.
Dunno, John. Extrasensory perception?

During the game the public-address announcer explained where to
pick up the ballots to vote for "your favorite Pilot." I thought it necessary to remind the people sitting near the bullpen that your
favorite Pilot did not necessarily have to be good.

Frank Howard drove in five runs with two home runs and a single
against us and we beat the Senators anyway, 6–5. It was three

straight over them, but all I got out of the evening was a marvelous nickname given to Frank Bertaina, a pitcher, by Moe Drabowsky, also a pitcher, when they were with Baltimore. Bertaina, Drabowsky decided, was not too smart, and was flaky besides. So Drabowsky called him "Toys in the Attic."

This is the kind of nickname that could be turned around into an offensive weapon. There is no bigger flake in organized baseball than Drabowsky. Once, out in the bullpen in Anaheim, he picked up the phone, called a number in Hong Kong and ordered a Chinese dinner. To go.

Boston

Off day for travel to Boston. As dusk fell Gary Bell and I went out to celebrate the fact that we've won five of our last six. We chose Sonny's as the ideal place, and it was, because when we returned to our hotel it was three-thirty in the morning and we were still able to have a long discussion about the world, the ghettos and civil rights (all of which we disagree about). We also decided that it would be a good idea, at each baseball game, to allow a fan to suit up and play in the game. Just announce on the public address that if there are any fans in the stands who think they could do a good job at any position, to come down and draw lots for the privilege. We could designate him as our wild-card fan.

And so to bed, after deciding that we are both promotional geniuses.

✣ ✣ ✣

Today I've been thinking about God and baseball, or is it baseball and God? In any case, this rumination was caused by the sight of Lindy McDaniel of the Yankees. Although I've never met him, I feel I know him pretty well because of this newsletter he sends out from Baytown, Texas, called "Pitching for the Master." One of the first I got from him—and all the players receive them—was a complete four-page explanation of why the Church of Christ was the only true church. The dogmatism of this leads to the kind of thinking you find in the Fellowship of Christian Athletes and in *Guideposts* and *The Reader's Digest*. The philosophy here is that religion is the reason an athlete is good at what he does. "My faith in God is what made me come back." Or "I knew Jesus was in my corner." Since no one ever has an article saying, "God didn't help me" or "It's my muscles, not Jesus," kids pretty soon get the idea that Jesus helps *all* athletes and the ones who don't speak up are just shy or embarrassed.

So I've been tempted sometimes to say into a microphone that I feel I won tonight because I don't believe in God. I mean, just for the sake of balance, to let the kids know that belief in a deity or "Pitching for the Master" is not one of the criteria for major-league success. But I guess I never will.

Eddie O'Brien has finally been nicknamed. Mr. Small Stuff. It's because of his attention to detail. Says Mr. Small Stuff: "Put your hat on." He said that to me today. Also to Mike Hegan. We were both running laps at the time.

Another thing Eddie O'Brien does is stand next to you when you're warming up. I think he does it so he can be near the phone when it rings. He has to answer it. One of these days I'll beat him to it and when Schultz asks for O'Brien I'll say, "He ain't here," and hang up. Add dreams of glory.

Oh yes. As I went out to pitch he said, "Throw strikes."

I don't think Eddie O'Brien understands this game.

Maybe nobody does. Like when I went out to do some throwing on the sidelines before the game Sal Maglie said, "Do your running before you throw."

"Gee, Sal," I said agreeably, "I don't like to throw when I'm plumb tuckered out from running. I'd rather throw first, then run."

So Sal said, triumphantly, "What if it rains?"

"If it rains, then I'd rather have had my throwing in than my running."

At which point Ron Plaza said, to no one in particular, "Aw, c'mon, let's go."

I went. But first I did my throwing. And it didn't rain.

Before we left the park today we were told that tomorrow's game would start at twelve-fifteen because of national television and that we'd have to take batting practice at ten-thirty. "Ten-thirty?" said Pagliaroni. "I'm not even done throwing up at that hour."

✣ ✣ ✣

Today Mr. Small came out to the outfield where the pitchers were running and said, "Gentlemen, from now on we can all run with our hats off. It's really silly for us to run with our hats on, because the band gets all sweaty and ruins the hat."

"How come you weren't able to think of that a few weeks ago?" I asked him.

"Well, it wasn't as warm then and we weren't sweating at the same rate we are now."

Oh.

✣ ✣ ✣

On the way to the ballpark tonight Ray Oyler, sitting in the back of the bus during a bumpy ride, discovered an erection. He promptly offered to buy the bus from the driver.

In the bullpen Talbot revealed an awful truth about Joe Pepitone. He has two different hairpieces. He's got a massive piece, which he wears when he's going out, and a smaller one to wear under his baseball cap. He calls it his game piece. On opening day he was wearing his game piece and hadn't put it on very well. So when he was forced to take his cap off, there it was, sitting on his head all askew. He was so embarrassed he tried to hide his head in the shoulder of the guy standing next to him. Kiss me, Joe baby.

Pepitone took to wearing the hairpieces when his hair started to get thin on top. And the hair he still has is all curly and frizzy when he lets it grow long. So he carries around all kinds of equipment in a little blue Pan Am bag. Things like a hot comb, various greases and salves, glue for the hairpiece, hair-straightener—and even a hair-dryer. He carries it wherever he goes, on the buses to the park, on airplanes. You never see him without that little blue bag. At any rate, one day Fritz Peterson and I, a bit bored during a game we were winning about 6–2, went into the clubhouse and filled his hair-dryer with talcum powder. Then we cleaned it up, left it where he had and went back to watch the game. By this time it was 6–3, and then they tied it up and we lost it, 7–6, in extra innings. And one of the reasons we lost is that Pepitone struck out in a clutch situation.

So everyone was tired and angry and upset and you could hear a pin drop in the clubhouse, because after a loss that's the way it's supposed to be. After a while Pepitone came out of the shower and turned his hair-dryer on. *Whoooosh!* Instant white. He looked like an Italian George Washington wearing a powdered wig. There was talcum powder over everything, his hair, his eyebrows, his nose, the hair on his chest. Of course, everybody went crazy. Loss or no, they all laughed like hell. To this moment, Pepitone never knew who turned on the powder. He always thought it was Big Pete Sheehy. Wrong again.

Ranew tells me that Vancouver sent Bob Lasko to Toledo, which is another Triple-A team in the International League. It burned me up because here's Lasko, a guy with ten or eleven years in professional baseball, most of it in Triple-A, bouncing around all over the country, playing for three, four, five different organizations in thirty or forty different towns, all without his family, and now, in the twilight of his career he gets a chance to play in his own home town and he gets sent to Toledo.

There's no justification for this. No one can tell me there wasn't another pitcher they could have sent to Toledo instead. I bet no one even realized Vancouver is home to Lasko. So one day, if Lasko ever makes it in the big leagues and has a good year, the owner will scream bloody murder if he tries to get an extra thousand in salary.

Don Mincher goes up to people, and asks for a cigarette. When they give him one he pulls out a pack, puts the cigarette into it and puts it back into his pocket. Then he walks off.

✛ ✛ ✛

I'm trying so hard to be one of the boys I'm even listening to country music. And enjoying it. The back of the bus is the country-music enclave, and most of the players are part of it. So far, though, we've not been able to swing over city boys like Tommy Davis, Tommy Harper and John Kennedy. I think we'll get them in the end, though. Maybe with a bull fiddle.

Back at the hotel, Gary and I talked about the relationship between country and city guys on a ballclub, which is intertwined with the relationship between whites and blacks. There are lots of walls built up between people, and I pointed out that if I'd never roomed with Gary I would still think, "Oh, he's just a dumb Southerner." So probably the solution is to have people live together. I mean we still disagree about a lot of things—religion, politics, how children should be raised—but because we've been able to talk about these differences, spend so many hours together, we've been able to at least understand them. How's that for a solution? Put people together in a hotel room in Cleveland.

Getting on the airplane in Cleveland we ran into the Kansas City Royals. There was a lot of conversation because we're both expansion teams and a lot of us have been rescued from the same junkpile. The funniest line was about Moe Drabowsky. They said he was sick on the bus the other night and puked up a panty girdle.

I tried to let Joe know that I haven't been pitching much lately. "I sure could use a workout," I said.

And Joe Schultz said, "If you need a workout go down to a whorehouse."

June

There's a promotion they run here in Seattle called "Home Run for the Money." If a listener has his name drawn, he is assigned a certain hitter. If that hitter hits a home run in the right inning, the listener wins the jackpot. Sometimes there are several thousand dollars in it. And if the right hitter hits a grand-slam homer at the precise moment required, there is a $25,000 bonus.

It so happened that, *mirabile dictu*, Fred Talbot hit a home run with the bases loaded tonight. And thus a man named Donald Dubois, who lives in Gladstone, Oregon, won $27,000. The applause in the stands had not yet died down when it was decided in the bullpen that tomorrow morning Fred Talbot would receive a telegram from Donald Dubois of Gladstone, Oregon, thanking him for his Herculean efforts and telling him that a check for $5,000 was in the mail as a token of esteem and friendship. Since the telegram was my idea, I had to send it. We agreed that my identity would be revealed only under penalty of death.

Freddy Talbot believes.

The telegram read: "Thank you very much for making our lives so happy, Mr. Talbert. We feel we must share our good fortune with you. A check for $5,000 will be sent to you when the money arrives." (I thought it was a clever touch to misspell his name.)

As soon as he read the telegram, Talbot called over his faithful roommate and asked him to step outside. "You know anything about this, Merritt?" he said. "You think it's a joke?"

"Looks legitimate to me," Ranew said, biting his lip to keep from laughing.

Later, Talbot showed the telegram to Ray Oyler. "You think it's for real?" Oyler said.

"Yeah, I think so," Talbot said. "If one of the guys had done it he wouldn't have misspelled my name."

"That's right," Oyler said. "And what are you going to do with the money?"

"I think I'll buy that boat I always wanted, one with a 95-horse-power motor. I'll tell my wife I won it in a raffle. Otherwise she'll want me to put the whole $5,000 in the bank. And whatever you do, Ray, don't tell the writers about it. If they put it in the paper I'll have to pay income tax on it."

Ray promised he wouldn't tell.

We came from behind three times tonight to beat the Tigers 8–7. I pitched a third of an inning, coming in with a man on second. I got Tom Matchick on a ground ball back to me on a 3-and-2 count. After the game I told Joe Schultz that the reason I went to 3-and-2 was that I needed the work. "I figured you were doing *something* out there," Joe Schultz said.

In the clubhouse Joe delivered his usual speech: "Attaway to stomp 'em. Stomp the piss out of 'em. Stomp 'em when they're down. Kick 'em and stomp 'em." And: "Attaway to go boys. Pound that ol' Budweiser into you and go get them tomorrow."

This stuff really lays us in the aisles.

Then there's the tale Jim Gosger told about hiding in a closet to shoot a little beaver while his roommate made out on the bed with some local talent. Nothing sneaky about it, the roommate even provided the towel for Gosger to bite on in case he was moved to laughter. At the height of the activity on the bed, local talent, moaning, says, "Oh darling, I've never done it *that* way before." Whereupon Gosger sticks his head out, drawls "Yeah, surrre," and retreats into the closet.

213

After he told us the story, "Yeah surrre," became a watchword around the club.

❖ ❖ ❖

In the bullpen during the game the conversation turned to many things (Fred Talbot on the American destroyer that was cut in half by the Australian aircraft carrier: "The bastards must have been playing chicken out there"). But especially the talk was about the strike in the spring and the players who signed their contracts despite it—like Pete Richert of Baltimore. He said he had to sign his contract because he was just buying a house and the story was that he'd borrowed the money from the club and if he'd borrowed it from the bank he'd have had to pay a high interest rate. O'Donoghue thought this was justification enough. I said I didn't think so. I said that *everybody* could use the money, and that those who didn't sign were risking the owner's getting angry at them besides. And what about the marginal players? And the rookies? A lot more was at stake for them than some high interest rate on a loan.

There *was* agreement about the large number of Atlanta Braves who had signed. And we agreed *that* was all Paul Richards' fault. He put a tremendous amount of pressure on his players and I guess I blame them a helluva lot less than I do Richert.

And then Carl Yastrzemski's name came up because he'd just ignored the strike and Gary Bell said, "Didn't surprise me. Carl Yastrzemski is for himself first and second and the hell with everybody else."

Gee, Gary, Carl Yastrzemski?

Yes. Besides, during the strike Yastrzemski called several superstars in an attempt to form a separate committee and settle things without the Players' Association. Fortunately they told him to take a hike, son. I don't think the only bad guys in this thing were the few players who caved in. Richards was particularly beautiful, calling Marvin Miller "a mustachioed fourflusher." And many others were willing to take a strike and use Triple-A players and flush the game right down the drain if necessary. These are the same guys who want us to think they're sportsmen who run the game out of civic pride. They're not in this thing for money. They're not. We know because that's what they tell us. And we believe. Like Clete Boyer once told me that Dan Topping, former Yankee owner, was all for the players and a wonderful man. I asked him how he knew. And he said, "Ralph Houk told me."

✤ ✤ ✤

After the game Joe Schultz said, "Attaway to stomp on 'em, men. Pound that Budweiser into you and go get 'em tomorrow." Then he spotted Gelnar sucking out of a pop bottle. "For crissakes, Gelnar," Joe Schultz said. "You'll never get them out drinking Dr. Pepper."

✤ ✤ ✤

In the bullpen it was can you top this on general managers. Bob Locker told this one about a contract argument with Ed Short, general manager of the White Sox. This was after Locker had had his best season in 1967—77 games, 125 innings and a 2.09 ERA. It was a year after Phil Regan of the Dodgers had had his super year—14–1 and a 1.62 ERA—in relief. Short had offered Locker $16,000 and he was asking for $18,000. Short said he was asking a lot and that what the hell, Regan had just signed a contract for $23,000. "If Regan is making only $23,000 then I'm asking too much," Locker said. "You check that. If he signed for $23,000 I'll sign for $16,000."

The next day Short called him and said, "I called Buzzie Bavasi (the Dodger GM) and he told me Regan was making $23,000 this year."

"All right," Locker said. "I'll take the $16,000."

After he signed he got to thinking about it and just for the hell of it he wrote Regan a letter. He asked if Regan would mind telling him about what he had signed for. And Regan wrote back saying he'd signed for $36,500.

"You know, you don't mind a guy deceiving you a little during contract negotiations," Locker said. "You get used to it. They all do it. But when a guy just outright lies right to your face, that's too much."

Brabender told about the generosity of Harry Dalton, the Baltimore general manager. When the minimum salary was raised from $7,000 to $10,000 he was making $8,000 and had a year-and-a-half in the majors. When he went to talk contract with Dalton he was told that he was getting a $4,000 raise, to $12,000. He felt pretty good about it—for about a minute. Then he realized that no matter what, his salary would have to go to $10,000, so he was therefore getting only a $2,000 raise. Dalton didn't think he'd see it that way.

And O'Donoghue chipped in with the one about Eddie Lopat, when he was GM of the Kansas City A's. O'Donoghue agreed to terms with Lopat over the telephone and went down to spring training. When he got there he was offered a contract for a lot less money. "But you agreed to a different figure on the telephone," O'Donoghue said. By this time, who knows, he may have been crying.

Said Lopat: "Prove it."

This kind of stunt was pulled on several players. It cost Talbot $500. He offered to throw Lopat through a closed window, but it didn't do him any good.

In the end Lopat must have been hurt by all of that. Because now no one will ever forget that when Tony Oliva first came up Lopat's pronouncement was, "The kid will never hit in the big leagues."

Jim Gosger was sent back down to Vancouver. "You know, I didn't think I was that bad a ballplayer," he said. "But they're making a believer out of me."

❖ ❖ ❖

Today in the visiting dugout at Yankee Stadium, Joe Schultz said to nobody in particular: "Up and at 'em. Fuck 'em all. Let it all hang out."

Joe Schultz is not like Sal with the pitchers. Gelnar was telling us about this great conversation he had with Joe on the mound. There were a couple of guys on and Tom Matchick was up. "Any particular way you want me to pitch him, Joe?" Gelnar said.

"Nah, fuck him," Joe Schultz said. "Give him some low smoke and we'll go in and pound some Budweiser."

❖ ❖ ❖

For a while I was getting almost no work at all. Now I'm getting plenty. I've been in 29 games and about eight of our last ten. But I suddenly realized *I never get in at crucial times*. I'm never in there if it's close and we have a chance to win. No wonder I have 29 appearances and only one win and one save.

Today there was a perfect example of what I mean. We're playing a doubleheader against Chicago and in the first game Timberlake (even he gets a start) is taken out in the second inning, losing 4–0, bases loaded, two out. I come in and get the first hitter I face on a fly ball. I then get the next nine-straight hitters, three scoreless innings. Now we've tied it at 4–4 and I come out for a pinch-hitter. We end up losing 6–4.

In the second game we're losing 4–2 in the fifth and O'Donoghue's in there, pitching in relief of Talbot. They let O'Donoghue bat for himself in the fifth even though we're two runs down, which I don't understand at all. Anyway he's out. Somebody gets a base hit and Comer hits a home run. Now if somebody had batted for O'Donoghue, we might have gotten three runs instead of two. Instead we have a tie game and O'Donoghue is still pitching. Pretty soon they're ahead of him 5–4 and then 6–4. And when we tie it at 6–6, who goes into this critical situation? The knuckleball kid? Nah. Diego Segui. He's in trouble right away with a walk and a base hit, but he gets out of the inning. By this time I'm warming up. But do they take him out? Nope. So he gives up a home run. Do they take him out now? Nope. Not until he gives up a double in the ninth. *Then* I go in. I need one out, I get it. One third of an inning. And we lose 7–6. I never got a real chance to save either game, and if I had we might have won both. I think I'll go bite Sal Maglie on the leg.

I read in the paper today that Richie Allen, who has left the Phillies, says he wants to be traded and will not play for them next year. Then I heard Van Patrick on the air complain that baseball ought to have some recourse against a player who simply walks out on a team during the season. Bullshit, I thought to myself, gently. Here's one of the few cases where a baseball player has enough courage or money or both to tell baseball to take its one-sided contract and shove it. How many times does a ballclub release a player without a thought to his future? The players have zero recourse, but Van Patrick wants to think up another weapon for baseball.

I've admired Richie Allen from afar ever since his second year in the majors when, after a great rookie season (.318, 125 runs, 13 triples, 29 home runs and 91 RBIs—I looked it up) he demanded a large salary, $50 or $60,000 and said he wouldn't play unless he got it. Philadelphia must have thought he meant it, because he got it. (I wonder if they told him there was a club rule against quadrupling salaries.)

The minute somebody refuses to work for somebody else at a particular wage, the onus, in the public mind, is on the person who chooses not to do the working. I'm not sure why this should be, but it is. Like the lady in my Wyckoff, N.J., bank who said to me during a plumbers' strike, "Well, they don't *have* to be plumbers if they don't like it." She probably thinks, well, Allen doesn't *have* to be a baseball player if he doesn't like it. Sure, he can always be vice-president of the Wyckoff, N.J., bank.

✧ ✧ ✧

I'm taking the family to Disneyland on our next trip to Anaheim and

I asked Marvin Milkes if he minded if I stayed with them in a hotel next to Disneyland rather than the team hotel. Actually, the guys prefer that you don't bring your wife on road trips and I thought this would be less awkward.

Milkes said I couldn't. "Nothing personal," he said. "You're doing a good job for us. If you weren't you wouldn't be here. I wouldn't want you to misconscrue [*sic!* baseball fans] my meaning on this. It's just a club rule and it has to be followed."

The reason for the rule, he said, was that he remembered when he was with the Angels and the Yankees used to come into town and stay out all night at those Johnny Grant parties. (Grant is what they call a radio personality in Hollywood.)

"But Marvin," I said. "The way I remember it we would stay out all night and then beat you guys anyway. I remember having a particularly good time at a Johnny Grant party and then pitching a two-hitter against you."

In fact I remembered more than that. I remembered doing a strip to my underwear to the theme song of *Lawrence of Arabia* and then treading water in the swimming pool with a martini in each hand and *then* going out and beating the Angels the next night. In fact, every time I hear the *Lawrence of Arabia* music my mind still snaps.

"Yeah, well, maybe," Marvin said. "But I could always count on you guys keeping late hours and I want to crack down on it."

"I'm more likely to go to bed early if my family is here than if I'm with the guys in the team hotel."

"That may be true. But we're going to stick to this rule. As I said, don't misconscrue it. Nothing personal.". . .

In the bullpen tonight Jim Pagliaroni was telling us how Ted Williams, when he was still playing, would psyche himself up for a game during batting practice, usually early practice before the fans or reporters got there.

He'd go into the cage, wave his bat at the pitcher and start screaming at the top of his voice, "My name is Ted fucking Williams and I'm the greatest hitter in baseball."

He'd swing and hit a line drive.

"Jesus H. Christ Himself couldn't get me out."

And he'd hit another.

Then he'd say, "Here comes Jim Bunning, Jim fucking Bunning and that little shit slider of his."

Wham!

"He doesn't really think he's gonna get me out with that shit."

Blam!

"I'm Ted fucking Williams."

Sock!

Today Joe Schultz said, "Nice going out there today, Jim."

The only thing I'd done all day was warm up.

"Joe, I had a fantastic knuckleball today," I said. "Just fantastic."

"Did you?" Joe Schultz said. "Did you have the feel of it?"

"I sure did."

Whereupon Joe Schultz grabbed his crotch and said, "Well, feel this!"

It's true that Joe Schultz does seem to have a firmer grip on reality than other baseball men. Example: Joe got into a terrible argument with an umpire at home plate about a checked swing and when it was over he stormed back to the dugout, still muttering. Just before stepping into the dugout, though, he spied a blonde sitting in the first row and said, "Hiya, blondie. How's your old tomato?"

There was a meeting in the clubhouse on the new contract negotiations between the players and owners, which should be taking place soon but probably won't until after the season. I suggested that if you apply the standard-of-living index to the base of $7,000 that was set up eleven years ago you come up with about $14 or $15,000 as a minimum instead of the present $10,000. So somebody said, "Why not $20,000?" and everybody broke up laughing. But when you really think about it, $20,000 is not out of line at all. Consider how hard it is to make a big-league club. If only the same proportion of the population were accepted as lawyers, the going starting salary would be a lot higher. When you overcome odds of better than 10,000 to 1 you ought to collect big.

I note today that the Topps Gum people have doubled their fee to players, from $125 to $250, for using their pictures on bubblegum cards. They explained that they were able to increase payments because of increased revenues. It had nothing to do with Marvin Miller and the players going to Topps and demanding the increase. Topps just happens to have a big heart. Yeah surrre.

Checking out of the hotel Wayne Comer called for a bell captain to send up a bellhop to pick up his bag. There was no bellhop around, and no bell captain either. So Don Mincher, who happened to be standing there, picked up the phone. When he heard it was Comer, Mincher said, "Now wait a minute. It's about time you guys started carrying your own bags down. All you prima donna cocksuckers are alike, always wanting people to do things for you. Why the hell don't you carry them down yourself?"

Comer didn't even splutter. He slammed down the phone and carried his own bags.

July

Oakland

Today I asked Joe Schultz for a start. I sat down with him on the bus and told him that I could help the team better if I started. I said I felt that being the ninth man on the pitching staff and being used as the mop-up man didn't help the team much. I reached into my pocket to show him my statistics and Joe Schultz said, "Aw shit. I don't want to see any statistics. I know what's going on out there just by watching the games."

"All right," I said. "I just wanted to show you that. I've only walked one man in the last 16 innings and only three in the last 21."

"I know you've been getting it over."

"That's all I wanted to say."

"Well, okay, Jamesy," Joe Schultz said.

Another Hovley story. He was standing by the clubhouse man's tobacco shelf opening up a can of snuff. (Just wanted to try it, he said later.) Joe Schultz walked by wearing nothing but a towel around his waist and hollered out, "Hey, men, look who's dipping into the snuff." Then he grabbed a paperback book out of Hovley's pocket. It was Dostoyevski's *The Possessed*. Schultz held the book up in the air and said, "Hey, men, look at this! What the shit kind of name is this?"

By this time there was a group of guys around him looking at the book like a group of monkeys might inspect a bright red rubber ball. Schultz read off the back cover—a sentence anyway—until he got to the word "nihilism." "Hey, Hy," Schultz said to Hy Zimmerman, "what the hell does 'nihilism' mean?"

"That's when you don't believe in nothing," Zimmerman said.

Whereupon Schultz, shaking his head and laughing, flung the book back at Hovley, hitched up his towel and strode off, amid much laughter.

If Hovley weren't 9 for 20 (.450) since he was called up I'd figure him to be back in Rochester in a matter of days.

Afterward Hovley said that this was, of course, anti-intellectualism at work, but that he didn't mind since he counted himself as anti-intellectual too—that is, if by "intellectual" we meant the academic community. Academic people bore him, Hovley said, and that while he wouldn't choose to spend all his free time with Joe Schultz, he rather enjoyed the company of players.

And Mike Marshall pointed out that Joe's act might have been more a tactic than an expression of his real feelings about college types. "You have to keep in mind that Joe's goal is to keep a loose clubhouse and that he uses this as a device to make people laugh," Marshall said. "I'd be careful not to put him down as merely a buffoon."

Well, I don't know. If it *is* an act, he's finding it awfully easy to play.

Seattle, WA

Mike Marshall was sent to Vancouver today. I'm having very bad luck with roommates.

I feel a little funny about him getting it because I know his wife warned him right from spring training about getting too closely associated with me. Not that she doesn't like me, but she knew my reputation and was worried about guilt by association. Now he rooms with me three days in Kansas City and gets cut. . . .

Minneapolis

Before the game Dick Baney and I were walking across the outfield grass to the bullpen, and the crowd was buzzing, and the organist was playing, and Baney looked around and said, "Hey, you know something? This is fun, walking across the outfield with all the people looking down at you."

And I thought, "It's true." You forget how much fun it is sometimes just to walk across the outfield. And then I remembered sitting up in the left-field stands in the Polo Grounds as a kid and thinking to myself, "Cheez, if I could only run out on the field and maybe go over and kick second base, or shag a fly ball—God, that would make my year. I'd never forget it as long as I lived if I could just run across that beautiful green outfield grass." And now, sometimes, I forget to tingle. . . .

When Dick Baney went into the game to throw his first major league pitch everybody in the bullpen moved out to the fence to watch him.

We wanted to see how he'd do against the Brew, which is what we call Harmon Killebrew. Inside I still think of him as the Fat Kid, which is what Fritz Peterson over at the Yankees always called him. I'd say, "How'd you do, Fritz?" and he'd answer, "The Fat Kid hit a double with the bases loaded." Well, the first time the Fat Kid faced Dick Baney he hit the second pitch 407 feet into the left-field seats.

After the game I was shaving next to Baney. "Welcome to the club," I said. "You lost your virginity tonight."

"The only difference," he said, "is that all you guys will still be here tomorrow."

✛ ✛ ✛

I made a terrible mistake today. I was chatting with Fred Talbot and said, "Hey, Fred, by the way, you ever hear from that guy you hit the home run for?"

Fred's eyes narrowed and he looked mean. "Were you the one who sent that telegram?" he said.

"What telegram?" I said, feeling my stupid face breaking up into a giveaway smile.

Now he was clenching his teeth. "I *knew* you sent the damn thing," he said, "and I'm going to get you back for that. I know you sent that paternity suit thing too."

"Fred, I did *not* send you the paternity thing," I said, all injured innocence. "I *may* have sent you a telegram. I don't know yet. What did the telegram say?"

And he said: "I'll get you back. I'm going to get you back on something, and when I do it's going to involve your wife, your whole family, your friends back home, everybody in the whole damn country."

After the game Talbot got back at me. It was still so hot that a lot of the guys didn't want to wait for the bus back to the hotel and grabbed air-conditioned cabs instead. We lined up for them, and when I started to get into one as the last man, Talbot, who was behind me in line, leaped in ahead of me and said, "Take the next cab, you Communist."

⁘   ⁘   ⁘

While we were losing the first game of the doubleheader—we were down 5–1 and it was going to be our third straight here—Joe Schultz called to John Gelnar, who was keeping the pitching chart. "C'mere a minute," he said, motioning Gelnar down to the other end of the dugout. Gelnar was sure he was going to get a big tip on pitching. And Joe Schultz, pointing up into the stands, said, "Up there near the Section 23 sign. Check the rack on that broad."

In the eighth inning, Joe Schultz said, "Well, boys, between games today we have a choice of roast beef, baked ham or tuna salad."

Jerry Stephenson was outrighted to Vancouver today just as he was moving into his new apartment. I know he lost a deposit and some rent money when he was called up from Vancouver, and I'm sure it will cost him again. Stephenson was here for seventeen days and pitched a total of three innings. He was on the road most of the time, and while he was away his wife had a miscarriage. Stephenson is all shook up. Now wait a minute. Bob Lasko lives in Vancouver and he's spending the summer in Toledo. Mike Marshall had to fight to get sent to Toledo instead of Vancouver. Why couldn't they just have been switched around? Because nobody thought of it. Because nobody cared. I agree with the title of a paper Mike Marshall wrote in college: "Baseball Is an Ass."

I was chatting with Fred Talbot about contracts and keeping statistics to use as negotiating arguments and he said, "Aw hell, I don't keep statistics. Whatever they send me, I just sign and send it back. Of course, I call them a few names first."

✤ ✤ ✤

Diego Segui pitched a marvelous ballgame. He was magnificent throughout and won it 2–1. As I watched the game I was torn between wanting him to get bombed and wanting him to do well, because we could use a win and because he's a good fellow. So there I was torn, and warming up in almost every inning. In the second game, same thing. And I never got into either game.

"You know something?" said Pagliaroni. "You looked great warming up."

I told him thanks.

Even winning we didn't do much to stop Rod Carew, who is now leading the league. He's the kind of hitter who puts the ball into a hole someplace, or bloops one, every time. "He can't miss," McNertney said. "If I were him I'd go looking for wallets."

Steve Hovley won the first game for us. It was a 1–1 tie in the last of the ninth, bases loaded, Hovley up and Ron Perranoski, the old pro, pitching. It was a classic confrontation; the graybeard, wily pitcher against the upstart young slugger. In the end, Hovley beat the old man at his own game. He worked the count to 3 and 2 and then fouled off a couple of borderline pitches. It was exciting. Me, I ran all the way down to the dugout so I could be closer to what was happening. And as I watched Hovley struggling out there against the best reliever in the league, I thought, how can a guy with friends like Dostoyevski be scared in this kind of situation? He wasn't. He hung in for another foul ball and then got the base on balls, forcing in the run.

As we walked down to the clubhouse I heard John Gelnar say, "You know, one good thing about having Hovley up there, he's too gooney to be scared."

In the second game Hovley hit his second home run of the season. I'm the proud owner of the first ball he hit out. I bought it from the kid who caught it. Hovley said he didn't want it. He said he didn't think it was particularly important. The year he hits 62 it may be my most valuable possession.

✛ ✛ ✛

After the game, Joe was patting everybody on the back, saying "Attaway to go" and "Nice job." When he got to me I said, "Joe, I really had it out there tonight in the bullpen."

"You did?" Joe said.

"Yup. Great knuckleball. Hellacious."

"Did you throw too much?"

"Hell no."

"Good. You're starting tomorrow night. Feel up to it?"

"Hell yes."

Well, what do you know? It's put-up-or-shut-up time for Jim Bouton.

Before I left the ballpark, Sal Maglie said, "Get your sleep, Bouton."

And I said, "Right, Sal. And I want to have a catcher out there five hours before game time so I can start warming up."

Driving home I found myself doing a lot of worrying. Should I take a sleeping pill tonight? Should I sleep late or get up early and take a nap later? What should I eat? At what time? Then I thought, "What the hell am I worried about all this crap for? I've started a lot more important games. World Series games, pennant-race games. And here I am acting like a kid." Foolishness. I'm just going to be normal. I'm going to sleep tonight and not even think about it. When I start the game I'm going to pretend that I'm in there for relief, that I'm just going to pitch a few innings the way I do almost every day.

Look at it this way. In a couple of days two men are going to land on the moon. How the hell can I be nervous about starting a baseball game? Even if it is against the Fat Kid and his wrecking crew.

✛ ✛ ✛

I went over the hitters with McNertney before the game. For me the only thing this involves is deciding which hitters we're going to throw fastballs to on what particular count. We know we're going to start everyone off with a knuckleball and we're going with it until 3 and 0. On the big hitters, like Killebrew, we decided to throw the knuckleball even on 3 and 0. We'd also throw the 3-and-0 knuckleball to any guy who was hitting in a game-winning situation, even if we walked him. I mean I'd rather give up a base on balls than a three-run homer.

My main concern was that Carew and Tovar would be stealing on my knuckleball, so we went over the pick-off signs carefully and hoped for the best.

It wasn't good enough.

In my first start of the year, on this day of July 19, 1969, A.D., I, James Alan Bouton, was creamed.

Five runs were scored off me before I was mercifully taken out of the game with two out in the fourth. There were two home runs, by Leo Cardenas and Ted Uhlaender. When Joe Schultz came out to get me I could only think of a line Fred Talbot delivered in similar circumstances: "What kept you?"

Not more than one out of every three knuckleballs I threw was doing its proper thing. Besides, my control was way off and I was behind on the hitters.

I started out in trouble and recovered. With two out the Fat Kid got on base because of an error. A single and a walk loaded the bases, but I struck out Bob Allison on a 3-and-2 knuckleball.

After that, oblivion. I blocked it all almost as quickly as I could shower, dress and join my family in the stands. That's the easiest way for me to forget. I crawl back to my family and use them for a crutch. Some guys drink. I talk about the kids needing new shoes.

I was glad to have the chance to start, of course. Yet now that I've fouled everything up so royally I'm thinking of excuses. Why did they have to start me against Minnesota? Maybe if I knew a few days in advance I could have prepared myself better. Maybe I should have taken a greenie. That's just kidding myself, of course. I had a start and I didn't win, and now I can look forward to the All-Star break.

Now that I think of it, I didn't lose either. We were losing 5–0 when I left the game. We tied the game at 7–7 and went sixteen innings before stopping on account of curfew. I think I'll remind Sal and Joe that I'm still undefeated as a starter.

And I just remembered something else. When my boy Mike was still a baby and he cried, I'd say to him, "Harmon Killebrew's little boy doesn't cry." Now I wonder if Harmon Killebrew ever thinks of crying.

✤ ✤ ✤

If you want to know what aspect of the moon landing was discussed most in the bullpen it was the sex life of the astronauts. We thought it a terrible arrangement that they should go three weeks or more without any sex life. Gelnar said that if those scientists were really on the ball they would have provided three germ-free broads for the astronauts.

Got a letter from Jerry Stephenson. Says that God is alive and surfing in Waikiki. He also said that he had a marvelous final conversation with Milkes. He complained that he hadn't had an opportunity to pitch and Milkes said he'd blown two starting opportunities.

"When were those?" Jerry asked.

"You were going to start the night it rained," Milkes said.

"I know," Jerry said. "When was the other one?"

"When your wife had a miscarriage and you had to leave the club for three days."

The next best thing about the way things broke was that on the very day he was sent down Jerry and his wife had moved into a new apartment. That afternoon they had to move out. "We felt groovy moving all that stuff," Jerry wrote. "By the end of the day we were working very well together as a team."

O'Donoghue was on the airplane flying east with Don Mincher

and Joe Schultz, who were going to the All-Star game, and said Joe was feeling hardly any pain when he left the plane and was mumbling his two favorite words—shit and fuck—in all their possible combinations.

It's still hard to get used to playing baseball again after the All-Star break. Three days off reminds you how much tension you live under playing baseball every day. During the break Harmon Killebrew can't get you. Reggie Jackson can't get you. It's peaceful. Like looking up at Mt. Rainier. That's the great thing about our ballpark. When a home run hit off you disappears over the fence your eye catches a glimpse of the majesty of Mt. Rainier and some of that bad feeling goes away.

Great thing happened today. Police arrested a twenty-two-year-old blonde who had climbed a tree outside our clubhouse and was peeping in at us in the shower. A female beaver-shooter.

The game was great too, largely because J. Bouton recorded his second win of the season. I started warming up when the score was 3–0 against us. That's still too close to put me in. It was 5–0 with a runner on when I got the big call. I needed one hitter in that inning and got him, mowed them down 1-2-3 in the next inning and, of course, came out for a pinch-hitter. Only this time it was when we were in the process of scoring six runs. The big hit was a three-run homer by McNertney. The final score was 8–5. Locker got the save and I got a pat on the ass from Sal Maglie.

Another infielder got racked up during the game. Ron Clark collided with George Scott of the Red Sox and had thirteen stitches taken in his lip. Ron's a tough, gutty little ballplayer. He has a baby face, two tattoos on his arm (one says "Mother" and the other is of a black panther), smokes big cigars—and when he has thirteen stitches in his lip he drinks beer out of the side of his mouth.

Greg Goossen played his first game and went 3 for 3, including a tremendous line-drive home run into the left-field seats.

from BALL FOUR

I love them, one and all. . . .

The last time Marty Pattin had a bad game—and he's had about eight in a row now—he came charging up the runway to the clubhouse breaking things on the way. He kicked over a couple of garbage cans and crashed the door into the clubhouse. So today Talbot said to him, "Marty, what are your plans if you don't win tomorrow?"

✦ ✦ ✦

Talbot has finally been able to talk about that fellow Dubois who won that $27,000 on his home run. "Never made a nickel out of it," Talbot said. "They flew me out to Gladstone to go on four different radio shows. I went for the ballclub and they didn't pay anything either."

"Didn't Dubois offer you anything at all?" I said. "What did he say to you?"

"He asked for the bat," Talbot said. "He wanted to have the bat I hit the home run with as a souvenir. And when the whole thing was over it ended up costing me $2.75 for parking."

Before the game tonight pitchers were taking extra bunting practice because we'd been having trouble moving the runner along. And Joe Schultz said, "Boys, bunting is like jacking off. Once you learn how you never forget."

August

I try, but it remains most difficult to convey the quality of the banter in the back of the bus. . . . Have an example from our trip to the Washington airport. Greg Goossen: "Hey, does anybody here have any Aqua Velva?" Fred Talbot: "No, but I gotta take a shit, if that'll help."

❖ ❖ ❖

When I got to the clubhouse I was confronted by Pagliaroni. "Did you send me the check, Bouton?"

"Check? Me? Money?" I said. "How much did I owe you?"

"No. You don't owe me. I got a check for $100 from the guy who won $2700 on Home Run for the Money because I hit one. I just figured it might be a phony from you."

I bit the check and pronounced it genuine. "Nope, I didn't send it," I said.

It was then calculated that if Pagliaroni got $100 for winning his man $2700, Fred Talbot should have gotten a thousand from Donald Dubois. Did he ever get anything? "Nope," Talbot said.

Gee, wonder what old Dubois would do with all that money.

Said Talbot: "I hope he gets drunk on it, wrecks his car and kills himself."

❖ ❖ ❖

Before the father-and-son game Sunday, Pagliaroni said to Wayne Comer: "Now, no fair giving your son a greenie."

Greenie or no, the Comer boy stole the show. When he came to bat he took the handle and knocked some imaginary dirt off the bottom of his little sneakers, then he rubbed dirt on his hands, gripped the bat, tapped the plate with it and showed all the mannerisms of the big-league players. Said Fred Talbot: "Comer's kid has a little hot dog in him, doesn't he?"

The kids beat the fathers 40-0, and Sibby Sisti said, 'Forty runs, for crissakes, and nobody gets knocked down." And McNertney said that he was standing next to Sal Maglie during the game and swore he heard Sal saying, "He's a first-ball hitter"—"a high-ball hitter"—"a fastball hitter"—and none of the kids was over four feet tall.

For some reason that reminded me of my manager in Amarillo,

Sheriff Robinson, who used to say about every hitter, "Jam him." And then later on we talked with some old-timers who'd played with Robinson and they said, "He was a pretty good ballplayer. But we used to jam the hell out of him.". . .

Bullpen humor:

The attendance at the Baltimore games was respectable, but we're back to not drawing much for the Tigers. It is decided in the bullpen that the people who came to see us play the Orioles are the same kind who went to see the lions eat Christians.

There's going to be a Day soon for Tommy Harper, so John O'Donoghue is reminded of the Day that was given to him in Kansas City. "All my family and friends were there," O'Donoghue says. "And they gave me a Legionnaire's cap, a *used* Legionnaire's cap. They also gave me honorary memberships to all the drinking clubs in town. They gave me two plaques. And then they gave me a wallet, a brand-new wallet. I practically tore that damn thing apart looking for the money. I know there *had* to be something more than a used Legionnaire's cap and a wallet. But there wasn't."

"Hey, Merritt," Fred Talbot says to Merritt Ranew. "Tell Bouton to his face what you said about him last night."

Merritt's face gets red and he says, "I didn't say a thing." And I say, "What'd he say, Fred? You can tell me."

And Fred says: "I didn't get it all. Something about your mother."

I'm telling Talbot and Comer about El Bodeon in Washington and Talbot says, "If Bouton recommends a restaurant, you can be pretty sure they got some good Communist dishes."

Talbot says to Hovley: "Hey Hovley, some of the guys are starting to talk about your hair." He pauses. "And I'm one of them."

Then he turns to me. "You know, writing notes like that, Bouton, it's worse than whispering."

Talbot and Ranew get into a deep discussion about the South. Ranew is from Georgia and Talbot is from Virginia. Talbot started it because he said that all the guys from the South are dumb.

"Well, where the hell are you from?" Ranew says, because he knows the answer.

"I'm from the north part of the South," Talbot says.

"It's better down where I live than it is where you are," Ranew says.

"Everything but the people," Talbot says. "The people are dumb."

I can't resist. I get into the discussion. "It's true, Merritt," I say. "What other state in the union has a governor that never even finished high school?"

"The reason they got this guy Lester Maddox," says Talbot, "is because he's so dumb. That's what they need to talk to all the dummies they got down there. They'd never understand a guy from Yale or Harvard or one of them colleges."

Ranew scratches his head. "I still think the South is better where I live."

"How can you compare which part of the country is better?" Talbot says. "I say mine, you say yours. How can you compare?"

"Why doesn't Bouton do some research on it tomorrow in the library and come back with some figures for us?" Ranew says.

"Nah, let's do it right here," Talbot says. "All right, let's start. How many dummies you got down there?"

By this time there is a lot of general laughter. I'm not prepared to explain why.

"I tell you one thing," Ranew says. "We got better-looking guys down where I am."

Talbot is shocked. "Better *looking*?" he says. "For crissakes, look at yourself. You've got hair like a sissy."

It's not a felicitous description. Ranew has his hair styled in the modern mode. It is not unattractive. Talbot wears his in an old-fashioned crew cut.

"Look at you," Talbot says, moving in for the kill. "You use hair spray and go to a goddam beauty parlor."

"With that hair *you've* got," Ranew says, "you could use a little beauty parlor yourself."

"I'll tell you one thing," Talbot says. "I don't walk around with hair spray and I don't look like a goddam sissy and I don't squat to piss, either."

Now the laughter has turned against Ranew and he is searching desperately for a counter. One can almost hear the file cards in his head fluttering.

"You know what you look like, Talbot?" Ranew says. "You look like a perch, a goddam perch."

"A *perch*?" Talbot says. "What the hell do you mean, a perch?"

"Well, you look like a perch," Ranew says. "Your head is square, you have hardly any nose at all, your eyes bulge out and you look like some kind of fish."

Now the laughter has turned on Talbot.

"But I don't look like a goddam sissy," he says.

I am afraid he is defeated.

That's not the funniest. The funniest is what happened to Ray Oyler. He was warming up Locker and caught a sinker right on the cup. It didn't even hit the ground first. Ding-dong! He went down on all fours and crawled around that way for a while. Then he limped into the dugout and vomited.

The boys were hysterical. We were getting beat a ballgame and we were *laughing*. Joe Schultz laughed so hard he had to take off his glasses, dry his eyes and hide his head in a warm-up jacket.

✢ ✢ ✢

The Orioles beat us for the fourth-straight time. The score was 15–3. Said Fred Talbot: "We got no business scheduling these guys." Then, "This Baltimore outfit can sure fluff up your ERA."

We can now look forward to snapping our losing streak on the road against such weak sisters as Baltimore and Detroit. Maybe something nice will happen in New York.

Baltimore–St. Louis

235

Maybe it will. But it won't happen to me. At nine this morning while I was asleep in my room at the Statler Hilton in Baltimore the phone rang. I picked it up and Joe Schultz said: "Jim, you've been traded to the Houston Astros."

There were two things I wanted to know. The first was, where was I? You travel as much as we do and somebody wakes you up in the morning, you don't know where you are. The second thing was, who for? You like to hear a big name on the other end. It's good for your morale.

"Who for?" I said to Schultz.

"Dooley Womack," he said.

Dooley Womack? Holy mackerel. The same Dooley Womack whose great spring I almost matched with the Yankees? Oh Lord! I hope there was a lot of undisclosed cash involved. I hope a hundred thousand, at least. Maybe it's me for a hundred thousand and Dooley Womack is just a throw-in. I'd hate to think that at this stage of my career I was being traded even-up for Dooley Womack.

Joe sounded as down as I felt. I know he's in trouble. All kinds of rumors in the papers about his being fired. So I tried to cheer him up. After all, he wasn't going to the Astros, I was. I told him I thought he was a helluva man and that I was sorry I couldn't do more for him. I told him that even though I disagreed with the way he used me, that looking back I think he did the right thing.

I was only lying a little. . . .

"Hey, Steve, wake up, wake up!" I said to Hovley. "Wake up. I've been traded to Houston."

And he sort of rolled over a little and said, "Ah, the dreams, the dreams." Then he said, sitting up, "You can't go to St. Louis today."

"Why not?"

"Because you're supposed to go to the Museum of Art this afternoon. You promised."

We speculated why Milkes would make a deal like that and Hovley said, "He's building a team for the future, and how long can a knuckleball pitcher last?"

It is possible to laugh at nine in the morning in Baltimore.

I thought of calling my wife right away but realized it was only 6 A.M. in Seattle, so I went down to breakfast instead and ran into Mike Hegan, who was just rejoining the club after two weeks in service. Opposite us was Curt Rayer, the trainer. They started talking about how tough it probably was in Houston, since they were only two-and-a-half games out of first place in a five-team race.

"Now you'll be with a real ball-club," Hegan said.

"Think of it, imagine the pressure on those guys," Rayer said.

"Hey, knock it off," I said. "I'm one of them now. I hope they have plenty of Titralac for my stomach."

And I thought, Jesus, the Houston Astros, a pennant race, my first since 1964. Pinocchio, you're a real boy now.

"The end of an era," Mike Hegan said, "and there goes the Seattle dynasty, slowly crumbling."

When I went back to my room to pack I started to feel a knot in my belly. What if I don't have the feel of the knuckleball when I get there? Christ, they'll kill me in that league. Well, I'm just going to have to tell the Astros that I'm still learning the pitch and they'll have to be patient and not expect any miracles. Lord, wouldn't it be awful if I couldn't get the feel of it? If it happened in Seattle, nobody would notice. But here the whole country is watching a pennant race, and I'm in it, and suppose I can't pitch? I took a Titralac and started to pack.

Marvin Miller

A WHOLE DIFFERENT BALL GAME

Until major league baseball players went on strike in 1972, most Americans considered athletes lucky to get paid to play a game. But under the leadership of union director Marvin Miller, baseball players began to get their due as employees and as entertainers. Here Miller remembers the strike that put the business of sports in full view, and for good.

'm always surprised when I read a baseball historian who writes about the 1972 strike as if it were inevitable. The last thing I expected in 1972 was a strike; it really caught me unawares. It was not only the first in baseball history—it was the first in the history of professional sports. The issue described as the cause of the stoppage was only a mask for the real issue. The owners had decided to bring the Players Association's progress to a halt either by provoking a strike, which they felt confident of winning, or by forcing the players to back down and accept their unreasonable position in the negotiations.

Only the benefit plan (pensions and health insurance) was open for negotiation. The cost of the players' health care had risen by about $500,000 a year since the prior settlement in 1969. The union wanted the owners to meet that rise in costs and wanted payments to the pension plan increased so that retirement benefits could be adjusted to match the 17 percent jump in the cost of living over the prior three years. It was a modest request, especially in light of the four-year television contract major league baseball had signed recently with the National Broadcasting Company for the World Series, All-Star Game, and Game of the Week. That contract was worth $70 million.

Negotiations had gone slowly, but with no sign of a crisis. John Gaherin had made an offer—$500,000 a year—on the health-care contribution, but management was reluctant to increase retirement benefits. There was, however, surplus income from the pension fund that could be used to fund an increase in the retirement benefits. This meant that it could be financed without additional cost to the owners. It seemed to me that a settlement was within reach. In fact, on my annual spring training trip in early March, I discussed the pension negotiations with seven teams without mentioning the possibility of a strike. And I'm not an optimist.

Things changed fast. The night before Dick Moss and I were set to meet the Chicago White Sox at their spring training facility in Sarasota, Gaherin surprised us. "The owners aren't going to increase pension benefits at all," he said, "and we're going to *reduce* our offer on health care." Reducing a bargaining proposal which Gaherin knew was inadequate in the first place was an unmistakable signal: Management was baiting us into a strike. Their position was, "Take it or leave it! There's nothing you or the players can do about it."

Before I could even consider a long-term plan, I was faced with an immediate logistical problem. Having already visited seven clubs, I had to backtrack to tell them about the threat without disrupting my scheduled meetings with the seventeen remaining teams—eleven more in Florida, five in Arizona, and one in California. I also had to find a way to continue pension negotiations, conduct the rest of the Association's business, and keep the press up to date on what was happening. All within a span of twenty-three days. That night Dick and I mapped out a strategy, making the necessary calls to rearrange our schedule.

The next morning we went to the White Sox meeting with an entirely different mind-set. "Negotiations will continue," I said, "and there's always the possibility we'll reach a settlement, but it's beginning to seem unlikely." Over the next ninety minutes I explained how important it was to keep retirement benefits on the same level as rising living costs; if not, inflation over the next twenty-five to thirty years (when the players would begin drawing benefits) would reduce the value of their pensions to a tiny fraction of the current worth. I explained what the options were (stand or fold), what each option would lead to, what would be involved if the players decided to walk out, and the procedures we'd follow until the benefit plan expired on March 31. Before leaving the meeting, I asked Jay Johnstone, the White Sox player rep, to conduct a strike authorization vote—the first in baseball since Robert Murphy's attempt to get the Pirates to walk out in 1946 was derailed by Commissioner Chandler's labor spies on the Pittsburgh ball club. The White Sox voted to support a strike, 25-0. (In the next eight days I met again with the seven clubs where no strike vote had been taken; the players unanimously endorsed a strike.)

As the March 31 deadline approached and the negotiating sessions produced no change, my hopes of reaching a settlement faded. If I still hadn't known which way the wind was blowing, all I needed to do was feel the hot air billowing from St. Petersburg, where, after an owners' meeting, Gussie Busch announced to the press, "We voted unanimously to take a stand. We're not going to give them another *goddamn* cent! If they want to strike, let them strike." Busch's war cry was heard throughout the spring training camps. Of all his confrontational statements, this may have been the dumbest. It became a rallying point for the players, a factor in their rapidly spreading solidarity against the owners' arbitrary, antiplayer position. As for Bowie Kuhn, his contribution to the governor's dinner at St. Petersburg was to deliver pious platitudes. "The club owners. . . are a group of sportsmen whose hearts are in the game we all love."

Busch, the "malty proprietor," as Red Smith labeled him, had become a caricature of the factory owner resisting unionization, but he was by no means acting alone. The Player Relations Committee in 1972 contained scarcely a "moderate." There was Reds owner Francis Dale, a publisher and later treasurer of CREEP—the Committee to Re-Elect the President (Nixon)—the organization whose activities were exposed at the Watergate hearings; brewery owner Jerry Hoffberger of the Orioles; Royals owner Ewing Kauffman, who made his money in pharmaceuticals; Dick Meyer representing the petulant beer baron Busch; Wall Streeter Donald Grant of the Mets; Twins owner-by-inheritance Calvin Griffith; and Dan Galbreath of the Pirates representing his father, John, who had amassed a fortune in construction and real estate. These hardliners didn't hide the fact that they were out to destroy the union. From 1971 to the spring of 1972, the rate of "disposal" of elected player reps had jumped dramatically. Of twenty-four reps, sixteen had been cut or traded.

The press generally followed the owners' read. The public heard that the players had the most generous pension plan in America and they were greedily grasping for more, even though what we were seeking was stable pension benefits. We endured editorials like "The fan goes from steak to hamburger while the ballplayer rides a golden gravy train"—as if we were taking steaks out of the fans' mouths! And they echoed management's line that the athletes were well paid for "playing a game." (In case anyone thinks allegations of players being overpaid began when salaries reached seven figures, major leaguers were averaging roughly $22,000 a year at the time.) I wondered how the same writers would have responded had newspaper owners asked why grown men demanded payment to *watch* games and *write* about them—and still expected decent salaries and benefits.

The more I read the more I was persuaded that the owners were not only out to break the union, but also intent on achieving a "victory" over me. After all, I had cost them a fair sum of money. Since 1966, the minimum salary had more than doubled, from $6,000 to $13,500, the players' various allowances had been substantially increased, the pension and medical benefits had grown by many millions, and the Association had demonstrated an ability to defend players' rights. I was portrayed in the newspaper as the villain, the union man who had introduced the evil serpent of money into baseball's Garden of Eden. Atlanta executive Paul Richards said that a stand must be taken or "there isn't going to be any baseball for a long, long time. The owners . . . simply aren't going to let Marvin Miller run over them any more."

The columnist who seemed most obsessed with me was Dick Young, who wrote, "Clearly, to the owners, the enemy is not the players, whom the owners regard merely as ingrates, misled ingrates. The enemy is Marvin Miller, general of the Union. The showdown is with him. It is not over a few more thousand dollars, not the few thousand demanded for some obscure pension inflation, it is over the principle of who will run their baseball business, they, the Lords, or this man Miller." Young was overstating the case, as usual, but he wasn't entirely wrong. I had every intention of making the Players Association into an effective, independent organization. I had no desire to "run" baseball, but I was determined that the players' importance to the game be fully recognized and the concept that they were property be eliminated.

On the sixteen teams I visited in Florida, only eight players voted not to strike. When I got to Winter Haven, in the middle of the trip, Carl Yastrzemski and Reggie Smith asked several questions, the tone of which indicated that they were opposed to a walkout. A Red Sox player since 1961, Yaz had already spoken out against Curt Flood's struggle to end baseball's monopolistic practices. Management had treated Yaz well, and he was close to Sox owner Tom Yawkey. Yaz and Smith influenced another two players, making a total of four negatives, but they were outvoted by their teammates, 26-4.

In his book, *The Wrong Stuff*, Sox pitcher Bill Lee wrote: "Reggie Smith stood up the day we took the vote, announcing that he was voting no because every week out was going to cost him four thousand dollars, while it would cost most of the other players less than eight hundred. I looked at him and said, 'Reggie, you didn't say that, did you? That didn't come out of your mouth?' But it had....The rest of the club voted strike and the brief discussion between Smith and me was forgotten. By everybody but Reggie. From that day on I was *numero uno* on his shit list."*

In the Dodgers camp there were other minor cracks. On March 17, St. Patrick's Day, Dick, my wife, Terry, and I arrived at Vero Beach, the site of Los Angeles's newly renovated sprawling spring training complex known as "Dodgertown." The meeting went well. It was a lively, interesting group, with veterans Frank Robinson and Maury Wills (later, baseball's first black managers); pitchers Don Sutton and Tommy John; and Davey Lopes, Ron Cey, and Steve Garvey, the nucleus of the club that would advance to four World Series in eight seasons.

Afterward, player rep Wes Parker reported the results of the vote: 21-4 in favor of a strike. While I was talking to a few sportswriters, a messenger interrupted in order to invite us to Walter O'Malley's annual St. Patrick's Day party that evening. Ordinarily I would have declined—nothing against St. Patrick, but Dick and I still had nine clubs to meet. But a thought came to me that this might be the best time to talk to Walter O'Malley. He carried a lot of clout and possessed a quality many other owners did not: He was a realist. Perhaps he could talk some sense into the rest of the owners and possibly avoid a strike. "We'd be delighted," I said to the messenger, "but could you ask Mr. O'Malley to set aside some time for a private meeting?"

The party was a big league bash. Everything was green: water, scotch, beer, potatoes, tablecloths, you name it. O'Malley had chartered a plane from Los Angeles with scores of season-ticket holders, and everybody was whooping it up. I hadn't been there very long before I began to feel uncomfortable—and not because I was wear-

---

*It's worth noting that all four Boston players came around to supporting the Association. Before a strike vote in 1980, Reggie Smith, then with the Dodgers, made an emotional speech about the value of a strong union. He told his teammates that he regretted his vote in 1972 and urged a unanimous vote to strike. He got it.

ing a green party hat. Ex-Dodgers Sandy Koufax and Roy Campanella were there, but none of the current players had been invited. Their absence dampened my spirits.

I was talking to team executive Al Campanis when Dick and I were summoned to meet with Walter and his son Peter O'Malley. O'Malley Sr., his party hat still perched on his huge head, was puffing on a fat cigar, laying a cloud of smoke throughout the room.

We got down to business quickly. "Walter, I don't really understand what's going on. This isn't a new issue. And we're not asking for anything out of the ordinary. The amount of money separating us isn't even that large, certainly not large enough to require a strike. Unless you confirm what I think—that the owners are deliberately challenging the players, the Association, and me—I don't get it."

Instead of discussing the issue seriously, O'Malley said, "Oh, well, don't worry. There's not going to be a strike. We'll resolve this."

I told him I hoped he was right, but that it was getting close to the deadline.

"A lot can happen in two weeks," he said, sipping a glass of green Scotch.

Either O'Malley was ignoring the facts, or he didn't understand them. I never really understood which. In any event, O'Malley's remark caused me to despair; if the most rational businessman among the owners didn't understand that their stance was about to force a strike, none of the owners did.

As I stood up to leave, O'Malley said, "I heard the strike vote was twenty-one to four. Who were the four?"

I thought he was kidding. He wasn't. "I have no idea," I said, "but I wouldn't tell you if I did. Why do you want to know?"

"A baseball team is only as good as its unity," he said. "I don't want players that cast themselves as management tools on my team." He explained, "Don't get me wrong. I'd prefer the players to vote unanimously not to strike, but if the majority decides to walk out, I don't want dissenters on my club opposing their teammates. A winning ball club is unified, not split."

I didn't know whether to believe him. But much later, after I learned their identities—Wes Parker, who told me about his vote; two veteran stars who were managerial candidates, and a utility catcher—I realized O'Malley had been telling the truth. Two were traded, and two retired.

I left the meeting with him and his son convinced for the first time that there would be a showdown by March 31.

Supported overwhelmingly by the clubs in Florida, Dick, Terry, and I flew to Arizona where Dick and I would meet with the players on the six clubs in the "cactus league." By the time we completed our tour out west, only two players had voted against a strike—a Milwaukee Brewer and a Seattle Pilot—pushing the final player vote to 663-10.*

Unfortunately, this impressive show of solidarity didn't persuade the owners to bargain in good faith. On March 29—two days before the pension agreement expired—I proposed that the dispute be decided by an impartial arbitrator in order to avoid a strike. Among other things, this proposal was an excellent way to determine whether the owners wanted the matter resolved or whether they were hell-bent on *not* finding a solution. I even suggested that the arbitrator be selected by ex-President Johnson, President Nixon, or former Chief Justice Earl Warren. My only stipulation was that he be a "professional" arbitrator. John Gaherin said no, issuing the stock alibi that baseball was a unique business and hence an outside arbitrator couldn't understand the issues. (When it suited the owners to admit it, baseball was magically transformed from a "game" into a "business.") Actually, Gaherin was partially right. Baseball's exemption from federal antitrust laws was *unique* in American industry; it was even unique among the other professional sports.

We scheduled a meeting for March 31 in Dallas to inform the player reps and their alternates of the latest developments. The night before,

---

*Two players abstained.

in a hotel in Scottsdale, Arizona, Dick Moss and I reviewed our options. The amount of money we wanted for health care and retirement benefits was chicken feed compared to the $70 million the owners were getting in television revenue, the traditional source of funds for the pension plan. Money was not the issue. That had been obvious for several weeks.

The real issue was power. Set on having their way, the owners believed the players would back down or, if they did strike, fold before you could say "pension plan payments." I suppose it was inevitable, given the Association's gains over the past six years, that management would eventually test us. We were armed with a vote of 663-10 in favor of striking, but the owners were checking to see if we'd be firing bullets or blanks. Management was certain it would be the latter.

To strike or not to strike, that, as one playwright almost said, was the question. It was a rough decision. The players were inexperienced (none had ever been out on any kind of strike), and the Association lacked the financial and public relations resources the owners had at their command. Postponing the conflict wouldn't damage the players in the long run, but if they struck and couldn't sustain it, the blow to the still young Association could prove disastrous.

After a long discussion with Dick and several phone conversations with player reps, I decided to recommend the strike be postponed. Before we shut down baseball, I wanted the Association to have a stronger base and better funding. I wanted the players to be better informed and prepared and the issues to be more meaningful to the players' long-term interests. As it was, I didn't like the odds.

So Dick and I worked on an alternate plan. We would negotiate during the season, a scenario that would also give us more time to educate the players. If we couldn't come to an agreement during the season, we'd be able to try again when the basic agreement (and the pension plan) were renegotiated in 1973. By then we would be in a stronger position to strike, if need be. Under no circumstances, however, would we accept an inadequate settlement. The old benefit plan agreement would remain in effect, and retirement benefits could be increased retroactively after we had come to terms. Dick set down our recommendation and the reasons for it in longhand.

The three of us flew to Dallas on the morning of the thirty-first. Sitting behind Terry and me on the plane were Chuck Dobson, Oakland A's player rep, and Reggie Jackson, the team's alternate rep. They had been following the negotiations in the Phoenix newspapers, and their view was that the owners thought the players were afraid to strike. Reggie and Chuck certainly didn't seem afraid. We arrived at the airport motel near Love Field around two P.M. and were greeted by a swarm of reporters and photographers. I had been involved in five nationwide Steelworkers' strikes, but I'd never seen anything approaching this. Such was life in baseball.

The meeting got underway. After reviewing all that had happened during the negotiations, I recommended that we delay striking. Hands shot up all over the room. The players were more committed to accepting the owners' challenge to strike than I had realized; in fact, they were positively militant. Soon I found myself playing the role of devil's advocate, trying to be as realistic (even pessimistic) as possible. I explained the hardships involved. I pointed out that we had no strike fund, no field offices, and no public relations staff; the press would likely be hostile; and on and on. To no avail. Player after player stood up to convince *me* that they were united, that *they* were hell-bent on taking the fight to the owners—even though it was impossible to know how long the strike would last.

Roughly four hours into the meeting, one of the player reps, impatient with the continuing discussion, started to chant: "Strike! Strike! Strike!" It was picked up by the others and repeated over and over. It reminded me of a scene from Clifford Odets's play, *Waiting for Lefty*, in which a group of cab drivers, preyed on by racketeers and exploited by corrupt taxi owners, have gathered for a meeting. They wait, but the union leader, Lefty, doesn't show, and they finally learn he has been murdered. The cabbies refuse to be intimidated and begin shouting in unison, "Strike! Strike! Strike!" The play presented an overly sentimental view of the labor movement in the 1930s, but that scene packed an emotional punch. I was similarly moved by the dramatic turn of events at the Dallas meeting, more so since this wasn't staged. For the first time in baseball history, the players wanted to fight management head on. Our new draft resolution would be a lot simpler—a declaration to strike immediately. The remaining exhibition games on or after April 1 would be canceled, as would the regular season games until a satisfactory settlement was reached.

The final tally was 47-0 in favor of a strike. Wes Parker, the Dodgers' player rep, abstained. Parker had been quoted several times as being opposed to players receiving "ridiculously high" salaries (such as $150,000 a year); not long after the meeting he was removed from office by his teammates, who described their action as "impeachment."

After the vote, we worked out a strategy to communicate with the rest of the players, who would soon be scattered around the country (and throughout Latin America). I announced that Dick and I would remove ourselves from the Association's payroll as we had when the Steelworkers Union went out on strike.

When I called John Gaherin with the final tally, he was flabbergasted. Then again, so was I. Both of us knew the odds were stacked against the players, but Gaherin and the owners had no idea how determined the players were. I could only hope the players' resolve would last—though the tenor of the meeting had made me a believer.

Meanwhile, the meeting had lasted much longer than anyone anticipated, forcing us all to scramble for new flight reservations. Unable to get a nonstop flight to New York, Terry and I were forced to stop in Baltimore. Around midnight, I stirred from a nap to find a dozen of the biggest men I'd ever seen boarding the plane. I sat up, looked closely, and focused on the familiar faces of the New York Knicks who, hours earlier, had been battling the Baltimore Bullets. The Knicks greeted us with cries of "Right on!" Bill Bradley, Dave

DeBusschere, Earl Monroe, Walt Frazier, Willis Reed, and most of the others came over to talk about the strike, which was how we spent the rest of the flight. It was a satisfying end to an emotional day.*

We returned home in the early hours on April 1. The morning newspapers would soon announce the unexpected. It might be April Fool's Day, but no one would be laughing. I slept for a few hours and called John Gaherin early in the morning to discuss resuming our negotiations. Over my second cup of coffee, I thought back on the events of the past six years, trying to understand the owners' fury against us. Soon I found myself thinking about their folly in bringing on baseball's first strike.

As soon as the 1972 strike was announced, the owners and the press sounded off immediately. Red Smith and Leonard Koppett of the *New York Times* provided, I thought, accurate and balanced reporting, but over all, the players were blasted. Some of the criticism bordered on hysteria. C. C. Johnson Spink, the editor of the *Sporting News*, called the walkout the "darkest day in sports history," adding, with breathtaking stupidity, that "the whole idea of pensions for major league players may have been a mistake growing out of a misconception of what constitutes a career." Paul Richards of the Braves said, "Tojo and Hirohito couldn't stop baseball but Marvin Miller could." When California owner Gene Autry learned that the Angels-Dodgers exhibition game had been canceled, he said: "We ought to close baseball down forever!" And he called *me* an extremist!

The press in Cincinnati was particularly virulent—no surprise considering that Reds owner Francis Dale also owned the *Cincinnati Enquirer*. Reds player rep Jim Merritt was concerned and asked me

*A few days later, Bill Bradley . . . wrote a letter to the *Daily News* in response to one of Dick Young's hateful columns. He called me and asked if I'd check his facts on the baseball dispute. It was an intelligent letter, and the paper ran it right away.

to talk to the players on April 5, the traditional Opening Day of major league baseball. I flew to Cincinnati.

Roberto Clemente called to ask if I would visit Pittsburgh as well after speaking to the Reds. The Pirates were a loose, fun bunch of guys. Dave Giusti was the player rep in 1972, but Roberto Clemente was the real leader of the clubhouse. He himself was known to stand up to the owners. Dave Giusti told me a Clemente story that I'll always treasure. Pirates owner Dan Galbreath was in the locker room talking to the players. The club would draw better, he said, if the players signed more autographs and made more public appearances. Galbreath piled it on, claiming that the players weren't appreciative enough of the fans. According to Giusti, the team had had enough, but nobody had the audacity to speak up.

Finally, Clemente said, "Mr. Galbreath, I had a dream last night about this. I had terrible neckache, and suddenly I had become so old and tired and injured that I could no longer play. But those *wonderful* fans out in right field banded together and said, 'Even if the Great One can't play, we can't let him go. He belongs in right field.' So the fans presented me with a rocking chair and said that I should sit comfortably between the stands and the right-field foul line and relax all through my retirement."

The rest of the Bucs didn't know what to think. Was he buttering management up? Had he gone loco?

But Clemente continued in his heavily accented English. "You know, Mr. Galbreath, what that dream is?"

Galbreath hesitated. "No, what?"

Clemente replied firmly, "It is *bool-sheet*!"

Everybody busted up. Except Galbreath.

❖   ❖   ❖

After meeting with the Reds and Pirates in the strike's first week, I stopped in Baltimore at the urging of club and American League player rep Brooks Robinson. Robinson had reason to be concerned.

After the walkout, Orioles owner Jerry Hoffberger had called a team meeting and blasted the players for hours. Hoffberger had two prominent allies on the team: manager Earl Weaver and pitcher Jim Palmer. Weaver told the players that the strike would ruin the club's chances of returning to the World Series. Palmer said I had "brainwashed" the players. (He must have been anticipating a column Dick Young later wrote, which read: "[Miller] runs the players through a high-pressure spray the way an auto goes through a car wash, and that's how they come out, brainwashed." Maybe Young brainwashed Palmer.) After the meeting, Weaver announced to the press that a poll he had conducted showed that twenty-one of the twenty-six Orioles were against the strike and sixteen of the twenty-one were willing to play a scheduled exhibition game against Atlanta.

I spoke with the team at Brooks and Connie Robinson's home in suburban Maryland. Brooks was one of the real heroes of the 1972 strike—not the only one, but one of the most important. Perhaps the best defensive third baseman of all time, he *had* been a hero in Baltimore until the virulent press (among the worst in terms of union bashing) turned on him like a traitor; after the strike was settled, the fair-weather fans showered him with choruses of boos. A kind and modest man who did a lot for the community, Robinson remained the same calm, level-headed person he had always been; undeterred, he carried out his duties as player rep superbly. He regretted the fans' reaction, no doubt, but he didn't show it. I never heard him criticize them. I did criticize them— publicly. Recalling their jeers still galls me.

The meeting at Brooks's house was a good one with a full airing of the relevant issues. I'm not sure why, but that Orioles team produced several of the Association's most vociferous supporters. Robinson's successor at third base, Doug DeCinces, went on to become the American League's player rep. Shortstop Mark Belanger, the O's alternate rep in 1972, became the club's player rep and a special assistant for the Association after he retired as a player in 1983. And some time after the 1972 strike, Earl Weaver, of all people, became a vocal and eloquent union stalwart.

The players surprised everybody during the walkout, even themselves. Players around the country kept in constant contact with their team reps; others worked out together at high schools; and many veterans invited the younger players to stay at their homes to lessen the financial strain. Twins pitcher Jim Perry was a case in point. Perry had grown up in a farm community in North Carolina. He had no experience with unions, and yet overnight he became an efficient, dedicated leader. He was the first to organize the housing of younger players with veterans, and he rented a school bus to transport players back and forth to a local gym which he had arranged to use for workouts. He telephoned me each day for reports on the negotiations and even put together a public address system in the gym so that I could report directly to all of the Twins working out there.

When there were potential cracks, players stepped forward to prevent them. Maury Wills led a meeting of thirteen players in Los Angeles and announced that they had voted to play the Dodgers' home opener on April 7, but Wes Parker—the lone abstainer from the strike vote one week earlier in Dallas—contacted the press to say that Wills didn't speak for the rest of the players, who would remain solidly on strike.

While Wills's conduct turned out to be an aberration, it did feed my biggest concern—division in the ranks. I had to keep reminding myself that the players had never struck. But then, in New York, Willie Mays addressed the players' executive board and my doubts disappeared like one of his towering home runs. Mays had always supported the union, but he hadn't been particularly outspoken—not strange, really, since Willie's career was winding down just about the time the union was solidifying. In 1971—Willie's twentieth big league season—owner Horace Stoneham had traded Giants player rep Hal Lanier and alternate Gaylord Perry. Mays, the forty-one-year-old superstar (he, too, would be traded in a few weeks to the Mets), became the acting player rep.

At the meeting in New York, Mays quieted any doubters with his speech: "I know it's hard being away from the game and our pay-checks and our normal life," he said. "I love this game. It's been my whole life. But we made a decision in Dallas to stick together, and until we're satisfied, we *have* to stay together. This could be my last year in baseball, and if the strike lasts the entire season and I've played my last game, well, it will be painful. But if we don't hang together, everything we've worked for will be lost."

The silence in the room spoke volumes. Mays's on-the-field brilliance had dimmed, but his influence off it remained strong. Sometimes I wish I had come to the Players Association ten or twelve years earlier, if only to see what Willie Mays (or Mickey Mantle or Sandy Koufax, among others) would have pulled in as a free agent near his prime.

As the standoff moved into its second week, negotiations progressed at a snail's pace. But on April 8, forty-eight hours after telling me the owners wouldn't contribute a dime more, Gaherin announced that the owners planned to add another $400,000—the "revised" estimate of the increased cost of insurance benefits.

He was only doing his job. Divisions had begun to appear among the owners. The White Sox, Pirates, and Phillies opened their stadiums to the players for workouts. When the league offices ordered them to stop, Sox owner Arthur Allyn barked, "Nobody is going to tell me what to do with my team!"

After a meeting of the owners in Chicago on April 10, Gussie Busch was reported to have said that the clubs should band together to raise a $1 million emergency fund to help the poorer teams during the strike. Supposedly, Walter O'Malley shot back, "You idiot, the Dodgers alone lose one million dollars each weekend the strike goes on!" That was the refreshing thing about O'Malley: You always knew his bottom line.

Charlie Finley, who had made his millions selling medical insurance to doctors, said after the owners' meeting, "Very few owners knew there was any surplus in the pension fund. That was the main problem. . . . The owners didn't understand what this was all about." (Apparently, they hadn't read the memorandum I sent to them documenting the surplus in the pension fund.) It was a far cry from his stance ten days earlier, when he claimed the players had forgotten two things: "First, they don't contribute one red cent to their own pension plan, and, second, they already have the best pension plan in America." Dick Moss noted Finley's turn-about by saying, "Charlie's going to be my hero yet." In ten days, Finley's consciousness had been raised 100 percent. If we could make a fraction of that progress with a few of the owners, we were home free.

Several hours after Finley's proclamation, the owners revised their offer by adding $500,000 for health-care benefits and agreeing to a cost-of-living increase in retirement benefits.

But no sooner had we settled that than another problem threatened to wreck the agreement. The owners wanted us to make up all the games lost during the strike *without* pay. The hardliners didn't give up easily. They suggested extra doubleheaders and games on scheduled off-days. The players scorned the plan.

At this point, Gaherin and I were in my office when I asked him, in total confidence, to think about an idea. I said, "What if we make up all the lost games due to the strike with neither the owners nor the players receiving compensation? Make admission to those games free as a way to make it up to the fans, and have the proceeds from concessions, parking, and radio-television go to mutually agreed upon charities."

Gaherin almost fell out of his chair. "Are you nuts?" he asked. "The owners would never go for it, and do you realize the lousy PR we'd receive if this leaked to the press?"

"Okay. Let's forget it," I said. "It was only an idea."

What followed was the one and only time Gaherin broke a commitment to me. After leaving my office, he told the owners and their lawyers the idea I had spoken of in confidence. Management exploded, just as he had predicted. Not only were they shocked, but they cleared out of New York *just in case* word leaked to the press. From then on, the remainder of the negotiations were conducted by phone to the owners' new headquarters in Chicago.

On April 10, I called Gaherin with our proposal: "No canceled games will be rescheduled, and the players won't be paid for the days we were out on strike." (I never expected that they would be paid for the struck games.)

The owners' answer was the same: "No dice."

On April 13, after three days of batting this back and forth, the owners okayed our proposal. Had they agreed to our proposal on April 10, only about half as many games would have been missed. The owners then refused to settle unless the players lost credited service for the nine days of the strike in the season. I rejected their demand out of hand. They folded, and the agreement specified that players would lose no credited service time because of the strike.

The strike lasted thirteen days (nine during the season) and forced the cancellation of 86 games. Some clubs played 153 games, others played 156. That twist of fate may have cost the Red Sox the pennant—they finished behind Detroit by one-half game. The owners lost an estimated $5.2 million. Major league players lost nine days' salary, or about $600,000. Starting in 1972, the increased pension benefits represented a gain of an even greater sum *each year* into the future. Pete Rose, who finished with 198 hits, sounded off by saying, "If there's another strike. . . the Players Association will not get my support.... Last year's strike cost me seven thousand dollars and a chance for two hundred hits." I'm happy to say that Pete changed his tune in 1981, backing the Association all the way. He did the same in 1985, even though he was a manager. Thanks to the Association, Pete became a free agent in 1978, signed a four-year, $3.2-million contract with Philadelphia, and earned more money *each day of the season, every year*, than he "lost" in the entire 1972 strike.

Baseball was back, and the Association—now stronger than ever—had successfully stood up to the owners. Leonard Koppett of the *New York Times* summed up baseball's first strike like this:

Players: We want higher pensions.

Owners: We won't give you one damn cent for that.

Players: You don't have to—the money is already there. Just let us use it.

Owners: It would be imprudent.

Players: We did it before, and anyhow, we won't play unless we can have some of it.

Owners: Okay.

Between the last two statements, thirteen days elapsed and eighty-six games went unplayed. Koppett was making a very basic point; the terms accepted by the owners on April 13 would have averted a strike had they accepted them on March 31.

In later accounts, Koppett provided an analysis of greater depth, pointing out that the real significance of the strike was that the owners never again would be able to exercise the control over players that had been the hallmark of the owner-player relationship for so many decades.

When a settlement was reached, I told the press, "All fans should be proud of the players. They showed courage and hung together against terrible odds. They made the owners understand that they must be treated as equals." I felt very hopeful. Weathering such a crisis, of course, would enable the Players Association to stand up against further assaults: the 1976 lockout and the 1981 strike. Of course, those battles were years away.

The 1972 strike was settled on April 14—my fifty-fifth birthday. The season was free to begin. I don't remember any other gifts I received, but I do remember celebrating late into the night.

Donald Hall with Dock Ellis

DOCK ELLIS IN THE COUNTRY OF BASEBALL

Poet and professor Donald Hall met major league pitcher Dock Ellis in 1973. Three years later the poet and the talented pitcher produced a unique account of a unique player's life in the game; at the time, Ellis was an outspoken, sometimes outrageous maverick, often referred to as "the Muhammad Ali of baseball." These two, strong-minded outsiders presented a truly fresh perspective on what it was like to be a black man in the 1970s playing major league baseball. The following excerpt includes a memorable episode during which Ellis declared war on the Cincinnati Reds.

Baseball is a country all to itself. It is an old country, like Ruritania, northwest of Bohemia and its seacoast. Steam locomotives puff across trestles and through tunnels. It is a wrong-end-of-the-telescope country, like the landscape people build for model trains, miniature with distance and old age. The citizens wear baggy pin-stripes, knickers, and caps. Seasons and teams shift, blur into each other, change radically or appear to change, and restore themselves to old ways again. Citizens retire to farms, in the country of baseball, smoke cigars and reminisce, and all at once they are young players again, lean and intense, running the base paths with filed spikes.

Or they stay in the city, in the capital of the country of baseball. At the mouth of the river, in the city of baseball, young black men wear purple leather maxicoats when they leave the ball park. Slick dressers of the twenties part their hair in the middle and drive road-sters. In old *barrios* everyone speaks Spanish. Kids playing stickball, and kids running away from cops, change into fierce adults round-ing third base in front of fifty thousand people, and change again into old men in their undershirts on front stoops.

Though the grass transforms itself into a plastic rug, though the players speak Arkansas or Japanese, though the radio adds itself to the newspaper, and the television to the radio, though salaries grow from workingmen's wages to lawyers' compensations, the country remains the same; everything changes, and everything stays the same.

The players are white and black, Cuban and Welsh and Mississippi farmers. The country of baseball is polyglot. They wear great mustaches and swing bottle-shaped bats, and some of them dress eccentrically. John McGraw's Giants play two World Series wearing black uniforms. Now the citizens' hair shortens, their loose uniforms turn white, their faces turn white also, and the white world cheers—while on the other side of town, black crowds cheer black ballplayers. Now the hair returns—beards, handlebar mustaches, long locks hanging beside the catcher's mask, now brightly colored knickers cling close to thick legs; now bats are scooped out at the thick end; now black and white play together again.

In the country of baseball the magistrates are austere and plain-spoken. Many of its citizens are decent and law-abiding, obedient to their elders and to the rules of the community.

But there have always been others—the mavericks, the eccentrics, the citizens of independent mind. They thrive in the country of base-ball. Some of them display with Lucifer the motto, "I will not serve." Some of them are known as flakes, and unless they are especially tal-ented bounce from club to club, to retire from the active life sooner than the others. Left-handed pitchers are reputed to be craziest of all, followed by pitchers in general, and left-handers in general. Maybe forty percent of the population in the country of baseball is flaky, at least in the opinion of the other sixty percent.

When Al Hrabosky meditates hate, in his public solitude behind the St. Louis mound, he perpetuates a great tradition.

The country of baseball begins to take shape at the age of six. Earlier, sometimes. Dock Ellis's cousin gave him a baseball to hold when Dock was in his crib. But Little League starts at six and stickball and cow-pastureball at about the same age. At seven and eight and nine, the players begin to reside wholly in the country of baseball. For the people who will live there forever, the long summers take on form—time and space shaped by the sharp lozenge of the base paths. Then high school, maybe college, maybe rookie league, Class A, Double A, Triple A—the major leagues. In the brief season of maturity, the citizens of this country live in hotels, watch movies, pick up women who lurk for them in lobbies, sign autographs for kids, and climb onto the team bus for the ride to the ball park at five in the afternoon.

In their brief season, they sit for a thousand afternoons in front of their lockers, pull on archaic stockings, set their knickers at the height they affect, and josh and tease their teammates. Tony the trainer measures a tender elbow, tapes an ankle. Then the citizens saunter without urgency onto the field, gloves under arms, and pick up a ball.

Richie Hebner sees Richie Zisk. "Hey," he says, "want to play catch?"

Baseball, they tell us, is part of the entertainment industry.

Well, money changes hands; lawyers make big money; television people and their sponsors make big money. Even the citizens make big money for a while. But like actors and magicians and country singers and poets and ballet dancers, when the citizens claim to be in it for the money, they are only trying to be normal Americans. Nothing is further from the country of baseball than the business life. Although salaries grow and contract clauses multiply, the business of baseball like the business of art is dream.

In the cardboard box business, a boss's expectations rise like a plateau gradually elevated, an infinite ramp leading to retirement on the ghost plains of Arizona. And in the country of cardboard boxes, the manners of Rotary proliferate: the false laughter, the bonhomie of contracts, the golf played with boss's boss. Few flakes survive, in the country of cardboard boxes.

But in the country of baseball, men rise to glory in their twenties and their early thirties—a garland briefer than a girl's, or at least briefer than a young woman's—with an abrupt rise, like scaling a cliff, and then the long meadow slopes downward. Citizens of the country of baseball retire and yet they never retire. At first it may seem that they lose everything—the attention of crowds, the bustle of airplanes and hotels, the kids and the girls—but as they wake from their first shock, they discover that they live in the same place, but that they live in continual twilight, paler and fainter than the noon of games.

Dock visits an old friend, Alvin O'Neal McBean, retired to his home in the Virgin Islands. In the major leagues, McBean was *bad*. The language of Rotary does not flourish in locker rooms or dugouts; the citizens' speech does not resemble the honey tongued *Reader's Digest*; eccentricity breeds with outrage. "McBean would as soon curse you as look at you," Dock says—even if you were his manager or his general manager; and he could *scream*. He was therefore not long for the major leagues. Now Alvin O'Neal McBean supervises playgrounds, the old ballplayer teaching the kids old tricks, far from reporters, umpires, and Cadillacs. "He's made the Adjustment," says Dock. "He doesn't *like* it, but he's made the Adjustment."

The years on the diamond are fantasy. The citizens *know* they live in fantasy, that the custom cars and the stewardesses and the two-inch-thick steaks belong to the world of glass slippers and golden coaches drawn by unicorns. Their fathers were farmers and one day they will be farmers also. Or their fathers loaded crates on boxcars for a hundred dollars a week and one day they too will load crates on boxcars for a hundred dollars a week. Just now, they are pulling down two thousand.

But for them, the fantasy does not end like waking from a dream or like a transformation on the stroke of midnight. They make the

Adjustment, and gradually they understand that even at a hundred dollars a week, or even on top of a tractor, they live in a crepuscular duplicate of their old country.

And most of them, whatever they thought, never do just what their fathers did. When they make the Adjustment, they sell insurance or real estate to their former fans, or they open a bar in the Missouri town they came from. They buy a restaurant next to a bowling alley in their old Oakland neighborhood, and they turn paunchy, and tilt a chair back behind the cash register, remembering—while they compute insurance, while they pull draft beer—the afternoons of August and the cold September nights under the blue lights, the pennant race at the end of the dying season.

The country of baseball never wholly vanishes for anyone once a citizen of that country. On porches in the country of baseball old men are talking. Scouts, coaches, managers; car salesmen, manufacturers' representatives, bartenders. No one would let them exile themselves from that country if they wanted to. For the kids with their skateboards, for the men at the Elks, they remain figures of youth and indolent energy, alert at the plate while the pitcher fidgets at the mound—a young body always glimpsed like a shadow within the heavy shape of the old body.

The old first baseman, making the final out of the inning, in the last year he will play, underhands the ball casually toward the mound, as he has done ten thousand times. The ball bounces over the lip of the grass, climbs the crushed red brick of the mound for a foot or two, and then rolls back until it catches in the green verge. The ball has done this ten thousand times.

Basketball is not a country. It's a show, a circus, a miracle continually demonstrating the Newtonian heresy that muscle is lighter than air, bodies suspended like photographs of bodies, the ball turning at right angles. When the game is over, basketball does not continue; basketball waits poised and immobile in the locked equipment room, like the mechanical toy waiting for a hand to wind it.

from DOCK ELLIS IN THE COUNTRY OF BASEBALL

Football is not a country. It's a psychodrama, brothers beating up on brothers, murderous, bitter, tender, homosexual, ending with the incest of brotherly love, and in the wounds Americans carry all over their bodies. When the game is done, football dragasses itself to a bar and drinks blended whiskey, maybe seven and seven, brooding, its mouth sour, turned down, its belly flowing over its angry belt.

In the country of baseball days are always the same.

The pitchers hit. Bunting, slapping weakly at fat pitches, hitting line drives that collapse in front of the pitching machine, they tease each other. Ken Brett, with the fireplug body, lifts one over the center-field fence, as the big hitters emerge from the dugout for the honest BP. "Did you see *that*?" he asks Wilver Stargell. "Did you see *that*?" he asks Al Oliver.

The pitcher who won the ball game last night lifts fungoes to a crowd in left field—outfielders, utility infielders, even pitchers who pause to shag flies in the midst of running. When they catch a ball, they throw it back to the infield by stages, lazy arcs linking out-fielders to young relief pitchers to coaches. Everyone is light and goofy, hitting fungoes or shagging flies or relaying the ball. Everyone is relaxed and slightly self-conscious, repeating the motions that became rote before they were ten. Some citizens make catches behind their backs, or throw the ball from between their legs. Behind the mound, where a coach begins to throw BP to the regulars, Paul Popovich and Bob Moose pick up loose baseballs rolled toward the mound, and stack them in the basket where the BP pitcher retrieves three at a time. Now they bounce baseballs on the cement-hard turf, dribbling them like basketballs. Moose dribbles, fakes left, darts right, jumps, and over Popovich's jumping body sinks a baseball in a wire basket for a quick two points.

Coaches slap grounders to infielders, two deep at every position. Third, short, second, first, a bunt for the catcher. The ball snarls around the horn. Third, short, second, first, catcher. At the same time, the rubber arm of the BP pitcher stretches toward the plate, where Bob Robertson takes his turn at bat. Two balls at once bounce

265

toward Rennie Stennett at second. A rookie up from Charleston takes his cuts, and a shortstop jabs at a grounder from Bob Skinner, and Manny Sanguillen leaps to capture a bunt, and the ball hums across the infield, and Willie Stargell lofts an immense fly to center field. Behind the cage, Bill Robinson yells at Stargell, "Buggy-whipping, man! Buggy-whipping!"

Stargell looks up while the pitcher loads himself with balls, and sees that Joe Garagiola is watching him. Tonight is Monday night. "Hey, man," he says slowly. "What are the rules of this bubble gum contest?" He whips his bat forward, takes a cut, tops the ball, grimaces. Willie has two fractured ribs from a ball thrown by a forty-one-year-old Philadelphia relief pitcher. Philadelphia is trying to catch Pittsburgh and lead the Eastern Division.

"What rules?" says Garagiola. "I don't have them with me."

Willie whips his bat forward with accelerating force. "How many pieces?" He hits a line drive off the right-field wall.

Garagiola shrugs. "Four or five," he says. "Something like that." He laughs, his laugh a little forced, as if he felt suddenly foolish. "Got to have a little fun in this game."

Nearer to game time, with the pitchers running in the outfield, the screens gone from the infield, five Pirates are playing pepper between the dugout and the first-base line. Dave Giusti holds the bat, and fielding are Ramon Hernandez, John Morlan, and Daryl Patterson. Giusti hits miniature line drives back at the other relief pitchers. Everyone laughs, taunts, teases. Giusti hits one harder than usual at Hernandez. Another. The ambidextrous Puerto Rican—who tried pitching with both arms in the same inning until they stopped him; who pitches from the left side now, and strikes out the left-handed pinch hitter in the ninth inning—Ramon drops his glove, picks up a baseball in each hand, winds up both arms as he faces Giusti head on, and fires two baseballs simultaneously. Giusti swings laughing and misses them both.

In the outfield, big number seventeen lopes with long strides, then idles talking to fans near the bullpen for ten minutes, then fields grounders at second base, says something to make Willie Stargell laugh, and walks toward the dugout. Seeing Manny Sanguillen talk with Dave Concepcion and Pedro Borbon, soft Spanish fraternization with the enemy, he throws a baseball medium fast to hit Manny in the flesh of his thigh. Manny jumps, looks around, sees who it is, laughs, and runs with gentle menace toward him. But Dock has turned his back, and leans on his folded arms at the top of the dugout, scanning the crowd for friends and for ladies, his high ass angled up like a dragster, his big handsome head solemnly swiveling over the box seats—bad Dock Ellis, black, famous for his big mouth, suspended in 1975 for a month without pay, the suspension rescinded and pay restored, Dock, famous for his Bad Attitude, maverick citizen in the country of baseball.

At Old Timer's Day in Cincinnati, Edd Roush is an honorary captain, who hit .325 in the Federal League in 1914, .352 in the National League in 1921, and played eighteen years. Lou Boudreau plays shortstop. His gut is huge, but he breaks quickly to his left and scoops a grounder from the bat of Pee Wee Reese, and throws to Mickey Vernon at first. I saw Lou Boudreau, player-manager for Cleveland, hit two fly balls into the left-field screen at Fenway Park in the one-game American League pennant play off in 1948. I discovered Pee Wee Reese eight years earlier, when I was twelve, and the soft voice of Red Barber on WOR chatted about the new shortstop up from the Louisville Colonels. Joe Nuxhall pitches, who pitched in the major leagues when he was fifteen years old, and still pitches batting practice for the Cincinnati Reds. And Carl Erskine pitches, and Harvey Haddix. Harvey Kuenn comes to the plate, and then Dixie Walker— who played right field for the Brooklyn Dodgers, and confessed to Mr. Rickey in the spring of 1947 that he could not play with a black man. Dixie Walker flies out to a citizen who retired last year, still limber as a squirrel, playing center field again—Willie Mays.

In the country of baseball, time is the air we breathe, and the wind swirls us backward and forward, until we seem so reckoned in time and seasons that all time and all seasons become the same. Ted Williams goes fishing, never to return to the ball park, and falls asleep at night in the Maine summers listening to the Red Sox on radio from Fenway Park; and a ghostly Ted Williams continues to play the left-field wall, and his flat swing meets the ball in 1939, in 1948, in 1960. In the country of baseball the bat swings in its level swoop, the ball arcs upward into the twilight, the center fielder gathers himself beneath it, and *Dixie Walker flies out to Willie Mays.*

✤ ✤ ✤

Dock Phillip Ellis, Jr., exercises his life in the pursuit of freedom. By freedom Dock means speaking his mind and doing what he needs to do without regard for consequence. This independence has not endeared him to fans. In the spring of 1975—to pick an example at random—a Pittsburgh newspaper printed a photograph of Dock running laps in Florida; his midriff was bare in the heat, and a dog was running after him. The photograph seems inoffensive, but someone in Pittsburgh took the trouble to cut it out of the paper, letter "No Good Black Rat" along the top, and mail it to Dock in Bradenton.

Of course when he makes the papers by screaming about the All-Star Game, or when he gets suspended, or when Commissioner Bowie Kuhn orders him to stop wearing hair curlers in uniform, then the hate mail piles up like slag. Some fans prefer their athletes docile, humble, grateful, clean-cut, and white.

So Dock—being proud, being black, and being his own man; possibly being eccentric—has more than his share of detractors. He can also count on some of the most devoted fans in the world, including most young black people in Pittsburgh, where he played his major league baseball until 1976.

All over the country, Dock is a roguish and spirited celebrity among black people, even among those indifferent to sports. *Jet* has so often printed photographs and news stories about Dock that it seems to have a Dock Ellis Division. *Ebony* has featured him. He is popular because he upsets white racists. He is popular like Muhammad Ali because he does what he pleases and gets away with it. He is popular because he is brave and stylish at the same time. He is also popular because he is loyal to black brothers and sisters everywhere, and spends his leisure in projects for black people—working at the rehabilitation of convicts, fighting sickle-cell anemia, and working with black youth. In these pursuits, he has avoided publicity. Readers of white sports pages know little of this side of him. He combines, in a way known only to himself, pizzaz with dignity.

Much of the public does not *wish* to accord dignity to men who pitch, field, and hit baseballs for a living.

I remember June 8, 1974. Dock was scheduled to pitch against the San Francisco Giants at Candlestick Park. It was a Saturday afternoon game, and the sun was bright, but high winds from the Bay made it cold. Candlestick is the worst park in the major leagues. Made for football, it suffers a baseball diamond—awkwardly tucked on acres of green plastic—the way a circus horse tolerates a monkey. And no one comes to the games, not since Oakland arrived, across the Bay.

This Saturday was Camera Day. For nearly an hour before the game, fans crowded along the rails of the lower deck with Nikons and Polaroids, Leicas, Instamatics, Hasselblads, and antique box Brownies. The Giants strolled on the dirt at the edges of the field, offering themselves for photographs. One of them led a llama on a rein, another a pony, another a dog, another a camel. A young man not in uniform led a huge tiger. Ballplayers strayed close, but not too close, to the tiger.

Which were the animals, and which the athletes? At the zoo, every day is Camera Day. At Candlestick, only once a year do the visitors come close enough to the animal-athletes to fill camera frames with head and shoulders. The creatures behind the rail, camel or outfielder, gradually melted into each other.

Dock would never have taken part in such a show. In 1971—the year after his no-hitter, the year he started the All-Star Game for the National League, and won nineteen games—Dock was bannered in a Pittsburgh paper, ELLIS PROBABLY MOST UNPOPULAR BUC OF ALL TIME. Sportswriters all over the country had already censured his Bad Attitude. In Pittsburgh, he made people angriest when he refused to sign autographs. That's not exactly what he did, but that's what he was accused of.

Before every Sunday home game at Three Rivers Stadium, selected Pirate players hand out autographed photographs of themselves. In 1971, the players were sitting inside little cages to hand them out. The cage was there, presumably, to protect the players from the fans.

But the metaphor of the cage did not suit Dock. "I went up there and looked at it, so I said, 'I'm not going to be in a cage. I'm no monkey in a cage.' So they said, 'Well, if you don't do it, we're going to fine you.' I said, 'I don't care.' "

He cared enough to pay two sequential one-hundred-dollar fines.

Newspapers and television stations throbbed with indignation. One TV commentator, calling Dock "an egotistical pop-off," rehearsed earlier incidents and mounted to this climax: "Now the Pittsburgh prima donna is refusing to take part in . . . signing autographs in special booths before game time. . . . This past weekend my eleven-year-old son got the autographs of Bill Mazeroski and Bob Veale at just such a booth. He was thrilled. . . . By his action, Ellis has labeled himself as too big or too important to be bothered with the kids who hold him as something to look up to, with the fans who pay his salary. I intend to teach my son that that is not the behavior of a champion . . ."

This one quote can stand in for a hundred others.

A year later, the Pirates changed the system.

Other players felt as Dock did, but did not speak out until he had provoked the usual abuse. Now the players sit at long tables while fans file by, and hand out photographs and sign yearbooks. A security guard stands by the table to protect them. Dock takes his turn.

Tomorrow he will sit at gate C. "I wish they would have me at gate B," he tells me. "I can sell more yearbooks there. Can I sell them! I must have sold at least fifty or seventy-five yearbooks. We don't sign *any-thing*, but . . . let me see, what do we sign? . . . We sign *yearbooks*, that's all we sign is *yearbooks*. They'll throw a piece of paper at you, or a ball, and I'll say, 'We can't sign that. You've got to get a yearbook. Go get your yearbook!'" Dock is helping to support his employers.

"But you *are* handing out autographed pictures?" I ask him.

"Oh, yeah, I'll hand them out."

"Already signed?"

"We don't sign them. Somebody else signs them."

After I have digested this information, I ask Dock to elaborate.

"They tried to get us to sign the autographs beforehand. Like if I'm signing autographs tomorrow, I should have signed all those pic-tures two and a half weeks ago. But a lot of guys wouldn't do it, so they just said, 'Forget about it,' and they hired a girl to write the names. She does it *close!*"

With his own right hand, Dock Ellis signed more autographs than anyone else on the Pirates.

Before almost every game, in every park, Dock loiters along the box seats, walking from the outfield where he has been running, or from the bullpen where he has been throwing. People yell at him. He sees old friends. He chatters and makes new ones. Kids lean out, holding their pads and pencils. He will sign ten or twenty, move on, sign ten or twenty more. Frequently, he will make conversation with rapid questions: "Is that your sister? What you doing up so late? You go to school? Where? What's your daddy's name? Don't you like the *Pirates*?"

It takes forty minutes, some days, to walk from right field to the dugout.

Dock complains about the new parks. "You're just not as close to the fans as you used to be. If you don't have the fans, what're you doing out there playing ball?"

I ask him if he's aware—if ballplayers are aware—of old fans who have been coming to the park for fifty years, who watch the players change while the team remains the same.

"The DIEHARD fans," says Dock, with new heights of emphasis. "They sit out there in the rain, snow, everything. They won't *leave*, unless they've got bad health. They'll be *right there*. Today, I saw—" we were talking after a game with Cincinnati at Pittsburgh "—it was two guys, their wives. They said, 'Do you remember West Mound Street Columbus?'" Dock spent two years at Columbus in the minor leagues. "I say, '*Yeah!*' That's where the ball park was. I remembered the guy's voice, and I remember his wife from her glasses.

"Oh, you should have seen me out there today, after the game. I must have signed a hundred autographs. Of course I was trying to get close to that girl. I made sure I signed all their autographs, so they would *get away*! Of course they were Cincinnati fans, hundreds of them—They went *crazy*. She just happened to be blonde."

All over the league there are fans that a ballplayer knows only at the ball park. When you go into San Diego, you know you will see the fat woman on the third-base line whose husband arrives in the fifth inning. In Philadelphia there is a black family named Eustace always in left-field boxes. "Take Chicago. I have a lot of friends in Chicago, I don't know their names but I know their faces; I could see them anywhere and I'd know them. They got this Japanese family there. She takes pictures, and she took a picture, an *original* picture of me in curlers."

It must be unpleasant, though, to be yelled at by obnoxious fans.

Dock's face gets serious. This notion touches a principle he lives by. "The fan's *privilege* is to say what he wants to say. That's the same privilege I want, to say what I want to say and to do what I want to do."

Of course there is abuse from the fans. "Ellis, you stink!" "Hey, Ellis, crybaby!" "Ellis, where your curlers?" "You suck!"

Once in Chicago he had a quarrel going with the bleacher bums, as they called themselves. "I even had a grown man crying. I was just wolfing. I was getting on them *bad*. A man just shut up, and started crying. Then they apologize. They say, 'We didn't *mean* it.' I say, 'Well, okay, then, don't *say* nothing.'

"That particular time, that's when they *challenged* me to come to the bleacher bums' bar. They was the only ones they let in, there. Behind the scoreboard in Chicago. I stayed about an hour and a half. They all wanted to buy me drinks. They were just *amazed* that I came in there."

Not all the abuse is so open. Besides anonymous hate mail, there is the telephone.

"You get a lot of crank calls. You see in the papers, guys saying that people want to kill them? They've been trying to kill me ever since they started writing about me in the papers. If I *told* them, every time somebody called to say he was going to kill me, they'd have to put a man with me every day. They call me and say, 'If you peek your head above that dugout again, we're gonna blow it off!'"

Loitering along the rails signing autographs, Dock mostly talks to the kids. "Well, what's happening, my man?" When he gets abuse from white adults, sometimes he counterattacks through their children, setting young against old to make his point.

"Ellis, you stink! Ellis, if you're going to wear curlers, why don't you get out of baseball?"

Dock searches for the source of the taunts, and finds a pair of white adults with their children, sitting near the field. "I *charge* them. I run over to them, and say, 'What's your phone number? What's your address? Because I'm coming to dinner.'"

While the parents gawk, Dock levels his finger at a child and says, "Is that all right? Am I coming?

"The child is excited anyway, by the fact of me being over there talking to them, because I'm a major league ballplayer. The kid is all happy about it and says, 'Yeah! Dock's coming to dinner.' The parents look like fools. What can the parents say? 'No?'"

And Dock telephones, and comes to dinner, and "They tell me they were booing only because they were going on what they'd read about me."

"How many dinners have you invited yourself to?"

"Three. It's a warm welcome. From there, we sort of become friends. They all still come to the ball park. It just tickles the hell out of me! . . ."

Years ago, newspapers started to call Dock a "militant," short for "black militant." The word annoys him, because it does not mean what it says.

In some ways, Dock is indeed a black militant, and wishes to be. When he was younger, during junior college, he read *Elijah Speaks*; in the minor leagues he went into "a heavy black thing" and isolated himself from whites. More relaxed now, he gets along as easily with whites as with blacks, travels in mixed company, and does not allow himself to be limited by any of the categories to which he belongs, "black," or "athlete," or "Californian." But he is alert to prejudice, he takes pride in his blackness, and he has been a particular friend to the young brothers on the team.

It irritates him that the press calls him "militant" when the term is inappropriate. When he complains about short beds or crowded airplanes, when he wears curlers or refuses to pitch relief, he is characterized as militant. If he complains about anything, he shows a Bad Attitude. If Dock Ellis returned a steak to the chef at Bonanza, complaining that it was too rare, a wire service would report BLACK MILITANT DOCK ELLIS REFUSES STEAK. When Richie Zisk started screaming to the press about the way the Pirates were treating him, Dock—who regarded Zisk proudly as his pupil in public relations—called him a "white militant."

When someone calls Dock Ellis "militant" because he complains that his hotel bed is too short, he is calling him "an uppity nigger."

In the country of baseball, pitchers are always throwing baseballs at batters. Some pitchers are better known for it than others.

If the pitcher has acquired a certain reputation, the batter may have other matters on his mind besides his batting average, his ribbies, his slugging average, and his team's place in the standings. As Sandy Koufax has remarked, "Pitching is the art of instilling fear."

Dock Ellis is moderately famous for throwing at batters. On May 1, 1974, he tied a major league record by hitting three batters in a row. They were the first three batters up, in the first inning. They were Cincinnati Reds batters. Dock's control was just fine.

Four days earlier, I had seen him at a party in Pittsburgh. I wandered around, talking to various people. Dock's attorney and friend Tom Reich was there, shaking his head in disapproval of a plan of Dock's. I met Dock in the kitchen fixing a drink. I asked him with some awe, "Are you really going to hit every Cincinnati ballplayer Wednesday night?"

He returned the awe. "How you know that?" he said.

We must now consider the history, philosophy, and psychology of hitting batters.

In the challenge between mound and plate, which is the center of the game, a reputation can be as effective as an extra pitch. Dock: "The hitter will try to take *advantage* of you. Like if you are a pitcher who throws a lot of breaking balls, a lot of sliding fast balls, or if you pitch *away*, the hitter will have a tendency to lean across the plate. Quite naturally, if they know that this is your routine, they'll be trying to go *at* the ball, to get a better swing at it. They'll be moving up closer on the plate. Therefore, when you throw in on them, you don't throw to hit them, you throw to brush them back. That means 'Give me some of the plate. Let me have my part, and you take yours! Get away! Give me some room to pitch with!'"

"As far as *hitting* a batter, there are situations when it is called for, like sometimes a pitcher might intentionally or unintentionally hit a batter, or throw two balls near a hitter. The other team, to retaliate, will either knock someone down or hit a batter."

Not all pitchers will throw at batters. If you are a batter, you want your pitchers to throw at *their* hitters, to protect you.

Bob Veale was the Pirates' best pitcher for years. Between 1962 and 1972, he won a hundred and sixteen games. But he had a flaw. Gene Clines, a Pirate outfielder at the time, talked to me after Veale was traded to Boston: "He can throw the ball through a brick wall, but everybody knew that he was a *gentle* giant. If Veale would knock you down, it had to be a mistake. He didn't want to hurt anybody." Clines shook his head in bewildered melancholy. "Who's going to challenge him? Nobody on the *baseball field* is going to say, 'I'm going to go out and *get* Bob Veale.' . . . Take a left-handed hitter. Take Willie. They going to be going up to the plate, and digging in, knowing that Veale is *not* going to knock them down. . . ." He shakes his head again, at the waste of it all.

"Blass was the same way." Steve Blass announced in 1973 that he would *not* throw at batters, even if management fined him for disobeying orders. "Now he was one guy that personally I really didn't like to play behind," Clines told me. "If they knock me down two or three times . . . well, if *he* throws at a batter, he's gonna say, 'Watch out!' . . . and I don't want that, because they never told *me* to watch out! They trying to knock my *head* off! Why go out there and play behind a guy that's not going to protect you?"

Manny Sanguillen: "I tell you about Veale. The only player Veale used to knock down was Willie McCovey. The only one. I was catching. Because McCovey hurt him so much." McCovey hurt Veale by hitting long balls off him. "You remember when McCovey had the operation here?" Manny, whose hands are as quick as the expressions on his face, jabs at his right knee. "Veale used to throw down at the knee!"

When Bruce Kison came up to the Pirates, Dock took to him immediately. Although Kison was six feet six inches and weighed only 155 pounds when he first reported (in the locker room, Dock says, when Kison breathed and filled his frail chest with air, he looked like a greyhound who could walk on his hind legs), he had acquired a reputation for hitting batters. If you hit batters, it is sensible to weigh 230 and look *mean* at all times.

"I was wild," says Bruce Kison, sprawled and smiling. "I've always had a reputation . . . I have a fastball that runs in, on a right-handed hitter. In the minor leagues in one game I hit seven batters." Kison laughs, as if he were telling about a time in high school when he attempted a foolish escapade, like chaining a cow in the women's gym, and the cow kicked him, but nobody got hurt. "I was just completely wild. I hit three guys in a row. There were two outs. The manager came out of the dugout and said, 'Bruce, I know you're not trying to hit these guys, but we'll have the whole stands out on the field pretty soon!'"

"The next guy up was a big catcher. *No*, he was an *outfielder*, but he came up to the plate with catcher's gear on . . ."

I want to make sure I understand. "But you do, on occasion, throw at batters?"

"Certainly." Kison is no longer smiling. He sounds almost pedantic. "That is part of pitching."

A pitcher establishes his reputation early. Dock came up to Pittsburgh in 1968, and in 1969 was a regular starter. He quickly established himself as mean and strong. "Cepeda is the *biggest*," says Dock. So it was necessary for Dock to hit Cepeda. "He was trying to take *advantage* of me because I was a rookie. He was trying to scare me. I let him know, then, that I was not the type dude to fuck around with. It was a *big thing*, because who would be hitting Cepeda? If you went for the biggest guy, it meant you would go for *anybody*. You weren't scared of *anybody*. I hit McCovey, and I really got up on McCovey that year. But he's not so big. Cepeda is the biggest. The rest of the season, from that point on, I had no trouble with the hitters. They were all *running*."

Sometimes one courts trouble, hitting batters.

In 1969, in Montreal, "I hit Mack Jones in the head, but I wasn't trying to hit him in the head. I was trying to hit him in the *side*."

"They had hit Clemente in the chest. So I said, 'The first batter up, I'm going to try to *kill* him. Mack Jones was the first batter. I threw at him. I missed him. I threw at him again. He ducked, and it hit him in the head. He came out to the mound, like he was coming at me." Players rushed out on the field. Enormous Dick Radatz, relief pitcher recently traded from Detroit to Montreal, ran in from the bullpen toward the mound. Dock addressed Radatz, "Hey, man, I'll turn you into a *piece* . . . of . . . *meat!*" Radatz stopped in his tracks.

The umpire behind home plate looked as if he planned to interfere, possibly even to throw Dock out of the game. "But Clemente," Dock remembers, "he intervened, and he told the umpire, 'You leave Dock alone. The motherfuckers hit me twice! Don't mess with Dock!'"

On Wednesday night, May 1, 1974, the Reds were in Pittsburgh. Dock was starting against Cincinnati for the first time that year. As it developed, he was also starting against Cincinnati for the last time that year.

Beginning in spring training, among the palm trees and breezes and gas shortages of Bradenton on the Gulf Coast of Florida, Dock had planned to hit as many Cincinnati batters as possible, when he first pitched against them. He had told some of his teammates, but they were not sure he meant it. Dock loves to sell wolf tickets ("Wolf tickets? Some people are always selling them, some people are always buying them . . .") and the Pirate ball club had learned not always to take him literally.

Manny knew he meant it. At the regular team meeting before the game—the Pirates meet at the start of each series, to discuss the ball club they are about to engage—Dock said there was no need to go over Cincinnati batters, their strengths and weaknesses. "I'm just going to *mow* the lineup down," he said. To Manny (who later claimed to the press that he had never seen anybody so wild), Dock said,

"Don't even give me no signal. Just try to catch the ball. If you can't catch it, forget it."

Taking his usual warm-up pitches, Dock noticed Pete Rose standing at one side of the batter's box, leaning on his bat, studying his delivery. On his next-to-last warm-up, Dock let fly at Rose and almost hit him.

A distant early warning.

In fact, he had considered not hitting Pete Rose at all. He and Rose are friends, but of course friendship, as the commissioner of baseball would insist, must never prevent even-handed treatment. No, Dock had considered not hitting Pete Rose because Rose would *take it so well*. He predicted that Rose, once hit, would make no acknowledgment of pain—no grimace, no rubbing the afflicted shoulder—but would run at top speed for first base, indicating clearly to his teammates that there was nothing to fear. "He's going to *charge* first base, and make it look like nothing." Having weighed the whole matter, Dock decided to hit him anyway.

It was a pleasant evening in Pittsburgh, the weather beginning to get warmer, perhaps 55 degrees, when Dock threw the first pitch. "The first pitch to Pete Rose was directed toward his head," as Dock expresses it, "not actually to *hit* him," but as "the *message*, to let him know that he was going to get hit. More or less to *press his lips*. I knew if I could get close to the head that I could get them in the body. Because they're looking to protect their head, they'll give me the body." The next pitch was behind him. "The next one, I hit him in the side."

Pete Rose's response was even more devastating than Dock had anticipated. He smiled. Then he picked the ball up, where it had fallen beside him, and gently, underhand, tossed it back to Dock. Then he lit for first as if trying out for the Olympics.

As Dock says, with huge approval, "You have to be *good*, to be a hot dog."

As Rose bent down to pick up the ball, he had exchanged a word with Joe Morgan who was batting next. Morgan and Rose are close friends, called "pepper and salt" by some of the ballplayers. Morgan taunted Rose, "He doesn't like you, anyway. You're a white guy."

Dock hit Morgan in the kidneys with his first pitch.

By this time, both benches were agog. It was Mayday on May Day. The Pirates realized that Dock was doing what he said he would do. The Reds were watching him do it. "I looked over on the bench, they were all with their eyes wide and their mouths wide open, like, 'I don't believe it!'"

"The next batter was Driessen. I threw a ball to him. High inside. The next one, I hit him in the back."

Bases loaded, no outs. Tony Perez, Cincinnati first baseman, came to bat. He did not dig in. "There was no way I could hit him. He was *running*. The first one I threw behind him, over his head, up against the screen, but it came back off the glass, and they didn't advance. I threw behind him because he was backing up, but then he stepped in front of the ball. The next three pitches, he was *running*. . . . I walked him. " A run came in. "The next hitter was Johnny Bench. I tried to deck him twice. I threw at his jaw, and he moved. I threw at the back of his head, and he moved."

With two balls and no strikes on Johnny Bench—eleven pitches gone: three hit batsmen, one walk, one run, and now two balls— Murtaugh approached the mound. "He came out as if to say, 'What's wrong? Can't find the plate?'" Dock was suspicious that his manager really knew what he was doing. "No," said Dock, "I must have Blass-itis." (It was genuine wildness—not throwing at batters—that had destroyed Steve Blass the year before.)

"He looked at me *hard*," Dock remembers. "He said, 'I'm going to bring another guy in.' So I just walked off the mound."

In his May Day experiment, his point was not to hit batters; his point was to kick Cincinnati ass. Pittsburgh was *down*, in last place, lethargic and limp and lifeless. Cincinnati was fighting it out with Los Angeles, confident it would prevail at the end. And for Pittsburgh, Cincinnati was The Enemy.

In 1970, Cincinnati beat Pittsburgh in the Championship Series for the National League pennant. In 1971, with Cincinnati out of it, Pittsburgh took the pennant in a play-off with the Giants, then beat Baltimore in a seven-game Series. In 1972, three months before Roberto Clemente's death, Cincinnati beat Pittsburgh in the Championship Series, three games to two.

"Then," says Dock, "they go on TV and say the Pirates ain't nothing. . . ." Bruce Kison adds, "We got beat fairly in the score, but the way the Cincinnati ball club—the players sitting on the bench—were hollering and yelling at us like Little Leaguers. It left a bad taste in my mouth. I remember that. When I do go against Cincinnati, there's a little advantage."

In the winter of 1973-74, and at spring training, Dock began to feel that the Pirates had lost aggressiveness.

"Spring training had just begun, and I say, 'You are *scared* of Cincinnati.' That's what I told my teammates. 'You are *always* scared of Cincinnati.' I've watched us lose games against Cincinnati and it's *ridiculous*. I've pitched some good games at Cincinnati, but the majority I've lost, because I feel like we weren't aggressive. Every time we play Cincinnati, the hitters are on their *ass*."

"Is that what the players are afraid of?" I asked.

"*Physically* afraid," said Dock. In 1970, '71, and '72, he says, the rest of the league was afraid of the Pirates. "They say, 'Here come the big bad Pirates. They're going to kick our ass!' Like they give up. That's what *our* team was starting to do. When Cincinnati showed up in spring training, I saw all the ballplayers doing the same thing. They were running over, talking, laughing and hee-haw this and that.

"Cincinnati will bullshit with us and kick our ass and laugh at us. They're the only team that talk about us like a dog. *Whenever* we play that team, everybody *socializes* with them." In the past the roles had been reversed. "When *they* ran over to *us*, we knew they were afraid of us. When I saw *our* team doing it, right then I say, 'We gonna get *down*. We gonna *do* the *do*. I'm going to *hit* these motherfuckers.'"

When Dock had announced his intentions, he did not receive total support.

"Several of my teammates told me that they would not be there. When the shit went down, they would not be on the mound. Bob Robertson told me that. It really hurt me. I *believe* he was serious."

"Why?"

"Because this was benefiting him. He wasn't hitting but one oh two. Pitches coming up around his neck."

From time to time a batter who has been hit, or thrown at, will advance on the pitcher, the dugouts will empty, and there will be a baseball fight. Mostly, baseball fights are innocuous. But Dick McAuliffe once dislocated Tommy John's shoulder, and Campy Campaneris threw his bat at Lerrin LaGrow. But Dock thinks and plans. "I talked to other pitchers who have dealt with them on this level, one being Bob Gibson. He hits them at *random*! In fact, Pete Rose and Tommy Helms tried to whip Gibson, and Gibson got in *both* of them's stuff, in the dugout. He just went in and got them."

"I took everything into consideration, when I did what I did. Because I had to figure out who would fight us. Manpower per manpower, it had to be them. That's the *only* team that I could see would really try to *deal* with us. I was thinking of the physical ability of the two teams, and that was the only one that was comparable to us. The only one I could think of that was physically *next* was Philadelphia, and they wouldn't want to fight us. No way would they want to fight us. If I hit twenty of them in a row, they ain't going to fight."

As Pittsburgh endured a dreary April, Dock's resolve intensified. "The team was down. I had to do something for the team. Everybody was complaining about this and that. We weren't winning, and every time I hear someone talk, he's talking about whose ass he's going to kick. On our own team, I mean." The defense was abominable—not just errors, but hits that could have been called errors, like the fly ball that drops in front of an outfielder, or the ground ball that an infielder seems unable to bend over for. Pitching and relief pitching were spotty, hitting streaky, with some of the team's best hitters looking sluggish and halfhearted. "So I said, 'I'm tired of hearing you talk of how *bad* everybody is. We're going to get the shit *on.*'"

One of the troubles with Pirate hitting was *fear;* batters were standing away from the plate; opposition pitchers were dusting them, moving them back, and then suckering them with balls on the outside corners. "My hitters weren't aggressive at the plate," Dock says. And a hitter would complain, "My pitcher wasn't protecting me," since retaliation is the best defense.

The game before Dock started against Cincinnati, a Houston relief pitcher hit Wilver Stargell on the head. If Dock needed fuel for his fire, this was sufficient. "They hit Willie in the head!" Willie Stargell and Dock were two of the tightest players on the club. "Houston had hit him on the head last year, and whether it was intentional or not, they hit him in the head again this year. And the next time I was to pitch was Cincinnati, and I had said *before* that I was going to get Cincinnati anyway, so everything more or less fell into line. I *could* have picked out the team that hit him on the head, but I took my anger out on the team that I felt *our* team was afraid of.

"Because now you had the team from the Western Division which was the champs, and the team from the Eastern Division which *should've* been the champs—both of them physically supposed to be strong, and on the field strengthwise as far as hitting goes. In the clubhouse I say, 'Well, we going to whip some ass.' It was a message I was trying to convey, to other teams throughout the league, to *leave my hitters alone.*" It was also a message Dock intended for the Pittsburgh Pirates.

Dave Meggyesy

OUT OF THEIR LEAGUE

In 1971, St. Louis Cardinal linebacker Dave Meggyesy wrote what was characterized by reviewers as "the harshest book yet written about sports in America." Out of Their League—which Meggyesy had to leave the game to write—is a startling document, when read against the backdrop of our own era of highly packaged and polished media. This passionate self-portrait of one player's love/hate relationship with professional football is a time capsule from the days when "The Sixties" was still very real, rather than just another television movie.

Chapter 13

We hadn't been in St. Louis more than a few weeks when Stacy was invited to a party for the players' wives at the home of Judy Randle whose husband, Sonny, was the Cardinals' all-pro split end. Stacy was nervous about going, and just after she arrived, she noticed that none of the black players' wives were there. When she asked Judy Randle why this was so, she got icy silence as an answer; and since she feared it might cause some problems for me, she decided not to press the point. But the other wives stayed away from Stacy for the rest of the party and when she got home, I could see she was upset. We talked about it, but I was not able to shed any light on the problem.

Stacy went to another wives' party a few weeks later, this time given by Joan Koman. Her husband, Bill, the starting right linebacker, was the person who had told me during training camp that I had a good chance to make the club because my competition was "two dumb nigger linebackers who are so stupid they have trouble tying their shoes." I'd told Stacy about this, so she didn't expect to find any black wives at the party, but she once again asked the hostess why this was so. Unlike Judy Randle, Joan responded with a curt, "They weren't invited." Stacy then asked, "Well, why not?" "They have their own things to do," Joan responded. "How do you know?" Stacy asked, pressing the point. "Have you asked them?" Joan answered with an emphatic "No" and walked away. Stacy did not attend another wives' party until five years later when Dee Ann Wilson—wife of Larry, the Cardinals' famous all-pro safety—had a party to which she invited all the players' wives, black and white.

My 30-day waiver period ended after the second regular season game, and, since no one had picked me up, I was formally put on the Cardinals' cab squad. All this waiver business meant little to me. I was getting my regular salary and practicing regularly with the team. The only restriction was that I couldn't suit up for the games. One of my jobs as a cab squad member was to allow two rookie linemen, Sam Silas and Bob Reynolds, to practice their blocking techniques on me. About three nights a week Ray Prochaska, the offensive line coach, would have us stay out after regular practice ended. At the time, I weighed 215 pounds while Silas and Reynolds were both about 260. Under Prochaska's direction, we'd line up eye to eye and tear into each other. Night after night we'd battle to a stand-off. To avoid being annihilated by these guys, I would work myself up to a fanatical pitch, and while we went at it like animals in a pit, Prochaska would stand there grinning. There's nothing football coaches love more than to watch two guys really pounding the shit out of each other. Some nights when we'd really get going at it, Prochaska would signal for head coach Wally Lemm to come over and watch the fun.

In the eighth game of the season, Ed Henke severely injured his elbow and was placed on the injured waiver list, so I took his spot on the active roster. My first pro game was to be against the Browns in Cleveland—the team I'd watched regularly in high school and whose star, Jim Brown, had once been my model. I didn't play in any scrimmage plays in Cleveland, but I was on all the bomb squads. On the opening kickoff, my assignment was to block Lou Groza, the Browns' ageless kicker. It was like blocking a myth: as I stood there watching him place the ball on the kicking tee, I thought of the time six years before, when I was a junior at Solon High and Groza had come down from Cleveland to give the feature address at our football banquet. He was an established NFL star then and now he was still going strong. It was my first game in the NFL, and I was intent on knocking him on his ass—yet I felt very uncomfortable about it. Groza put the ball in the air and came lumbering down the field. My football fanaticism took over and I really gave him a shot. As I trotted off the field, I was feeling a little guilty, but I also knew my block would look good in the game films.

John Brown, one of Cleveland's offensive linemen, had been one of my teammates at Syracuse. On one fourth down, when Cleveland was preparing to punt, I was lined up across from Brown, whose nickname at Syracuse had been "Big Daddy." As we were both getting down in our stances, I said, smiling, "Hi there, Big Daddy, how're you doing?" John seemed surprised to hear anybody break the taboo and address him in a friendly manner on the field. He glanced up and I could see the look of recognition on his face, but he said nothing. Then we smashed into each other on the snap of the ball.

I finished out the season on the bomb squads and felt I had a good year. Every Tuesday during the viewing of the game films, I would invariably get a number of "good jobs" and "good hustles" from Wally. When I'd come home from practice on Tuesday nights, Stacy would always jokingly ask me, "How many 'good jobs' and 'good hustles' did you get today?". . .

As soon as the season ended, I got a job as a medical research assistant working for Doctors Armand Broduer and Leonard Fagan at Cardinal Glennon Memorial Hospital for Children in St. Louis. I worked at the hospital weekday mornings and took pre-med courses at Washington University in the afternoons. I was still planning to enroll in medical school after a few years in the league. Working at the hospital affected me deeply, especially seeing the dedication and commitment of the medical staff—particularly the two men I worked for. By choosing to be medical researchers, both Fagan and Broduer had given up the opportunity to earn easily four to five times as much as they were making. The other thing that left a lasting impression on me was watching the poor women who would come into the free clinic and wait, many times four to six hours, to get medical treatment for their sick children. I couldn't help but realize the perversity of spending thousands of dollars on a football player with a sprained ankle while many poor kids were not getting adequate medical care.

During the off season, one or two evenings a week I would go out on the speakers' circuit organized by the Falstaff Brewing Corporation, at that time a large stockholder in the Cardinals. They would set up speaking engagements for the Cardinal players who lived in the St. Louis area, paying us $35 a night and supplying us with a movie projector and a Cardinal highlight film with a few Falstaff Beer ads spliced into the action. We would usually speak before such groups as the Rotary, or the Lions Club, high school sports banquets, and Boy Scout functions. It was clear what these people wanted to hear from me and the other players. I wasn't only to be a professional football player talking about my craft, but—especially when youngsters were present—I was supposed to give an inspiring talk about sports, patriotism and mental hygiene. I had the spiel down pretty well. I had never been taught it, but it is next to impossible to play football without it becoming part of you. I told the kids they should always obey and respect their coaches and parents and to study and work hard. "Football is just like life," I would explain, "those of you who work the hardest and are the most dedicated will be the most successful. The competitiveness of football is excellent preparation for the competition of life." I would conclude by emphasizing that playing football would develop in them the right values and attitudes.

Even then, I only half believed it myself, and it wasn't too long before I saw it was absolute bullshit.

Chapter 14

Because I had recaptured some of my enthusiasm for football, my first year as a pro was in many ways very much like my sophomore year at Syracuse. But just as under-the-table payments there had started a process of disillusionment with college football, so Commissioner Pete Rozelle's decision to play the regularly scheduled games while the country was in mourning for President John Kennedy began to disillusion me with the pros. It also led me to think about the role football was beginning to play in the national imagination.

Like everyone else, I remember precisely where I was when Kennedy was killed. I was on my way to a meeting of defensive players at the old Country Day School where the Cardinals practiced during the regular season. Bill Simmons, our equipment man, had his radio on and I heard the first flash announcement that the President had been shot, but it was not until after practice that I found out he was dead. As the country went into mourning, there was suddenly a lot of discussion about whether or not the NFL would play their regularly scheduled football games. But the conclusion was never in doubt. The Cardinals, like all the other NFL teams I knew of, continued to practice, fully expecting to play our regularly scheduled game against the Giants in New York that weekend. Amidst all the gossip about possible cancellation of the games, Commissioner Rozelle issued a statement on Saturday saying the Sunday games would be played.

When we arrived in New York I was certainly in no mood to play football, and agreed with many of the other players that the game should be postponed. Many of the guys were pissed; they knew it wouldn't have been hard to extend the season for one more week as a gesture of respect But what was most galling was Rozelle's justification for his decision: "It has been traditional in sports for athletes to perform in times of great personal tragedy. Football was Mr. Kennedy's game. He thrived on competition."

During the pre-game meal that Sunday, many of the guys were openly talking about refusing to suit up. But they were afraid of reprisals—getting fined or possibly being banned from the league. So we wound up warming up for the game on a cold, blustery New York City day. Then we went back into the locker room and said a prayer led by Prentice Gautt. After a moment of silence for the dead President, we trooped out through the tunnel in Yankee Stadium, through the dugout and lined up for the National Anthem.

The players were pretty bitchy and they couldn't get with it. The fans too were listless at first, the quietest fans I'd ever heard anywhere. But I realized the power of football that day, for within a few minutes of opening kickoff they had forgotten the national tragedy and were yelling their heads off. It was frightening as hell.

Near the end of the season, Jack Drees, a CBS sportscaster, spoke about Rozelle's decision at the St. Louis Quarterbacks Club annual dinner, when awards are given to the football team. He said he felt that playing out the NFL football games that weekend provided a cohesive force, binding the country together when there were many doubts about our internal and international security. He thought the country had been rapidly disintegrating and that football and the NFL had met the challenge to pull the country together.

Drees was, in a manner of speaking, correct. And if I'd known then a fraction of what I know now, I wouldn't have been either shocked or surprised by the talk that led up to a business-as-usual for the league. There is, of course, a simple economic explanation for keeping to the schedule: various owners would have lost their huge profits from gate receipts if they had postponed games, and I imagine CBS, which had a contract with the league, exerted tremendous pressure to stick to normal procedures.

This whole dialogue suggested a deeper connection between football and our society that I would become aware of later on when I became involved in the anti-war movement. By then it would be impossible for me not to see football as both a reflection and reinforcement of the worst things in American culture. There was the incredible racism which I was to see close up in the Cardinals organization and throughout the league. There was also the violence and sadism, not so much on the part of the players or in the game itself, but very much in the minds of the beholders—the millions of Americans who watch football every weekend in something approaching a sexual frenzy. And then there was the whole militaristic aura surrounding pro football, not only in obvious things like football stars visiting troops in Vietnam, but in the language of the game—"throwing the bomb," being a "field general," etc., and in the unthinking obligation to "duty" required of the players. In short, the game has been wrapped in red, white and blue. It is no accident that some of the most maudlin and dangerous pre-game "patriotism" we see in this country appears in football stadiums. . . .

✢ ✢ ✢

Chapter 17

During the off-season after my second year, my biggest worry in terms of football was Dave Simmons, a linebacker from Georgia Tech, who was the Cardinals' number two draft choice and was slated to be Dale Meinert's back-up. I felt the Cardinals would now surely trade me, and I hoped it would be soon. With the competitive bidding between the AFL and the NFL, I knew Simmons would surely receive a multi-year no-cut contract, and that if I wasn't traded, I'd have a hell of a time making the team because the four veteran linebackers, Larry Stallings, Dale Meinert, Marion Rushing and Bill Koman were sure to stay.

By the opening of training camp in 1965, my fortunes looked very bleak. My contract was for $12,000—a $2,500 raise which I considered significant, although not particularly generous considering the fact that I had come so cheaply during my first two years. I started out fast because I was in my usual good shape and I came to camp a super-hustler and fanatic football player. Dave Simmons was down in Evanston at the All-Star training camp and would not report to the Cardinals until after the first week of August, which gave me almost three weeks to establish myself as the number two middle linebacker.

At the last team meeting before our first exhibition game in St. Louis, while Wally was going over the details for the game, it occurred to him that this would be our first home visit in five weeks. We were scheduled to arrive in St. Louis about noon the day of the game but we didn't play until eight that night and Wally justifiably suspected that many of us would be jumping in the sack with our wives that afternoon. He was concerned that this pregame action would sap our energy and keep us from playing good football and was pissed off that the schedule had put him and us in this predicament. So, at the end of the meeting, he launched into an impassioned speech about how we were playing in St. Louis for the first time since last season and had to look good for the home town folks. Working his way to the climax of the speech, Wally concluded, "Now guys, I know you're going to St. Louis. I know you haven't seen your families in a long time and I know you haven't seen your wives for a long time. But for godsakes guys, when you get home this afternoon, please use your heads." This literally broke up the whole meeting. Guys just doubled over in their chairs laughing. Wally, his face red, dismissed us quickly.

Throughout training until ten days before our last exhibition game up at Green Bay, Dave Simmons was playing defensive end instead of linebacker and hating every minute of it. He not only hated it, but he was doing horseshit. Dave was a great athlete but, as he admitted, one of the things he hated most was getting down into a three-point stance. He became the kind of athlete who played only at the level needed to survive in the league. He wasn't a hustling ball player, and like any other sane person, he didn't particularly like to

293

hit or be hit. But as the pro football cliché goes, "A player has got to want to love to hit."

. . .I got a chance to start in the game against Cleveland which at that time had the greatest running back in the league, Jim Brown. I was getting psyched up all week for him, as were all members of the Cardinal defense. I knew a lot of people who had followed my career at Solon High School and at Syracuse would be at this game, and for awhile I held my own. One of Brown's favorite plays was a sweep to the strong side of the formation. On this particular play, the tight end would "tailor-block" the linebacker—that is, he would come out of his stance slowly and attempt to get the linebacker to commit himself either to the inside or the outside; once the linebacker started to move, the tight end would block him, and the pulling guards would then take the play either inside or outside the tight end's block. This kind of play developed one time and I got hold of John Brewer, the Browns' tight end. Instead of committing myself, I wanted to string Brewer down along the line of scrimmage, making the guards take the play outside, where the cornerback could handle it. On this particular play I could see Brown with the ball about even with Brewer and me. Suddenly Brown came flying up the field straight at my inside. I slipped Brewer's block and lunged for Brown, hitting him with my helmet and shoulders. I felt like I'd grabbed hold of a steel telephone pole charged with 220 volts. Brown ran over me, hitting me so hard I was looking out the earhole of my helmet with my nose mashed against the side of my face when the play was over. I had a hell of a time twisting my helmet around straight. . . .

During the second quarter we had a blitz on. As I was flying into the Cleveland backfield, I saw that Brown was the guy I'd have to run over to get to Frank Ryan, Cleveland's quarterback. I had been under the illusion, probably from reading the newspapers and listening to league gossip, that Brown was not a good blocker. (Actually, in the game films we saw, Brown did little blocking, most of the time swinging out to the flat as a safety valve.) As I went in toward Ryan, revenge was on my mind for the way Brown had almost kicked my head in on that sweep. I was thinking, "I'm going to really drill him and test the son of a bitch." As I hit him with everything I had, Brown moved backwards about six inches and I watched stars from the blow of his forearm.

Later on in the quarter, Dale Meinert, our middle linebacker, again called the same blitz. As a linebacker, you can attempt to put a move on the back assigned to you, faking him and getting ahold of him with your hands, instead of trying to run over him. Since I had tried to drill Brown on the previous blitz, I had him partially set up for a fake. As I was flying in the second time I lowered my shoulder as if to try and run over him again, and then grabbed him by the shoulder pads and spun him around. Much to my amazement, I got by him, and although slightly out of the play, I managed to get a piece of Ryan along with Chuck Walker and Don Brumm.

During the '66 season we were playing Cleveland at Cleveland and we had put in a special blitz where the right outside linebacker, instead of shooting straight in from his position, would swing around the defensive tackle and end on his side and come flying up the middle. During the game Dale Meinert had called this blitz and Bill Koman was going full speed when he hit the hole in the middle of the line, eyes closed and arms pumping. Bill was about two yards in the backfield when Brown slipped up—out of nowhere it seemed—and unloaded his right forearm into Koman's head. Bill stopped dead in his tracks, sliding down in front of Brown like a steer whose head had been slammed by a sledge hammer at a slaughterhouse.

Much of the talk about Brown's inability to block was racist in nature, coming from people who knew they couldn't say anything about his ability as a ball-carrier. But those, like Bill Koman, who ran into Brown, quickly found out how wrong they were.

✛ ✛ ✛

DAVE MEGGYESY

Chapter 19

As the 1966 season progressed, I began to play a fair amount, mainly on second and third downs when the coaches saw a sure passing situation. They knew I could cover halfbacks flaring out of the backfield and play pass defense much better than Bill Koman could because of my speed. During the season I played about 40 per cent of the defensive plays for the Cardinals.

When the season was over I returned to my graduate studies at Washington University, switching to the Department of Sociology. I continued my political work and became increasingly involved in the anti-war movement. In April of 1967, I attended the big peace march in New York with over 300,000 other people. A few weeks after I returned, I received a post card from Rick Sortun, saying he had driven down from Seattle to San Francisco to attend the companion peace rally held in Kezar Stadium.

About this time a good friend of mine, a student, stopped by our house on his way to his home in New York City and proceeded to introduce me to the business of smoking marijuana. I thoroughly enjoyed it. Later that spring my brother Dennis came out from Ohio. He was deep into psychedelics and brought an ample supply with him. One beautiful spring evening in St. Louis, I dropped my first tab of acid. It was exhilarating. Dennis stayed with me for about a week, and we dropped acid a couple of more times. During that same week, I gave a couple of Falstaff speeches. The contradiction between where my head was at while I was experimenting with acid and the location of the collective head of one of the St. Louis neighborhood Lion's Clubs was a real mindblower.

Although I was becoming more conscious politically, I hadn't yet fully understood football as a political phenomenon, or the way it resembled a circus for the increasingly chaotic American empire. But I was feeling my way in that direction. Dr. Horowitz, my advisor at Washington U., was helping me to rewrite my senior thesis on football because he felt it could be suitable for publication in *Trans-Action*. Meanwhile, Jim Gillespie, a friend who was studying at

from OUT OF THEIR LEAGUE

Southern Illinois University in Edwardsville, Illinois, invited me to speak about the war at two meetings he had set up with some fraternities and sororities on his campus. Southern Illinois is located in what might be called the heart of Middle America. Its students come from nearby small towns, and although the sons and daughters of this conservatism were stunned to hear a professional ball player criticize our involvement in Vietnam, they nevertheless listened to what I had to say.

About three weeks later, "Stormy" Bidwell, the Cardinals president, called me and asked me to meet him at his office at the stadium concerning something he refused to discuss over the phone. When I went to see him, he said he'd received some letters from people around SIU at Edwardsville who were quite irate, and he wanted to know what anti-war groups I belonged to. I told him I'd appeared as a private citizen, not as a representative of the football Cardinals or of any specific political group. He was most concerned about my being a member of SDS. I told him that, although many of my friends in the movement were members of SDS, I was not. Stormy said he respected my right to protest the war but he warned me various groups would try to use my name because I was a professional player. We parted without animosity, although this was by no means the last I would hear of the matter.

Life as a football player makes one a victim of enforced schizophrenia. I was a football star half the year and another person for the rest, and I could not give myself completely to either identity. After my sophomore year at Syracuse, I'd quickly recognized that in order to grow emotionally and intellectually, I would have to divorce myself as much as possible from the "football mentality." I realized that spending time on the football field earned me a scholarship, and that this scholarship had to be the most important thing to me during my years at Syracuse. This is not to say I was immune to the football ethic; on the contrary, football gave me my identity, such as it was. Before I could quit playing football I had to learn what it was to be an individual. This won't seem very

297

momentous to people who have grown up outside the world of athletics. But for a jock, becoming somebody real, getting involved in life off the playing field, is a significant problem. I imagine that in some small way it resembles what a priest who has always lived in a cloister must feel after he goes out, gets married, and tries to go on from there.

Early in July, 1967, Stacy and I bought an old funky townhouse in St. Louis. My two younger brothers, Dennis and Joe, came to help us move, and when we were done Dennis informed me he had some acid. He and Stacy had decided to take some and he asked if I would too. I thought about it for five minutes, but finally declined. Making the down payment on the house had left us almost broke, and I had to make the football team in order to make myself solvent. Training camp was only about week away, and I felt that taking the acid might diminish the football psych I'd been working to get up since the middle of May.

Because the Cardinals led the league in defense in 1966 and because I'd played well at linebacker, I received a $21,000 contract for 1967. Larry Stallings, our regular left linebacker, had been called into the Army to fulfill his ROTC commitment, and I expected to play regularly. But other things were on my mind. I felt guilty about spending my time playing football, and for the first time, I was not mentally prepared for training camp. I was losing the will to hit and this distressed me. In some ways I thought of myself—to quote Dylan—as "a pawn in their game." Yet, despite my strong feeling that I should step up my political activities and move farther away from football, the game was my only source of income. There was another complication: if I completed the '67 season, I would become a five-year man entitled to the benefits of the pension plan available to all vested NFL players. . . .

Chapter 20

In 1967, the racial tension that I'd seen simmering for years on the

Cardinals finally reached the boiling point. What I saw around the locker room made me expect a race war at any moment.

I was first introduced to racism on the team, as I've said, in my rookie year, 1962; room assignment, wings of the dormitory, and the dining hall were all segregated. In the half hour between the end of practice and dinner, all the white ball players would head up to the town's only bar, the Lantern. I never saw a black football player in the Lantern at any time during my first five years with the team. The Cardinals had a strong southern clique, out and out rednecks who were the team leaders, including such guys as Sonny Randle, Bill Koman, Irv Goode, Joe Robb, Don Owens, and Ken Gray. Robb and Koman were the most vitriolic. Long before things came to the surface in 1967, Koman would continually tell me and anyone who'd listen that niggers were generally too dumb to play pro football, that pro clubs were giving niggers a break by having them around, etc.

Racism was not a matter of individual quirks in the St. Louis organization; it was part of the institution. For example, during my first six years with the Cardinals, the Falstaff Brewing Corporation gave parties for the players at Falstaff Inn. The Inn was two fairly large rooms separated by a large archway. One of the big surprises of my first year was the discovery that almost no blacks attended these parties, although Falstaff provided a free meal and all the beer you could drink after the games. When the blacks did begin to attend over the next few years, the squad usually broke up so the whites were in one room and the blacks in another.

Flying to the Dallas game in 1964, rookie Willis Crenshaw was sitting in the back of the plane with an empty seat next to him. Occasionally one of the stewardesses would sit down in the empty seat next to Willis. They talked casually throughout the flight. Sitting four rows in front of them were Joe Robb and Bill Koman. Koman began to turn around and stare at Willis nudging Joe Robb to bring this "affair" to his attention. Our plane landed in Dallas and all the players and coaches were standing in a group in the Dallas Airport lobby waiting for the team buses. In front of the entire group, Robb singled out Willis and began chewing him out for trying to date white girls. I was standing halfway across the lobby, heard the noise and came over. "If I was you, I wouldn't try to make a white girl in front of the team. You are in Texas now," Robb was almost shouting. Robb berated him for a few more minutes and eventually walked away. Throughout Robb's tirade, Wally Lemm and his entire coaching staff did nothing.

Blacks who "knew their place" on the Cardinals were generally not harassed. This group was labeled "the decent niggers." Bill Koman told me that, "Prentice Gautt is the only really decent nigger on the Cardinals, and I might even have him out to my house for dinner." Even so, Koman, a church-going Catholic, couldn't accept the sincerity of Gautt's religious beliefs. Gautt, an active member of the Fellowship of Christian Athletes, was nick-named "Elmer Gantry" by Koman.

Black ball players are selected even more stringently on the basis of "correct attitude" than whites. Blacks are in an especially difficult position; if they act like Toms, they will be completely dominated by the white ball players and lose respect for themselves and each other. But if they are too "militant" and try to assert their basic manhood by attempting to break out of the whites' stereotype of the shuffling, dumb, insensitive jock, they are immediately under suspicion and often cut from the squad.

Ed McQuarters, a defensive tackle from Oklahoma, was perhaps the best example of this dilemma. Ed was one of the quickest defensive linemen I have ever seen anywhere in football. But Charlie Winner said he felt McQuarters didn't have the correct attitude on the field. Actually, McQuarters' attitude was beautiful: he refused to take any shit from the whites. He carried himself with great dignity and certainly had the respect of his black teammates. Ed refused to smile at the cracks about black football players which were customary in training camp—white ball players talking about blacks' inherent ability to run fast or their congenital insensitivity to pain. In my opinion, and in the opinion of many other veterans, McQuarters would have been a great defensive tackle in the National Football League. But because he refused to demean himself, Winner cut him from the squad. When Ed was in camp, the coaches' complaints had nothing to do with his ability as a player, but with his aloofness and his inability to "laugh and joke along with the other players."

. . .One night in the spring of 1967, I arrived home after making a Falstaff speech and Stacy told me a guy by the name of Jack Olsen from *Sports Illustrated* had called and wanted me to return his call as soon as I could. I returned his call at his hotel in downtown St. Louis, and he asked if I could talk to him that evening.

I met Olsen around 10 o'clock that night. He was then doing research for his five part series on the black athlete and wanted to interview various Cardinal players about the racial situation which had flared briefly into the press at the close of the previous season. We established rapport immediately. Within five minutes, he was telling me about a phone conversation with Bill Koman. He said Koman was one of the worst racists he had ever talked to. "You wouldn't believe what that guy told me," he said. "I was down at El Paso, Texas, and the coaches and the townspeople down there were not as bad as Koman." We sat down with Olsen's tape recorder and rapped about the racial situation on the Cardinals for over two hours. I told him about the unconscious racism of the coaches and about the practice throughout the NFL of letting blacks play only in certain positions. (Very few blacks hold positions which are popularly thought to require a great deal of intelligence rather than a great deal of strength—such as linebacker, offensive guard and quarterback.) In our talk, I helped Olsen develop his thesis about the prevalence of stacking and racism throughout the National Football League. I was pleased to see that much of the information used in the last two parts of Olsen's series came from the football file I had accumulated since my senior year at Syracuse.

. . .Near the end of the 1967 season, these tensions had become so intense that there was almost no communication between black and white ball players. It was a miracle we weren't forced to field two separate teams. The black players met secretly and drew up a list of grievances that had their unanimous support. These were presented to Charley Winner at the end of the season, and the next spring he called a meeting of all the players in St. Louis to discuss the racial situation. I was afraid Winner only wanted information about various players' attitudes, so I declined to go. I had been through these phony soul-searching sessions, and I knew that when the coaches were there, very little ever got said because each man feared that a misplaced phrase might mean disfavor.

News of this action by the Cardinals' blacks appeared—very briefly—in the St. Louis papers. The club made no formal statement, but the rumors were rampant, mainly that the blacks had pointed to a certain racist coach. After that season, three assistant coaches left the football Cardinals one by one, and each time rumors flew that this was the racist coach. Jack Olsen's article, however, revealed that the man the black players had in mind was Chuck Drulis. Even so, Head Coach Winner—the only coach with the authority to correct the situation—did nothing until the racism on the Cardinals was revealed publicly. . . .

During my last few seasons, a few black ball players got together for what they call "sets." This consisted of a mass sex scene at one of the player's apartments with several prostitutes, beginning immediately after practice and extending well into the night. These scenes were not unlike those organized by a prominent white player each year after the Cardinals broke training camp following the Chicago Bears game. He too would hire prostitutes and invite Cardinal ball players to "work out" in front of certain of his business associates in St. Louis who were excited by the spectacle.

Even in its orgies, the Cardinals team was Jim Crow all the way.

✤ ✤ ✤

Chapter 22

About two weeks before the end of the '67 season Bernie Parrish had asked Jim Bakken, our player representative in the National Football League Players' Association, to call a meeting at one of the motels in St. Louis. That night Parrish and Harold Gibbons, vice-president of the International Brotherhood of Teamsters, gave a presentation favoring a union—the American Federation of Professional Athletes—that Bernie was attempting to form with the Teamsters.

Bernie Parrish began pro ball with the Cleveland Browns in 1959 and had been nominated as an all-pro and played in the Pro Bowl game. After seven years, he wanted to leave the Browns. He asked to be released outright, rather than being put on waivers, because he knew Atlanta, starting its first year in the league, would pick him up. Parrish felt he had contributed much to the Browns' success and wanted to play for another NFL team other than the Falcons, but prior to the opening game of the 1966 season, Bernie Parrish was waived out of the league. It was unusual, to say the least, that not one club was interested in an all-pro defensive back at the peak of his career with seven years experience.

As an officer in the Players' Association, Bernie had begun to look into the financial condition of the National Football League. After 13 months of research, he had come up with some startling facts showing that the athletes were incredibly exploited. He decided the first step was to get rid of the fiction that the Players' Association—a sort of company union—had any leverage, and he approached AFTRA and the Screen Actors Guild before finally contacting Harold Gibbons of the Teamsters. Parrish and Gibbons then entered into an agreement to begin organizing all professional athletes in one pro players' union. Parrish's first concern was football players, but because he didn't want to be accused of upsetting players at the start of the season, he waited until mid-season to begin contacting clubs, and even then chose only those teams with absolutely no possibility of winning the championship.

DAVE MEGGYESY

When Parrish and Gibbons met with members of the Cardinals, they brought out some rather startling facts. Perhaps the most amazing statistic was this: during the period 1956-1967, the profits of the National Football League owners had increased 4,300 per cent but the player salaries had gone up only 73.6 per cent. If you subtract rises in the cost of living during those years, our actual salary increases amounted to only 48.4 per cent.

Gibbons outlined the relationship between the Teamsters and the new Association, and he emphasized that the players would not be tied directly to the Teamsters. At the close of the meeting, he passed out authorization cards and applications for membership in the American Federation of Professional Athletes. About 15 of the 20 guys there signed the cards. By the end of the season Parrish had seen all but five clubs in the National Football League and had authorization cards from more than 30 per cent of the players in the league.

At the annual Players' Association meeting, held during the first week of January 1968 in Miami (before the Runner-Up bowl game between Los Angeles and Cleveland), it was clear there was going to be a tremendous fight between certain interests in the Players' Association and the Parrish-Gibbons team. The issue was simply whether the Players' Association could conceptualize itself as a union and enter into collective bargaining with the league, or whether it was merely an association, as Norm Van Brocklin put it, to "enhance communication between the players and the owners."

Gibbons and Parrish had a debate with Clayton Miller, the Players' Association attorney, in the presence of the Los Angeles Rams and many of the player representatives from other NFL clubs. Miller was eventually so embarrassed in the confrontation that he got up and walked out in the middle of the meeting. The LA players were shocked and many were hollering at him, "Wait a minute, you can't walk out, you're our attorney." The following day a majority of the players' representatives who had seen this asked Miller to resign, which he did. That same day, Dan Schulman, a good friend of Players' Association President Mike Pyle, was hired as the new attorney.

304

from OUT OF THEIR LEAGUE

Later that afternoon, the owners recognized the National Football League Players' Association as collective bargaining agents for the players in the NFL. Because of Parrish, the Players' Association was forced to take a militant stand. And the owners, fearing that the players would vote to affiliate with the Teamsters, agreed to bargain for the first time. It was the pressure that Parrish and Gibbons generated that forced the owners into collective bargaining with the Players' Association. Up until this time, the owners had adamantly stated that they would never enter into collective bargaining negotiations with the players.

Those players who opposed the Gibbons-Parrish unionization plan based their argument on the claim that they were not workers. Players like Jim Bakken felt that we should conceive of ourselves as professionals, and that it would have been degrading to be unionized. It's strange: pro ball players will allow their coaches to totally dominate their lives even to the extent of telling them when they have to go to sleep, but they still claim to be professionals. The workers that ball players look down their noses at don't take that kind of shit from the bosses. For that matter, even college co-eds have organized and rebelled against bedtime restrictions. . . .

It was good to see John Mackey's outspoken leadership during the 1970 players' strike, but it's depressing that the players' primary concern was just for money. While it is true the players are being ripped off compared to the enormous profits most owners are making, in reality the ball players are being paid pretty damn well for six months work. What is wrong with professional football is not that the players are not getting a decent wage, but the dehumanizing conditions they are required to work under. Players are naive to expect sportswriters or the public to support their demands for more money; however, there are many who could actively support them if they struggled to be treated as grown men. What is needed is a strong union, for it is obvious that the Players' Association—even after its hollow 1970 contract "victory"—does not have sufficient strength or political savvy to challenge the owners' total control over the players' lives and identity. Every player is aware of the racism that exists throughout the league, yet the Players' Association never forces the owners to correct this situation, or at least honestly admit that it exists. The Association was heading in the right direction, however, when it identified and challenged Rozelle as the owners' agent. When Rozelle regularly involves himself in scrutinizing players' off-the-field activities but fails regularly to do the same for the owners, there should be no question about who owns him. If any more proof is needed, it should be recognized that the owners, not the players, can have him fired.

No matter how much ball players like to picture themselves as professionals, they are still workers who can be fired, traded, or black-balled out of professional football at the whim of an owner; workers who make good money but are subjected to incredible psychological conditions. In their desire for greater profits, owners will do whatever is necessary, regardless of the effect it may have on individual ball players. Perhaps some day professional ball players will realize that there could quite easily be professional football without owners, who are the only irrelevant party to the sport. It was amazing to me that during the 1970 Players' Association strike, no one suggested the Players' Association conduct the regular season games itself. The Association could have negotiated a TV contract, rented stadiums and played the games. Among other things, cutting out the owners' tremendous profits would allow the players to still get adequate salaries, while at the same time allowing for a drastic reduction in the price the fans must pay for tickets.

Chapter 23
In the spring of '68 I returned to my graduate studies at Washington University. I was still working on my study of football, but my community organizing had increased so much I was spending almost all my time working in the movement in St. Louis. In April '68 the local SDS held a regional meeting. After gathering initially on the campus,

the meeting adjourned to my house for discussion groups. There were probably about 150 people milling around inside, in the front of, in the back of, and on the side of my house. The neighbors seeing all the wild-looking longhairs were really getting uptight. At one point, I went upstairs in search of my daughter Jennifer, thinking she was in my son Chris' bedroom. When I turned the knob and tried to go into the room, I met surprisingly strong resistance. I managed to open the door a crack and poke my head in and there, under clouds of blue cigarette smoke, sat about 25 women in heated discussion. The talk stopped and all eyes focused on me. I was informed that this was a caucus of Women's Liberation and that I could go now. . . .

I had been going through some changes—feeling extremely guilty about my $25,000 house, worrying that I was contributing too little to the movement and thinking that my life had little meaning. I was getting ready to make a major decision about football when, in February 1968, my third child, Sarah, was born. She was a severe microcephalic—a condition which will require custodial care all her life. Placing her in a private home cost over $3,500 a year and so I felt more trapped than ever and with no chance of resolving the contradiction in my life. I needed money but had no prospects other than football. I resigned myself to going back again.

That spring my house was constantly filled with movement people. It was large and comfortable, and an ideal central meeting place. But Stacy, who was under great emotional strain because of Sarah, soon had to field 25 calls a day and I began to feel that old need to isolate myself from a reality that greatly threatened my desire to play football. So, on May 1st, I decided to drop out: I changed my phone number, stopped going to meetings and stopped having them at my home. I lived as a recluse trying to get my football psych back, going outdoors only to work out. . . .

I went to training camp in 1968 without having agreed on a contract. This was also the first year I went in with the veterans instead of going in early with the rookies. The linebacker coach, Don Shroyer, had a meeting the evening we arrived in training camp following Charley Winner's general meeting. I waited around until all the guys had left and asked Don point blank what the Cardinals planned for me. He informed me that he wasn't sure where I fit in with the Cardinals' plans. I was stunned and outraged. I immediately went up to Coach Winner's office. He could see I was really pissed and admitted I'd be fighting it out with three other guys for the swing spot behind Stallings and Ernie Clark, who had come to the Cards in exchange for Joe Robb. I left the meeting in almost tearful rage. I couldn't believe the Cardinals had done this to me. I had played for five years behind Koman and done a credible job. When he retired, I expected at least to be given the opportunity to handle the starting position.

Coming off a fairly hectic off-season of political organizing combined with Sarah's birth and the business of facing the ugly reality that football was now inextricably a part of my life, Winner's news really blew my mind. Everything seemed to be going against me, and I felt the Cardinals were only keeping me around because they needed an experienced back-up man for Larry Stallings, whose Army obligation wasn't over. My response was to stop worrying about whether or not I was going to make it. I reckoned that one of my problems in earlier years was continually worrying about gaining the coaches' approval. And for the first time I just went out and worked—with my usual fanaticism but without thinking too much of how the coaches assessed my performance.

I was really at odds with my world, and the irony was that football gave my life structure. At times, I felt I was really flipping out, and that I'd be in the loony bin if it wasn't for the simple regularity of training camp. I could always depend on how practices would go and how stable the football routine was. It was the only time I was ever grateful for the game's authoritarianism.

Three days before the fifth part of Jack Olsen's "The Black Athlete: A Shameful Story" hit the newsstands, an advance copy was sent to the Cardinals because it dealt solely with the racism in their organization. At the eight o'clock meeting that evening, Charley

Winner passed out Xerox copies of Olsen's piece, told us to read it and then be back in the meeting room by nine o'clock to discuss what it said. When I returned, I found the coaching staff, owners and the entire squad there. The Cardinal organization naively believed the players would let their hair down and openly discuss the contents of Olsen's article in front of the owners and coaches. The assumption was that we were one big happy family of professional football players and could freely discuss the exceedingly volatile contents of Olsen's article.

Winner's opening speech went something like this: "You know newspapers and magazines always need to find something, some bit of information that they can sensationalize." He said flatly that the problems pointed out in Olsen's piece did not exist and that *Sports Illustrated* had exaggerated a few minor points of normal player friction only to sell more copies. Mike Strofolino immediately got up and seconded Winner with a mealymouthed speech about how he had experience with the Baltimore Colts, the Rams and Cardinals, and our team had nothing more than normal tensions. At that point, Ernie McMillan, the Cardinals' veteran black tackle, stood up, threw down his notebook and screamed, "That's bullshit. It's all bullshit. Every word of that story in *Sports Illustrated* is true." He accused Winner and Strofolino of trying to play down real problems. He said, "I will personally stand on every word that's printed in that article." At this point Winner became almost paralyzed because honest emotion was threatening to get loose. He assured Ernie that he was not only aware of some of the problems but indeed had gone to great lengths to correct them and admonished him not to be so passionate. Winner kept insisting that we could handle these problems ourselves. He felt that after the black players had presented him with their list of grievances, he had done much to correct the racial attitudes of assistant coaches and the various players that were mentioned then. Cid Edwards got up and said, "The real problem is how white football players feel blacks always want to jump in the rack with their wives and any white woman they see on the street. You white guys ask any of us here who we like, and I'm sure that, to a man, every black football player will say he prefers black women." He continued, "That's the reason why you guys get upset—because you think that we want to screw every white woman we see." The squirming throughout the room indicated that Edwards had indeed struck one of the sensitive nerves of white football players' racism.

Willis Crenshaw cited Olsen's article in mentioning our safety, Jerry Stovall, a Southern Baptist who held Bible meetings at the training camp. Stovall denied the racism Willis accused him of, closing his argument as follows, "Why, I even took Prentice Gautt [the Cardinals' black halfback] into my parish church in Monroe, Louisiana . . ."

Throughout the meeting, Winner was in a constant state of agitation. He kept coming down heavy on anybody who showed signs of real discontent and disagreement and after a while the players got fed up and realized no honest dialogue would take place in that meeting and any player who spoke the truth would surely face reprisals. Winner was trying to whitewash the whole problem. His closing line was that we must be a football team and that our prime concern was to go win a championship. He suggested we skip the regular football meeting that night and that all of us, black and white, should go down to the Lantern and have a few beers. At this point I almost fell out of my chair; Rick Sortun and I looked at each other incredulously. Winner hoped to solve a ten year problem of racist behavior among coaches and white ball players by having the guys go down to the Lantern, a place from which black players had been informally banned until recently, and drink a few beers together.

On the field, training camp was going very well for me. Yet when Larry Stallings came back from the Army for a week of practice, I was demoted to second team and resented the indignity of the move. All this time I was still haggling contract with the owners. I felt that if I continued to have good scrimmages I would be able to approach the salary that I wanted. After each scrimmage, I would go talk to

Charlie Shea, the club treasurer, who was negotiating my contract. I kept doing well, and the amount he offered kept increasing. Finally, on the day of the first exhibition game in St. Louis, I signed for $24,000 base salary with a $6,000 bonus clause. The bonus clause was broken up into four parts. If I played in $17\frac{1}{2}$ per cent of the defense plays, I would receive $1,500 and it would go up until I reached $6,000 at 75 per cent of the scrimmage plays on defense.

I was completely satisfied with this contract and began playing half of each exhibition game. Larry Stallings was able to play in most of the exhibition games and rotated with me and Ernie Clark. We played Kansas City for the first time in Kansas City for the Governor's Cup, a newly created award for the champion professional football team of Missouri. Kansas City beat us but I had a great night.

On one particular play, Mike Garrett attempted to run a pass pattern on me, but I wasn't faked into coming up for the run and chugged him as he got to the line of scrimmage. As he caught the ball, I tackled him for a two yard loss in the backfield. When we saw the films the following Monday, Dick Voris, our newly acquired defensive line coach, was ecstatic about my play. I still wasn't convinced that I'd won a starting berth but felt that I had made a great stride toward it. I also watched how Ernie and Larry did and I must admit I was pleased when they made mistakes and fucked up.

My contract made it financially important to me to play as many defensive plays as possible during the regular season. At the same time, the team, including myself, was attempting to win a division championship. So, where I was able to pick up a particular tip on the opposition, I was confronted with the dilemma of whether or not to share it with the other linebackers. Coaches constantly talk about team spirit but I've always wondered how the hell there can be team spirit if I know that the more other linebackers screw up, the more I'll be able to play, and the more I play, the more money I make. Owners keep writing contracts with performance clauses such as the one I had, though these can only work to create divisiveness on the team, for these clauses create a situation where the amount of money a player

311

gets is dependent on how badly his teammates at his position play. A second string player who will not get his bonus unless he plays at least 40 per cent of the plays will not be upset if the guy ahead of him screws up badly. The owners introduced these bonuses with the idea that they would extract better performances from the players and result in more victories. In reality, just the opposite usually happens. Rumors began to spread around the league during the 1969 season that receivers who had bonus clauses for the number of passes they caught were paying kickbacks to the quarterbacks.

This dual level of competition is built into pro football. On one hand, the player is competing against his opponent, the guy across from him, and wants to do a good job to further the club's success. At the same time, I was constantly aware that my every move would be on movie film and would be scrutinized closely by the coaching staff the following Monday when they decided between me and my competitors on the team for the starting role. This competition involved not only linebackers, but also halfbacks that I had to cover in practice: if they looked good it meant that I wasn't doing my job and that could get me demoted to second team.

Players bullshit the press on how they help the various rookies. I have rarely seen this happen—certainly I received no help at all when I was a rookie. Quite the contrary, rookies generally received constant abuse from the vets, designed to intimidate them and break their confidence. The new player must not only prove himself on the field, he must also prove he can take their harassment. It's survival of the fittest from beginning to end.

Chapter 24

. . . I had won a starting job at right linebacker. We lost our first game of the season to Los Angeles. The next game was played in San Francisco. Gary Lewis was in the 49er backfield with Ken Willard; together they were the biggest backfield we were to face all year. The former Cardinal halfback, John David Crow, was starting at tight end and Sonny Randle, another ex-Cardinal, was starting at split end for the 49ers. In the first quarter San Francisco had the ball on a third down with one yard to go. The 49ers ran a 37 slant—a play designed to go right over my position. I easily shed John David's block, slipped the pulling guard and hit Lewis with the front of my head, catching him about six inches above his knees. He went down like a bag of wet cowshit and didn't make the necessary yard. I went down on my hands and knees and "smelled the grass." (When I'd get hit really hard on the head, the grass would have a peculiarly pungent odor and I knew I'd been dinged pretty good when I smelled the grass that particular way.) I went over to the sideline and got an ampule of ammonia from the trainer and it seemed to clear my head.

That Sunday turned out to be a long day for the defense. We were in almost 80 plays and it was fairly hot in San Francisco. In the fourth quarter, Gary Lewis (who weighs about 230 pounds and has massive legs) ran a 37 flow to my side. As he started, he could see we had closed off all running room for him and reversed his field. I went after him, having eliminated in my mind all San Francisco players who could block me. I was closing in on Lewis going full speed when the 49er's Howard Mudd blindsided me. It was one of the hardest blocks I'd ever been hit with in professional football, and I literally went flying through the air, landing on the back of my head. I remember from watching the films and reflecting on the game that after I hit the ground I rose slightly, saw Lewis was going to be tackled, and lay back down on the field. I wasn't knocked out or dinged, just stunned by the impact of Mudd first hitting me and then me hitting the ground.

On our ride to the airport after the game, I began to feel nauseous, and when we arrived, I went behind the bus and threw up. I had the dry heaves. They first put me on the airplane, but then held up the plane and called an ambulance to rush me to St. Mary's hospital in San Francisco because the team physician thought I had a severe concussion. The dry heaves lasted a couple of hours; then I was finally able to sleep. The x-rays showed no broken bones in my head, and the next evening I flew back to St. Louis with Dr. Fred Reynolds, the team physician, who had stayed over to watch my progress.

On Tuesday, when watching the game films, I noticed the coaches were a little cool toward me, even though the films showed I had played an excellent football game. Dr. Reynolds told me I would be unable to play the following week against New Orleans. That week I didn't practice at all, although I did come to practice and attended the meetings. I missed the New Orleans game in which the Cardinals scored their first victory of the season. The headaches I'd been having subsided by Tuesday of the following week. I practiced all week and started the game against Dallas. I was nailed fairly hard a couple of times on my head, particularly when tackling Don Perkins, the toughest running back in the league since Jim Brown retired. I'd played a good ball game, but immediately after it was over I was wracked with severe headaches which continued until Friday of the next week. I went to visit Reynolds and he was clearly worried. I'm sure he felt I'd returned to duty too soon and that I might have aggravated the concussion I had incurred in San Francisco. He put me through a maze of exams and tests and found nothing. I remember that week as about the dingiest of my life: with the steady headaches and a hazy feeling of unreality, I had a difficult time remembering where I was or what I was doing.

The game after Dallas was against Cleveland. I stayed home and watched it on television. The week after the Dallas game was very strange. Although I was attending the meetings, the coaches refused to speak to me. Finally on Thursday, Drulis asked me how I was. Clearly, they were suspicious about my injury—because it wasn't evident, couldn't be put in a whirlpool or strapped with an analgesic pack. It had something to do with the head and the mind and football coaches are very suspicious about such things. They would be very happy if the mind could be as mechanical and predictable as a bicep. They thought of me as a little freaky anyhow and weren't sure that the dings I'd received in San Francisco and Dallas wouldn't render me too freaky to accept the routine of professional football. They evidently decided to leave things alone. After the Cleveland game, which the Cardinals won, I resumed my regular starting role and played great football throughout the remainder of the season.

That year we played Baltimore, and for the first time in my pro career I was able to go against John Mackey, my former teammate at Syracuse and now an all-pro tight end and the best blocking end in the National Football League. I'd been itching to play against him since we both entered the league in 1963, yet except for a few isolated exhibition games, we had not had a chance to square off. On one particular sequence of plays, Baltimore had the ball on our three yard line going in for a score. In watching game films all week, I'd learned that Baltimore's favorite goal line play was a 37 straight to take advantage of Mackey's tremendous blocking. This play went directly over me. Mackey came up and dropped into his stance; he tilted his weight a little bit forward and his forearm was shaking slightly. That was all the clue I needed, for I knew the play was coming right over me. I dropped into a slightly lower stance, and as soon as Mackey's head moved a fraction of an inch, I unloaded with my left forearm and caught him in the chest, picking him up off his feet and driving him two yards into the backfield. John grunted, "Good hit, man." On second down Baltimore ran a play in toward the center of the line and drove the ball to the one yard line. On third down I saw Mackey go into his stance again, arm trembling. This time I crouched a little lower because I knew I had surprised him the first time. My eyes were glued to his helmet because John, like many tight ends in the league, dips his head slightly before he charges at the snap of the ball. So, as soon as I saw the little nod, I unleashed my forearm and was able to get underneath John's block. I drove him back about a yard and the play was thrown for no gain. Finally, on the last down, Baltimore scored on a play pass to Tom Matte. When reviewing the films the following Tuesday, Dick Voris, who had been coaching in the western division and watching Mackey's play since he came into the league, said that was the best play he'd seen by any linebacker made against John. I was immensely pleased. I had gone against the very best and, in that sequence of plays, had been the victor.

In 1968 I played well because I needed to prove to myself more than anyone else that I could play in the National Football League. After a shaky start, in which we lost three of our first four ball games, we went on to win all but one game the rest of the season, and that was against Baltimore which went on to win the NFL championship.

After the season, I picked up my $6,000 bonus and reflected on my uncertainty of only a few months earlier. I had proven myself to the coaching staff and I knew that I had overcome my fears and anxieties about playing in the National Football League. Now it was time to move on to other things. To celebrate my success, Stacy and I took a two week vacation in the Virgin Islands. I still had no idea of what I was going to do, but was living in the glow of having had a good year. The one disturbing thing was my feeling that a good part of my life was still unfulfilled and that to continue playing football with the total dedication that I had shown in 1968 would be a great compromise.

The only thing I had going for me after my return from the Virgin Islands was being enrolled in graduate school at Washington University. I began my studies again, yet felt the university setting added less and less meaning to my life. Though I'd done a lot of thinking about who I was, I never seemed able to know my real feelings about many things. There was, in short, much ambivalence in my life. Then, in the last week of March '69 I attended a five day workshop at Esalen Institute led by Seymour Carter. My experience at Esalen was, to make an understatement, significant. I saw very acutely the contradiction between the feelings I had during my experiences at Esalen and the experiences I had working within my craft, which was football. Since high school, I had been using the mask of "football player" to confront the world. It was both my main line of defense and my main source of gaining approval and recognition. I also realized, paradoxically, how cut off and removed I was from my body. I knew my body more thoroughly than most men are ever able to, but I had used it and thought of it as a machine, a thing that had to be well-oiled, well-fed, and well-taken-care-of, to do a specific job. My five days at Esalen left me with an immensely good feeling. I had glimpsed a bit of myself and realized that the "me" behind the face guard was alive and well and could feel and think.

I felt more than ever that my role as football player was a sham. It kept me from responding and communicating on a human level with other people. Esalen was a benchmark and in many ways a beginning for me.

Sam Dardick, president of DGH & Associates, a St. Louis city-planning firm, had a contract to do advocate planning for the Kansas City Model Cities proposal. Sam hired me as a consultant. We had an office in a ghetto of Kansas City and my special project was to develop—that is articulate—the needs and desires of various young guys who lived in the Model Cities target areas. The proposal we wrote was accepted in total by the Model Cities director. When I returned from Kansas City, I went down to the Cardinal offices in Busch stadium to pick up my shoes and sweatpants to begin working out. I was sitting in the office of Joe Pollack, the public relations director, when Dick Voris, the defensive line coach, walked in. I looked up and smiled, and said, "Hi, Coach, how's everything doing?" He took one look at me and said, "When are you going to get your hair cut?" My hair wasn't outrageously long but I'd let it become a little shaggy during the offseason. I was unable to respond to his question with the scorn it deserved and realized I wasn't completely free from worrying about the coaches' approval.

Late in the spring, when I went down to the stadium to pick up a new pair of football shoes, I ran into Voris again. This time he grabbed a hold of me and began shaking my hand. He pulled me close and I felt his left hand running over my body. I had two very strange feelings go through me while he was touching me and asking, "How's your weight, you workin' out, you gettin' in shape, you look a little thin." The first one was a repugnance at being handled like a piece of meat; the second was a warm feeling because he was expressing "fatherly" concern about me. It was a sort of psychological civil war.

As a way of trying to convince myself that I really wanted to play, I was getting myself in fantastic shape for the 1969 season. For the first time I arrived in training camp under 225 pounds, weighing 220. I had tried to put all my doubts about playing out of my mind and worked like a demon to get into great shape.

That spring, I got to know Chuck Drulis, Jr., the son of our head defensive coach. Chuck had been an outstanding end at Duke but got a serious shoulder injury and didn't make it in the pros. Chuck and his wife, Ripple, went with Stacy and me to some music scenes over at Southern Illinois University. Chuck had some Nepalese hash which really lifted my head up. I found that being in condition was really great for smoking dope—with my lungs in shape, I could inhale a tremendous volume of smoke. I also found I could go out the next day and run without experiencing any bad after-effects. I had smoked cigarettes on and off throughout college and in the pros and found they really cut down my wind, but smoking marijuana or hashish didn't affect me at all.

This year, the Cardinals only had seven linebackers in camp because Don Shroyer, the linebacker coach, said he knew who was going to play and didn't want a lot of dead weight around. I reported with the rookies as did Larry Stallings, Jamie Rivers, and Rocky Rosema. When I first saw Shroyer, he was mildly surprised, but said he was glad because it showed we were interested in dedicating ourselves to making a team of championship caliber. Shroyer said, "Dave, if you don't make all-pro linebacker, I'm going to kick your butt."

There's nothing wrong with being an all-pro, and I would have liked being named all-pro during my career; but my feeling at the time was more one of measuring up to the coaches' expectations than of doing well for myself. More than in any of the preceding years, I felt great pressure to avoid thinking of my doubts about playing football. But no amount of effort could rid me of the knowledge about myself which had led me to understand that football was no longer necessary in my life.

Rick Sortun came in with the veterans, and I went over to his room before the six o'clock supper. We looked at each other almost as if to say, "What in God's name are you doing back here?" We shook hands and began to talk about what we'd done in the off-season. Finally, I turned to Rick and said, "What the hell are we doing here?" He said, "I don't know, but I'm pretty sure this is my last year." I said I'd done a lot of thinking and had pretty much decided the '69 season would be my last one too. We looked at each other and said, almost simultaneously, "Let's shake on that." So we made a pledge to each other, shook hands and walked over to the chow hall for supper.

Dennis Rodman

BAD AS I WANNA BE

As the culture of sports slowly opened its doors to the female athlete in the seventies, Dave Kopay and Renee Richards also raised their voices for homosexual and transsexual athletes. The valued presence of the cross-dressing, outspoken Dennis Rodman on many championship NBA teams proves that their courage made a difference, as Rodman himself has also done, in widening the once-narrow definition of the professional athlete. Here Rodman, the most visible sports rebel of his generation, discusses his own concepts of gender.

Basketball is a man's sport." "Sports is a man's world."

Everybody has an image in their mind of what it means to be an athlete in our society.

I paint my fingernails. I color my hair. I sometimes wear women's clothes.

I want to challenge people's image of what an athlete is supposed to be. I like bringing out the feminine side of Dennis Rodman. I like to shock people, to have them wonder where in the hell I'm coming from. To hang out in a gay bar or put on a sequined halter top makes me feel like a total person and not just a one-dimensional man.

I'm always looking for new ways to test myself, whether it's on the court or off. There are no rules, no boundaries—I'm trying to get deep into who I am. I'm trying to truly discover who I am. I don't think any of us really know who we are, and most people are afraid to let themselves go. They're afraid to take the chance, because they might find out something about themselves they don't really want to know.

Tomorrow I could bring a whole new, totally different dimension to myself. If I want to wear a dress, I'll wear a dress. I'm up for just about anything; I'm still finding my way through the tunnels, looking for that light that gets me into the next version of the state fair.

Immediately, people are going to say: he's gay.

No, that's not what it means. I'm not gay. I would tell you if I was. If I go to a gay bar, that doesn't mean that I want another man to put his tongue down my throat—no. It means I want to be a whole individual. It means I'm comfortable dealing with different people in different situations. It means I'm willing to go out there in the world and see how different people live their lives. There's nothing wrong with that.

I grew up in a house of women—my mother and two sisters. I thought when I was growing up that I was going to be gay.

I thought that all along, because I had women around me and I wasn't accepted by girls. They thought I was unattractive, and I was so shy around them, it didn't really matter what they thought of me.

That's not to say I repressed my sexuality and now, all of a sudden, I've decided I really want to be gay. I didn't get money and a little bit of power and decide to let the real me loose.

Everything I do is about confidence. After years of struggling with my identity—who I was, who I was going to be—I've become totally confident about being who I am. I can go out to a salon and have my nails painted pink, and then go out and play in the NBA, on national television, with pink nails.

The opinion of other players doesn't make any difference to me. Most of them think I'm insane anyway, so nothing I do now is going to change anything. They look across at me with my painted fingernails and it gives me another psychological edge; now they're looking at me like they really don't know what I'm going to do next.

I have a pink Harley-Davidson, and I don't care what anybody thinks or says while I'm riding it. My pickup is pink and white. I'm confident enough that I couldn't care less if somebody thinks I'm gay. What I feel inside is this: I know who I am, and there's nothing you can say or think about me that's going to affect me.

It took me a while, but I have the same feeling of confidence and power in my personal life as I have on the basketball court. I took a lot of wrong turns and made a lot of mistakes, but I feel that I'm finally running my own show. Nobody's going to tell me it's not manly to drive a pink truck or wear pink nails. I'll be the judge of my own manliness.

There might be some players in the NBA who are gay. Would that shock people? Probably, but it shouldn't. There might be some players in the league who are bisexual. There are people in any profession who are gay and bisexual, so why should basketball players and athletes be any different? Statistically, it would be almost impossible for the entire sports world to exist without gay or bisexual people.

I'm not pointing the finger at any one guy, because I don't know about other players' personal lives. Also, I don't think it's something you stand around and point fingers about. You don't blame people for this, or ridicule them. If I was gay, I would stand up and say that I am. I would let everyone know that I am gay and existing in what is supposed to be a man's sport.

There is so much hypocrisy in sports, bro. Everyone is supposed to be tough and macho. Everyone's a man's man, tough and mean. But if you look closer, there are so many homosexual aspects of sports. It's all swept under the rug, though, because no one wants to admit the reality of things. Everybody says, "No way, that's just teamwork." Sure, we're all part of a team. Everything we do is all in the group, all in the family—man on man.

Just look around. You'd be blind not to see it. Watch any basketball game. Watch any football game. What's the first thing guys do when they win a big game? They hug each other. What does a baseball manager do when he takes his pitcher out? He takes the ball and pats him on the ass. He could shake his hand or punch him on the shoulder, but he doesn't. He pats him directly on the ass. Isiah

Thomas and Magic Johnson whispered into each other's ears and kissed each other on the cheek for years before games.

Man hugs man. Man pats man on ass. Man whispers in man's ear and kisses him on the cheek. This is classic homosexual or bisexual behavior. It's in the gay bible. You tell people this and they're like, "Oh, no it's not. It's just a man's thing."

And I say, "You're damned right. It *is* a man's thing."

I'm not saying you have to be gay to do these things, but you have to accept that it falls in the large confines of homosexual behavior. You just have to accept that. I do those things on the basketball court—hug a guy, pat a guy on the ass—and if you want to call me homosexual or bisexual because of that, that's fine. I accept that. Then I guess you can take the next step and say I want to sleep with a man.

After *Sports Illustrated* came out with the article in May of 1995—the one where I talked about fantasizing about being with another man—people have assumed I'm bisexual. I don't do much to discourage that, since it fits into my idea of keeping people guessing. I went to a T-shirt shop in West Hollywood during the off-season before I was traded to the Bulls, and I bought two shirts. On one it said, *I don't mind straight people as long as they act gay in public*. The other said, *I'm not gay but my boyfriend is*.

I wore the first one out to a club in Newport Beach the next night, and this girl came up to me and said, "You're cool. You speak your mind, and that's what I like about you." Then she said, "I'm bisexual too—just like you."

I just laughed at her, and I didn't argue. Who knows? Maybe I am bisexual, but if I am it's in my mind only. I've never acted on it. Maybe I have this fixation that I want to be with another guy, but is it so wrong to think that? I don't believe so, especially when most people think about the same things—even if they don't act on their thoughts.

If you ask a man if he's ever thought about being with another guy, he'll probably say, "Oh, no. That's disgusting. I could never be with another guy."

Then you say, "Wait, have you ever thought about it?"

"No way. I can't believe you're even asking me. I've never thought about it."

To that I say, "Yeah, you have. If you didn't want to be with a guy, or if you never thought about it, you wouldn't be so quick to say it's disgusting. If you had never thought about it, you'd have to think about it before you gave me an answer."

I let people think what they want to think about me. I color my hair and paint my fingernails, and sometimes I wear women's clothing. I do it and watch people's reactions. Let them think what they want.

Gay men come up to me—and *on* to me—all the time. I'm very popular among gay men. I think I've done more to recognize them than any other professional athlete. When I put the AIDS ribbon on my head during the play-offs against the Lakers in 1995, I think that opened a lot of eyes. These people were finally seeing somebody openly recognize them. For the first time they saw someone openly show some support—with no embarrassment at all. It let them know there's someone in the sports world who understands and isn't going to pretend they don't exist.

I think I'm naturally drawn to people who are out of the mainstream. The people that society says aren't with the program are the people I'm most comfortable being around. No matter what city I've been in, I've always felt more at home when I go into a bad part of town and talk to some homeless people than when I'm sitting in some stuffy-ass restaurant with a bunch of people wearing ties.

The same holds true for gay people. They aren't fully accepted, and I don't think I'm fully accepted. We have something in common.

It came out in that same *Sports Illustrated* article that I go to gay bars. I do. I'm not afraid to do that, and I'm not afraid to say that. These people shouldn't be avoided or ignored. I think we can all learn something from them and from what they've been through.

Gay men always come up to me and say, "Thank you. Thank you for recognizing that we're not just a piece of dirt on the ground. Thank you for recognizing that we do exist."

I've found these people want to be recognized as individuals and not just as a disease. They're not a traveling, walking disease—what some ignorant people consider a curse from God. They shouldn't be looked upon as people who shouldn't be here just because of one thing they do.

Whenever I'm staying in Orange County—which is whenever the basketball schedule allows—I go into Los Angeles and hang out in the gay community of West Hollywood. I love it there. I love going into that community. I love being in the gay atmosphere, because it gives me something I don't find anywhere else. It's free, it's open—it's wide open. That appeals to me. There's only one danger about being in the gay community: those people have no fear of anything.

I think that comes from being through so much hatred and so much abuse. When I went through all the racist bullshit in Oklahoma, it changed me. It changed the way I thought about people, and it made me tougher. It also made me look for something that could provide me with safe, solid ground. I found that with the Riches, and when I got some wealth and fame I got the safe feeling in—of all places—the bad parts of town.

Gay people are the same way. They create communities where it's safe for them, but they aren't afraid of anyone, and they aren't surprised by anything.

When I was young, I don't think I had a fear of being gay. I didn't really know what was going on, or what any of it meant. If I was going to be gay, it would have happened back then. I didn't run from it or keep it bottled up inside me.

I was already fucked up, and having trouble deciding who I was going to be sexually was just another worry to throw on top of everything. I didn't really have to worry much about girls coming on to me when I was in my teenage years; I was already an ugly, big-headed klepto kind of guy.

My curiosity about my sexuality has followed me to this point, this big stage. Just because I can play a game and make a lot of money doesn't mean I suddenly have all the answers. I'm open to everything, and I'm always asking questions. That's just part of who I am.

I can't say I haven't experimented with other men, but I guess it depends on what you mean by experimenting. I've kissed men, but it's like saying you kissed your little boy or your teenage son on the lips. I'm not afraid to go up to a good friend of mine and give him a hug and a kiss. There's nothing wrong with that, and I don't care who sees me do it. It's showing that I care about somebody. People think homosexuality is bad, evil. It's not bad at all, but people make it out to be just the worst thing in the world.

I've questioned my sexuality, but I've never found myself forced into a position where I have to decide whether to enter into a homosexual relationship. It's never been like that.

Mentally, I probably am bisexual. I've thought about a lot of crazy things, and I've fantasized about a lot of crazy things. I don't know if I'll ever be physically bisexual. Someday I might be, but I haven't been to this point. I haven't acted out on any of the things that have run through my mind.

I fantasize about being with another man, and I'm not afraid to admit it. You can't help but fantasize about it, if you ask me. If you're a free thinker and willing to let your mind explore like it wants, then you have to think about it. I believe it's natural for your body to go and explore anything it wants.

But you don't want to just jump into something because you've been thinking about it. It has to be something you can live with afterward.

When I go into a gay bar, I get approached by other men. Of course I do. They figure you're in there, so there's got to be a reason. But it's not like gay people come up to me and say, "If you feel the need to have sex with a guy, I hope I'm the one." It's not like that. If it ever happens that I do have a homosexual relationship, or encounter, it's not going to be a situation where I just decide I'm going to do it just to do it.

And here's something about the craziness of the sports world that I just don't understand: Whenever a sports figure does something that isn't manly, or if he does something in a way that is not considered manly, everybody gets all upset. It's like, "Oh, God—no way, not *him.*"

Why are athletes treated differently than people in everyday society? It seems that people feel threatened when an athlete does something that is not considered manly. It's like they've crossed over some imaginary line that nobody thinks should be crossed.

Entertainers and actors are not treated the same way. If an entertainer is gay, it's accepted. People accept that without a second thought. But somehow it's always a scandal when an athlete comes out of the closet.

There haven't been that many examples, and I think it's because athletes are afraid of what might happen if they do come out. A baseball player named Glenn Burke had his career ruined because the Dodgers apparently found out he was gay. The team couldn't handle it, they couldn't deal with it. Teams can deal when a guy has a drug problem or an alcohol problem, but not when they find out someone's doing something they don't like in the privacy of their own bedroom. It doesn't make sense.

Maybe when an athlete comes out, people start to wonder: is the world of sports turning into a gay world? I guess athletes are supposed to be completely different from any other walk of life. If a guy who works in your office is gay, it's no big deal. He's just gay. But if a guy who plays basketball or baseball or football comes out and says he's gay, everybody looks at him funny. Nobody can believe it. That doesn't make any sense to me. We're held to a different standard.

People look up to us, and why? I think I have an answer: more than anything else, people play sports and listen to music when they're looking to escape their lives. Or they watch sports and read about sports and talk about sports. So with so many people interested in sports, there's no way it can be accepted if somebody within that community comes out and says he's gay. People trip on that.

This isn't something I can talk to other players about. I can't open up and say, "Have you ever thought about being gay?" There's not a player out there who would say, "Yeah, you know I have. I wish I was gay. I wish I could be." No way a player would ever tell you that, even if it was true.

I'm not trying to encourage kids to be gay, but it shouldn't keep them from being in athletics if they are. You can't say I'm less of a man because I've given some thought to being with another man. I'm not trying to steer kids into saying being gay is cool. You go with your heart, your feelings, and what you desire. Like anything, don't let what other people think decide who you are.

When I go on road trips, I sometimes laugh to myself when I think about everybody's luggage coming off the plane and down the conveyor belt to the baggage claim. Everybody's luggage is there, with all their fancy clothes, and then there's mine, carrying my jeans, T-shirts—and some women's clothes.

There might be a sequined halter top in there. There might be some women's leggings in there. There might be some tight leather shorts in there. You never know what might be in there.

I'm guessing here, but I imagine I'm the only guy in the NBA who packs these kinds of clothes on the road, then wears them out to bars and clubs. And I know I'm the only one who would come out and admit it.

I've got no problem admitting it. I can be the only guy in the world doing it and it wouldn't stop me. I don't think many people think about who's cross-dressing after the game when they look out there and see all these guys running up and down the court, playing this man's game.

Nobody I've ever played with knows I go out and dress in women's clothes. They know I dress in wild, crazy clothes, but when they're looking at it, they don't know if it's women's clothes or just gay clothes.

Sometimes, I admit, it's hard to tell. When I made a presentation at the MTV Music Awards, I was cross-dressing. I wore a woman's top and my fingernails were painted. It wasn't obvious that I was wearing women's clothes, but if you looked closely you would have known.

The first time I painted my nails was on Halloween of 1994. I had them painted orange and black, and people looked at it as more of a stunt than anything. Just Rodman being Rodman again. Now I don't even think twice about my nails; I get them done all the time. About once a week I'll go into a salon and have them done. It's just something different, and I like to look down and see the different colors.

I don't think painting my fingernails is a big deal. It's not like I'm sitting home by myself, trying on lingerie. That's not my style. I don't do lingerie. I think cross-dressing, the way I do it, is more accepted than people think. Look at all the clothes now that are made for both men and women. You go into a store and sometimes it's hard to tell whether you're in the men's or the women's section.

It wasn't that long ago that everyone freaked out when they saw a man wearing an earring. . . . As a kid I would sometimes dress up as a girl. You play house, you play doctor—everybody does that, but some people like it more than others. You play by dressing up and acting like a woman. I think a lot of kids have done that. I used to go through the whole routine—dress up, wear makeup, act like a girl.

When I cross-dress now, it's just another way I can show all the sides of Dennis Rodman. I'm giving you the whole package. I'm becoming the all-purpose person. I'm like the running back that can break one to the outside and also go over the middle to catch a pass.

I'll do this wherever I feel comfortable doing it. It doesn't matter where. If I feel like dressing up, I pick my time and place. I've done it in New York, Los Angeles, Chicago, Detroit, and Dallas. I go into straight bars, gay bars, it doesn't matter. I'm not afraid of doing it anywhere.

In New York I go to the Channel Club or the Tunnel. Those are two of the places I feel comfortable wearing my clothes. I'll go out with friends I know from different cities, but never players. Other than Jack Haley I'm not hanging out with any players on the road.

Cross-dressing is like everything else in my life: I don't really think about it, I just do it. I don't remember the first time I decided to do it as an adult; there isn't one time that really sticks out. It was more of a gradual thing, where it progressed from earrings and fingernails to halter tops and tight leather shorts. I've done it since my early days in the NBA, but I've started to do it more often since I made the decision . . . to live my life the way I want to live it.

I haven't worn a dress, yet, but I did buy one to wear on the Howard Stern show one time. It ended up that I didn't get out of bed in time to get it on. I had to rush out of the hotel and get to the interview, which was at seven in the morning.

I like to wear tight stuff, and I like sequins. I usually wear shirts and shorts and jewelry. I wear different earrings when I wear a halter top. I wear women's leggings under my clothes, but no lingerie. I haven't gotten to the point of wearing high heels either. I just wear my normal leather construction boots, the ones I wear all the time anyway.

You'd be surprised the kind of clothes you can get in my size. I buy all the stuff myself. Nobody does it for me. I go into women's clothing stores; I don't have a problem with that. I'm not going to call somebody and have everything custom-made, because that's not my style. Besides, that's sort of like hiding it. I could have someone come out to my house and measure me and all that, but half the fun is seeing the looks on people's faces when I go into the stores and try things on.

The salespeople love it. They can't believe there's a big, macho basketball player coming in and buying women's clothes—and buying them for himself.

There's another thing I found out right away: girls love it. They *love* it. Guys say, "I wouldn't wear it, but it looks good on you," but girls go crazy over it. They love to see a guy who's not afraid of his manhood. They love it when a guy has all the confidence in the world, enough to paint his fingernails pink or ride a pink Harley-Davidson. They love a guy who can wear a sequined halter top and be very comfortable.

Everything depends on how I feel. I'm not more likely to cross-dress after we've won, or after we've lost. I don't choose my spots like that. I just go by what I'm feeling at the time, and what kinds of emotions I want to express. If you want to dress, you dress.

It's total freedom. Totally. It's the freedom to be who the fuck you want to be, and nobody else matters. It's just another side of me, one that most people are afraid to show. There are all these sides I'm discovering, and I don't know how many are still out there, waiting to be discovered.

Roone Arledge

THE PLAYBOY INTERVIEW

The concept of sports "Up Close and Personal", of building into the coverage the drama

of instant replays, of miked action, and of outspoken commentators, all come from

Roone Arledge, former President of ABC Sports. In this 1976 Playboy Interview *with*

Sam Merrill, Arledge explains how many of his innovations came about—innovations

that changed not just sports, but all media.

PLAYBOY: You once described the Olympic-experience as "communal." What did you mean?

ARLEDGE: There's a desperate need for total reliance on other people during an Olympic production. We take over the entire prime time of the network for two solid weeks of *live television*. And the audiences are unprecedented. In Munich, 49 of the 50 top-rated half-hour segments each week were the Olympics. So I just have to *know* that if someone goes out to do something, he is going to get it done correctly, get it done the way I want it *and* add something of his own creativity as well.

PLAYBOY: You must get to know your people pretty well in a situation like that.

ARLEDGE: That's why the Olympics are so great for an organization. You get to watch people in action, see how they react under pressure.

And, as a communal experience, the absolute worst thing that can happen to a producer is for him to walk into the video-tape room and be treated like a VIP—the chairman of the board making his tour of the studio. There's got to be an equality of roles.

PLAYBOY: At Innsbruck, some ABC executives criticized you for demonstrating too *much* equality by barricading yourself in the video room when you should have been out pressing the flesh with the sponsors.

ARLEDGE: The network brought a lot of guests to Innsbruck. They stayed at one of the most beautiful hotels in the world up in Zeifel and spent their days skiing and their nights partying. Meanwhile, the production people were working day and night, many of them never even getting out of the video room to see what Innsbruck looked like. I decided to stay at the Holiday Inn with the basic troops and didn't go to a single cocktail party. The advertising people were a little angry.

PLAYBOY: Wasn't that as much for psychological reasons as for convenience?

ARLEDGE: I suppose so. I didn't want the people who actually make the shows good—which is why the sponsors buy them in the first place—to think I was living it up in the Alps while they were sweating it out in the tape room.

PLAYBOY: Doesn't that point up the biggest problem you've had in recent years, the schizophrenia of being an executive producer? What *is* an executive producer, anyway—an executive or a producer?

ARLEDGE: Both, usually both at the same time. The image that ultimately appears on the tube is what TV is all about, so for me, the most rewarding and exciting part of my job is making pictures and words that move people. Not selling time or buying rights or making schedules. But the bane of this industry—the problem we face that magazines and newspapers don't, the problem that leads to so much of television's gutlessness—is that we have to buy the rights to an event before we can produce anything. So I end up spending more and more time on rights and scheduling each year. Which is a shame because during a major sporting event, the action isn't in the commissioner's box, where every other TV executive sits, but in the mobile unit. That's the place to be.

PLAYBOY: Speaking of the technical end of the business. let's discuss some of the electronic wizardry for which you originally became known. The instant replay, for example. How did that happen?

ARLEDGE: In 1960, I was doing a survey for a college football game in the Los Angeles Coliseum with an engineer named Bob Trachinger—

PLAYBOY: Bob Trachinger? Isn't he that bearded guy in the commercials?

ARLEDGE: That's him. "More chief engineers choose blab-blah-blah than any other color TV." Trach is one of the most brilliant guys in the business, our head man on the West Coast now; but at the time, he was just a working engineer. Anyway, after the survey, we went over to a place called Julie's for a few beers. I asked him if it would be possible to replay something in slow motion so you could tell if a guy was safe or out or stepped out of bounds, and Trach immediately began sketching on the napkins. We talked and sketched and drank beer that whole afternoon and when we were finished, we had the plans for the first instant-replay device.

PLAYBOY: The top people at ABC must have been pretty excited when they saw those napkins.

ARLEDGE: On the contrary. Trach's superiors at ABC engineering thought he was crazy. They were opposed to the idea and wouldn't give him any development money. So he literally took funds that were supposed to be used for something else and developed the system. Incidentally, Trach is also the guy who developed the underwater camera for me. He's just an extremely creative guy.

PLAYBOY: Do you remember the first time you used the instant replay?

ARLEDGE: The first use was during a Texas–Texas A & M football game. It was a lousy game and the instant replays were justifiably unmemorable. But the first important use came the following weekend, during a Boston College–Syracuse game. That was a terrific game and, at one point, Jack Concannon, a sophomore quarterback, was trapped in the pocket but ended up running 70 yards for a touchdown. Six or eight people had a shot at him and we replayed the whole thing in slow motion with Paul Christman analyzing the entire play as it unfolded. Nobody had ever seen anything like that before and the impact was unbelievable. That moment changed TV sports forever.

PLAYBOY: Back in the early Sixties, when you were producing the old A.F.L. football broadcasts, you used to pull all sorts of weird technical stunts.

ARLEDGE: I'd prefer to call them experiments, but, yes, I guess we did play around a lot. Since nobody was watching, anyway—particularly when the N.F.L. was on opposite us—we had the freedom to try new things. That's how we invented the isolated camera, just by fooling around during one of those early A.F.L. broadcasts. Much of the space-age coverage we supposedly pioneered on *Monday Night Football* was actually developed on our A.F.L. telecasts in the early Sixties. Nobody knew about them because nobody was watching.

PLAYBOY: You were also the first guy to put sound into TV sports.

ARLEDGE: It's hard to believe now, but back in the "golden age" of the N.F.L., you couldn't even hear the ball being kicked. Yet sounds are very much a part of the experience of a game: the clatter of the lines converging, the sound of the quarterback barking signals. So when I began producing football for TV, I knew I had to get those sounds on the air.

PLAYBOY: But not *all* the sounds of the game are acceptable to the FCC.

ARLEDGE: That's true; and, at first, we used a two-second tape delay; but I never liked that, because you'd see the huddle break and they were halfway up to the line by the time you heard them clap and say, "Let's go." So finally I just said the hell with it and went live.

PLAYBOY: Have you ever gotten into trouble for any of those live sounds?

ARLEDGE: A couple of times. You know how a stadium will sometimes quiet down all of a sudden until, for a brief moment, there isn't a sound? That happened to us once in the Cotton Bowl. Absolute dead silence. Then some guy in the stands started screaming, "Get going, you motherfuckers!" It came over the air with better quality than we were getting from our announcers. Another time, a Florida A & M running back named Bob Paremore was taken out of the North–South Shrine game and said, "Awwww, sheeee-it!" But when that sort of thing *does* happen, the complaints usually come from league and network officials, not from the fans. Fans know what a game is supposed to sound like.

PLAYBOY: No one would deny that by wiring sports for sound you brought the TV viewer a lot closer to the stadium experience. But haven't you also gone overboard occasionally? We've heard rumors that, in 1972, you put a miniature microphone in the Olympic torch to catch the sound of the flame being lit at the opening ceremony. Is that true?

ARLEDGE: It is true, and perhaps we did go a *little* overboard with that one.

✤ ✤ ✤

PLAYBOY: Do you, personally, *like* television?

ARLEDGE: Let's say I don't think its potential is being properly utilized. I mean, do Mac Davis, Tony Orlando and *Laverne and Shirley* really represent the ultimate use of this medium?

PLAYBOY: But commercial TV as we know it is a mass medium. Look at your own career. You do the Olympics every four years. You do demolition derbies somewhat more often.

ARLEDGE: I believe we've proven in our best sports coverage, and I *know* it's been proven in certain areas of the news, that you can appeal to a mass audience without appealing to the lowest common denominator.

PLAYBOY: In general, what do you think of TV news?

ARLEDGE: I think news, like entertainment, is done better elsewhere. It is my understandably biased opinion that TV does sports better than sports is done anywhere else but that everything else is done better in other media.

PLAYBOY: What would a Roone Arledge news program be like?

ARLEDGE: The first thing I'd do as a news producer would be to hire a staff of investigative reporters. Television did nothing with Watergate, perhaps the biggest news story in the history of our nation. That's because Watergate was essentially an investigative story. John Mitchell didn't hold a press conference to reveal he was one of the co-controllers of Nixon's secret fund, so naturally, television newsmen had to read that in the papers. Also, I'd try for a more interesting format. Newspapers are always wrestling with their formats in an attempt to enhance reader interest. But TV thinks news has to be dull to be credible. Another thing I'd do as a news producer is personalize world leaders the same way I personalize sports figures.

PLAYBOY: Presumably, the networks do that on their panel shows.

ARLEDGE: Right. Three discussion programs that are carbon copies of one another. I simply cannot believe the only format in which a world leader can be presented to the American people is around a desk with three people asking him questions at one o'clock on Sunday afternoon.

PLAYBOY: What would you suggest?

ARLEDGE: I'd do one-minute press conference-type interviews on the six-o'clock news and hour-long documentaries on prime time. That way, on a daily basis, we could get to know who these people are. During our Olympic coverage, we routinely run documentary profiles of the athletes. The next morning, Americans know not only what people like Olga Korbut and Dorothy Hamill look like but where they come from and, to at least some extent, what kind of people they are. But until the Senate hearings, 90 percent of the American public didn't even know what Bob Haldeman looked like, let alone what he did and thought. He was the second most powerful man in the country and we had the most powerful medium in the country, yet somehow, a man like that was able to remain anonymous.

PLAYBOY: The most powerful man in the country was also America's number-one football fan. Did you ever meet Richard Nixon?

ARLEDGE: On several occasions. The first was at a Texas–Arkansas game for the national championship. I was supposed to meet my wife in Hawaii that weekend, but when Nixon decided to attend the game,

I felt I *had* to produce it personally. I would never have forgiven myself if something had happened to the President and I wasn't there.

PLAYBOY: Because you felt you could have helped prevent an assassination?

ARLEDGE: No, because I wouldn't have wanted anyone else making the decisions on how to cover one.

PLAYBOY: You are nothing if not professional.

ARLEDGE: Incidentally, stranding my wife in Hawaii like that proved to be the last straw in our marriage. Soon afterward, she divorced me. But getting back to Nixon, Texas won the game and after congratulating the team, the President went into the Arkansas dressing room to give the players a little talk. It started out with the usual locker-room clichés, just another politician giving another speech. But then something happened and Nixon began discussing defeat in the most intensely personal terms. It was extremely moving, since, as we all realized, he was actually talking about himself. But the next time I met Nixon, just four days later, it was plain weird.

PLAYBOY: What happened?

ARLEDGE: The afternoon before a football dinner Nixon was attending, I got a call saying the President would like to see me. I went up to his suite in the Waldorf Towers and everyone said, "Oh, yes, the President is expecting you." So I walked into this huge room, figuring there would be about 100 other people in a reception line. But the room was empty; just an American flag, the Presidential flag and one man: the President of the United States. It was a rather awesome experience. We spent more than half an hour together, talking about sports. At first, I thought, This is awfully nice of him. He wants to put me at my ease by talking about something I'm familiar with. But after a while, I began trying to change the subject to other things that interest me a lot more than sports: music, theater, the problems of our cities. But Nixon kept coming back to sports. Finally, I realized that he wasn't trying to put me at ease, he was trying to impress me with his knowledge of sports trivia. While he was rattling off the times of quarter-milers in the 1936 Olympics, I remember saying to myself, I can't believe it. The President of the United States is trying to impress *me*. But the third time I met Nixon was the strangest experience of all.

PLAYBOY: Why?

ARLEDGE: The President had agreed to come on *Wide World* and be interviewed by Frank Gifford. We did the show and, during a break, Nixon took me aside and said something I'll never forget. He said, "When Frank Gifford was a big star with the Giants and I was living in New York, he used to have parties after the games and I was up to his apartment many times. I know Frank Gifford. He remembers me." I thought, I do not believe what I am hearing. It has now become fashionable to discuss Nixon's so-called inferiority complex. But I think it went far beyond that. Here was the President of the United States trying to impress people, first, because be remembered some Olympic records and second, because he knew Frank Gifford. And because Frank Gifford knew *him*!

PLAYBOY: Let's go back a moment to your development of innovations in televising games: Did you run into much opposition from the sports establishment?

ARLEDGE: Sure. Techniques that are now considered standard, such as the instant replay, slow motion, showing the faces of the players, even superimposing the names of the players on the screen after a good play, were called gimmicks when we introduced them.

PLAYBOY: Do any particular incidents come to mind?

ARLEDGE: The first time we put a camera in the dugout was at Yankee Stadium. Before that, no one was doing field-level shots. But I wanted the kind of dramatic close-up from a human perspective—not foreshortened because the camera is in the upper deck—that has become standard now. Well, Red Barber was doing the local telecast for the Yankees and he turned his cameras on us and did a whole editorial on the air. He announced to his viewers, "Ladies and gentlemen, you are witnessing something that has never happened before in the history of baseball. The sanctity of the dugout has been violated."

PLAYBOY: You've had a lot of problems with the U. S. Golf Association over the years. That organization seems especially resistant to sports coverage Roone Arledge style.

ARLEDGE: When they were trying to get the P.G.A. tour on television, we said they'd have to go to sudden death in the event of a tie. We simply couldn't promise to do four hours of programming that the kids and housewives who are home on Monday afternoon wouldn't watch anyway, just so two guys could have an 18-hole play-off in the Dallas Open. We argued about it for days and days. Finally, they gave in and now they really like the sudden-death system. In fact, a couple of years ago, we were doing a tournament from the Coast and we preferred a play-off the next day. But the golf people refused. They wanted to get the hell out of town on Sunday night. But I don't want to rap the U.S.G.A. Even though I've had many disagreements with them, they are absolutely honest and straightforward. And the U.S.G.A. is the *only* organization that is willing to trade dollars for something it thinks will be good for the game—like fewer commercials and TV coverage of the U. S. Amateur. In an era of commercialism, the U.S.G.A. feels its responsibility is to the 50,000,000 people who play golf for fun, not to the handful who play it for money.

PLAYBOY: While revolutionizing the visual aspects of sports broadcasting, you were also making some important changes in the way events were announced. You have even been quoted as saying that sometimes sportscasters talk too much.

ARLEDGE: That's why Dick Button is so good. He's an expert who knows when not to talk. When something is truly beautiful to look at, a play-by-play becomes an irritating intrusion between you and the event. It would drive me crazy to watch Baryshnikov dance and have to listen to somebody babbling in my ear: "Now watch his left foot. He's going to jump and, as he turns, listen to the music change key."

PLAYBOY: But because of the size and variety of the TV audience, sometimes an announcer *has to* explain something that for millions of sophisticated viewers might seem academic.

ARLEDGE: Would you believe that when we first covered Wimbledon, very few Americans knew even the basic rules of tennis? It was embarrassing, but Jim McKay had to go on the air and explain that love means zero and the object of the game is to keep the ball inside the white lines. Can you imagine how that must have offended veteran tennis fans?

PLAYBOY: *Wide World of Sports*, which premiered in 1961, was really the show that made you and . . . it's been your proving ground for the techniques you use in covering the Olympics. How did that show get started?

ARLEDGE: In 1960, the major-league baseball owners still clung to their old blackout rule. They restricted the telecasts of major-league games to minor-league markets. As a result of that great humanitarian gesture, which contributed to the destruction of the minor leagues, the three networks were fighting over only 40 percent of the country, since 60 percent was in the big-league markets. ABC decided that was silly and assigned me to come up with a year-round sports show that could fill the void and not have to worry about the blackouts. That show was *Wide World of Sports*. The idea was to travel to the world's greatest events and try to capture whatever it is that makes those events fascinating. We combined the techniques of documentary film making—so viewers could get to know the performers personally—with coverage designed to make you feel as though you are there.

PLAYBOY: *Wide World of Sports* has covered some pretty weird events over the years. How do you find them all?

ARLEDGE: It's easy now, because people come to us with them. But when we were starting out, that was one of our biggest problems. I knew NBC had a large microfilm library with a lot of the information I needed and I gambled on two things: first, that nobody there knew I was gone and, second, that nobody there knew what I looked like. So I sent Chuck Howard, who was then a production assistant and is now vice-president of ABC Sports, over to NBC to go through their files and list all the sports events we might be interested in. I told him whenever anyone asked who he was, to say he was me. It worked, and so I began traveling all around the world signing up events for *Wide World of Sports*.

PLAYBOY: And that's how *Wide World* got started?

ARLEDGE: Not exactly. Because when I returned to New York with the rights to everything from the Japanese All-Star Baseball Game to the British Open, to the 24 Hours of Le Mans, no sponsor wanted to buy the show. At ten minutes to five on the afternoon of the day the show was going to be canceled, Ed Sherick, who was then the head of sales for ABC, had the guts to use N.C.A.A. football as a sledge hammer to sell time on *Wide World of Sports*. He made R. J. Reynolds Tobacco Company buy the new show before he'd let it have a quarter of college football. So *Wide World of Sports*, now the longest running sports show in television history, came within ten minutes of never getting on the air.

✛ ✛ ✛

PLAYBOY: You mentioned the kind of news show you might present. What other kinds of programming would interest you?

ARLEDGE: Well, considering my addiction to ballet, I can think of ways to produce that that would make it exciting.

PLAYBOY: How?

ARLEDGE: Well, apparently Baryshnikov and Nureyev had never met before a year ago January, when they were in New York at the same time. I think that, if we'd been given the opportunity to explain the rudiments of dance—as we explained gymnastics and figure skating at the Olympics—people would have really gotten into a kind of big-money shoot-out between two top stars. And the result would have been a piece of video tape that people would be watching 100 years from now.

PLAYBOY: When you say shoot-out, surely you're not implying that you'd open with a blimp shot of Lincoln Center, then cut to an isolated camera on Nureyev's big toe.

ARLEDGE: Of course not. And neither am I implying that after every leap, three judges would hold up signs saying 5.6, 6.3 and 5.8. As in sports or news or anything else, producing ballet would simply mean getting the shot the viewer really wants to see, not the shot that proves you are an electronic wizard.

from THE PLAYBOY INTERVIEW

PLAYBOY: But some of the shots you've gotten over the years *have* required a lot of electronic wizardry. How do you determine when you are getting the shot the viewer wants and when you have gone beyond it to become, in Cosell's words, "a bunch of kids playing with cameras"?

ARLEDGE: The answer is simple: You must use the camera—and the microphone—to broadcast an image that approximates what the brain perceives, not merely what the eye sees. Only then can you create the illusion of reality.

PLAYBOY: In other words, you distort reality in order to make it seem real.

ARLEDGE: Exactly; but, one must exercise the restraint to stop before it becomes surreal.

PLAYBOY: This is beginning to sound a little circular. Let's cut to a concrete example.

ARLEDGE: Take auto racing. When you're at Le Mans, the entire atmosphere is charged with the vivid sensations of speed and danger. But put a camera in the middle of the Mulsanne Straight, where the cars are traveling well over 200 miles per hour, and all you see is this dot that gets a little bigger as it approaches. The perception of speed is absent. So we put slave cameras much closer to the track than any spectator could ever get. They give the television viewer that zip and roar, the sensation of speed the live viewer would perceive simply by watching that little dot grow larger. That way, we are not creating something phony. It is an illusion but an illusion of reality.

PLAYBOY: *Wide World of Sports* routinely compresses three-hour events into eight-minute segments. And people seem to love it. But that doesn't seem to be even an illusion of reality—just a snippet.

ARLEDGE: There's certainly some truth to that, but it depends upon the setting. People eagerly watch the long, nonaction segments of the Olympics, heavyweight championship fights and the World Series. But in sports they aren't that familiar with, or in events that aren't that important, people do enjoy the knowledge that something different will be coming on every ten minutes.

ROONE ARLEDGE

PLAYBOY: In addition to catering to an ever-shortening attention span, do you feel you are oversaturating the airwaves with sports?

ARLEDGE: Oversaturation is a danger faced by everyone in the media. *Playboy* now has to compete with all its would-be emulators and TV is glutted with 43 cop shows that have replaced 43 Westerns. In every area of every medium, you can reach a point of surfeit, when numbness sets in.

PLAYBOY: Has sports numbness ever set in on you?

ARLEDGE: I must confess that it has. On the weekend after New Year's, you generally have at least two N.F.L. championship games and four or five—sometimes six or eight—bowl games. And by the end of that weekend, I have this composite image of 47 tumbling catches in the end zone, 26 explanations of why you've got to have both feet in bounds and, really, it's all just a blur.

PLAYBOY: Would you say, then, that sports have peaked on television?

ARLEDGE: No. In fact, I'd say the TV audience for sports will continue to grow for quite some time, but there's going to be a lot of weeding out. Some bowl games have already vanished. A football league and a basketball league both folded this year. Tennis went from being wildly underexposed to being wildly overexposed. There may never even be a TV audience for hockey.

PLAYBOY: But hockey is such a successful sport.

ARLEDGE: Not on television. NBC and CBS made big mistakes with hockey and I'm not knocking them. I could have made the same mistake. I enjoy watching hockey and every time I go to Madison Square Garden, there are 17,000 people there. But it's the same 17,000 people all the time. In the New York TV market, you need 1,000,000 viewers, not 17,000. So, you see, the weeding-out process is already under way.

PLAYBOY: But don't you think television has the power to create tastes, even create in entire sport, if it's left on the air long enough?

ARLEDGE: No.

PLAYBOY: Many media experts have credited you with creating the sudden American taste for gymnastics.

ARLEDGE: Gymnastics came along when Americans were just beginning to become aware of their bodies, and the personality of Olga Korbut came along when the women's movement was getting into athletics. TV *can* create a personality, but it *can't* create a taste the public isn't ready for. Americans were ready for golf when Arnold Palmer appeared on television. He was the swashbuckling hero who would be six strokes down, hitch up his pants and charge. People who didn't know a putt from a sand blast could root for him. But, like Bobby Fischer, Palmer would have soon faded into obscurity if an interest in the game didn't underlie an interest in the personality.

✛ ✛ ✛

PLAYBOY: You're almost as well known for business acumen as for technical expertise and your income is reputed to be awesome. Would you mind telling us where you invest your money?

ARLEDGE: Lately, I've been investing rather heavily in divorce.

PLAYBOY: On second thought, perhaps we should go elsewhere for financial advice. But we will ask you who your favorite athletes are—and why.

ARLEDGE: Bill Russell is probably number one. Not only did he exhibit total mastery of his sport but he was also an innovator. Due solely to his presence, the game of basketball Russell left when he retired was different from the game he found when he began playing. And Russell is also an important person in America. I've been after him for years to run for office. I think he'd make a great Senator, or President, for that matter. Another favorite is Jack Nicklaus and for similar reasons: his dominance of the game he plays and his personal qualities.

PLAYBOY: Nicklaus is an unexpected choice. The two of you are hardly friends. He has generally sided with the U.S.G.A. in your frequent disputes with that organization.

ARLEDGE: Nevertheless, I admire Jack's integrity. Golf is, in many respects, the purest sport, because it is the only one in which the player must penalize himself. If your caddy moves the ball in the rough, you must call it on yourself. That happened to Byron Nelson in the U. S. Open and he lost the tournament by one stroke. You just know that Nicklaus would do the same thing, even if no one on earth could possibly have seen his ball move. It's interesting to ask yourself what you'd do in a situation like that.

✛ ✛ ✛

PLAYBOY: Of all the shows you've produced, what would you consider the greatest moment, the single most important image you have ever beamed out to the world?

ARLEDGE: The word important may seem to require some justification in this context, since individually, both sports and television are essentially trivial. But when the two are combined, they can become very important. And I think my most important moment came during the 1963 U. S.–Russia track meet in Moscow. In those days, the meet was a titanic international struggle, with the conflict between the two systems as the underlying motif. And in that particular year, the U. S. and Russia were trying to put together the first meaningful arms agreement of the Cold War. Khrushchev and Harriman were negotiating day and night, but at the very end of the meeting, the two of them came out to Lenin Stadium to watch Valery Brumel, the great Russian high jumper, try for the world's record. It was getting dark and a light rain had begun falling. Brumel was down to his last attempt. He sprinted toward the bar, leaped and made it. There was a momentary lull as 90,000 people waited to see if the bar would topple. It didn't, and the crowd exploded. I turned our cameras on the chairman's box and Khrushchev and Harriman were jumping up and down, screaming, hugging each other. That was the single most important image I have ever broadcast. Two old men. Enemies who spoke different languages and couldn't even agree on a way to prevent the world from blowing itself up. Yet there they were, embracing like brothers on world television at the simple act of a man jumping over a bar.

ACKNOWLEDGEMENTS

"The Major Leagues" from *I Never Had It Made* by Jackie Robinson, as told to Alfred Duckett. Copyright 1995 by Rachel Robinson. Reprinted by permission of The Ecco Press.

Excerpt from *Veeck...As In Wreck* by Bill Veeck with Ed Linn. Copyright 1962 by Mary Frances Veeck and Edward Linn . Reprinted with the kind permission of Mary Frances Veeck and Ed Linn.

Excerpt from *In The Ring and Out* by Jack Johnson. Material taken from edition Copyright 1977 by Proteus (Publishing) Limited.

Excerpt from *This Life I've Led* by Babe Didrikson Zaharias. Copyright 1955 by A. S. Barnes and Company, Inc.

Excerpt from *Jesse* by Jesse Owens and Paul Neimark. Copyright 1978 by Jesse Owens, Paul Neimark. Reprinted by permission of the Curtis Management Group.

Excerpt from *Dick Button on Skates* by Dick Button. Copyright 1955 by Prentice Hall, Inc. Reprinted by permission of Simon & Schuster, Inc.

Excerpt from *Halas by Halas* by George Halas. Copyright 1979 by George Halas. Reprinted by permission of the Harold Matson Agency.

Excerpt from *Billie Jean* by Billie Jean King with Kim Chapin. Copyright 1974 by Billie Jean King. Reprinted by permission of HarperCollins Publishers.

Excerpt from *The Long Season* by Jim Brosnan. Copyright 1960 by Jim Brosnan.

Excerpt from *The Way It Is* by Curt Flood with Richard Carter. Copyright 1971, by Curt Flood and David Oliphant. Reprinted by permission of Simon & Schuster.

Excerpt from *Ball Four* by Jim Bouton. Copyright 1970. Reprinted by permission of the author.

Excerpt from *A Whole New Ballgame* by Marvin Miller. Copyright 1991 by Marvin Miller. Reprinted by permission of Carol Publishing Group.

ACKNOWLEDGEMENTS

Excerpt from *Dock Ellis in the Company of Baseball* by Donald Hall with Dock Ellis. Copyright 1976 by Donald Hall. Reprinted courtesy of the Gerald McCauley Agency, Donald Hall and Dock Ellis.
Excerpt from *Out of Their League* by Dave Meggyesy. Copyright 1971 by David M. Meggyesy. Reprinted by permission of the author.
Excerpt from *Bad As I Wanna Be* by Dennis Rodman with Tim Keown. Copyright 1996 by Dennis Rodman. Used by permission of Dell Publishing, a division of Random House, Inc..
Excerpt from the *Playboy* Interview: Roone Arledge, *Playboy* Magazine (October 1976). Copyright 1976 by *Playboy*. Reprinted with permission. All rights reserved.

Despite our ongoing efforts, there are cases where we have been unable to determine the copyright holder before our press deadline. Those with information regarding copyrights please contact Balliett & Fitzgerald, Inc.; we will be pleased to rectify any ommissions.

PHOTO CREDITS